DOWNHILL SLIDE

DOWNHILL SLIDE

Why the Corporate Ski Industry

Is Bad for Skiing,

Ski Towns, and the Environment

Hal Clifford

SIERRA CLUB BOOKS
SAN FRANCISCO

The Sierra Club, founded in 1892 by John Muir, has devoted itself to
the study and protection of the earth's scenic and ecological resources—
mountains, wetlands, woodlands, wild shores and rivers, deserts and
plains. The publishing program of the Sierra Club offers books to the
public as a nonprofit educational service in the hope that they may enlarge
the public's understanding of the Club's basic concerns. The point of view
expressed in each book, however, does not necessarily represent that of
the Club. The Sierra Club has some sixty chapters throughout the United
States and Canada. For information about how you may participate in
its programs to preserve wilderness and the quality of life, please address
inquiries to Sierra Club, 85 Second Street, San Francisco, California 94105,
or visit our website at www.sierraclub.org.

Published by Sierra Club Books, in conjunction with the University
of California Press

Library of Congress Cataloging-in-Publication Data

Clifford, Hal.
    Downhill slide : why the corporate ski industry is bad for skiing,
ski towns, and the environment / Hal Clifford.
        p.   cm.
    Includes bibliographical references and index.
    ISBN 1-57805-071-5 (alk. paper)
      1. Skis and skiing—Environmental aspects—United States.
    2. Skis and skiing—Economic aspects—United States.   I. Title.

    GV854.4.C55   2002
    796.93—dc21   2002070570

Jacket and book design by Frances Baca
Printed in U.S.A.

10 9 8 7 6 5 4 3 2 1

To Lou for her patience, Anne for her presence,
Simon for his companionship

CONTENTS

PREFACE

I took up skiing about the time I entered first grade, and it has been a lifelong pleasure. My love of the sport led me to attend college in northern New England and to seek a home, and a life, in the Colorado Rockies. I have lived in or near ski towns since I was eighteen years old. It's hard to imagine any other existence.

Much of my career as a journalist has been focused on chronicling these two things, skiing and mountain towns, and they are not faring very well. The unavoidable reality is that alpine towns that have risen around the sport of skiing—once full of heart, soul, and character—increasingly resemble the crowded, polluted, sprawling, and undistinguished landscapes that characterize so much of modern America.

An old colleague, Amory Lovins, is fond of repeating the aphorism "If we don't change the direction we are headed, we are likely to end up where we are going." Where many ski towns are headed today is toward a future in which they lose the very elements that made them attractive, a future in which they are affordable to a smaller portion of society—and have less to do with skiing—than ever before. Many ski industry executives seem mystified that skiing is not growing. They evidently are unwilling to consider the possibility that skiers may not want what they are being offered.

Skiing once was a way to get close to nature and experience it on its own terms. Today, the ski industry is a highly developed form of industrial tourism that exacts an enormous toll on the natural environment through the process of selling experiences. The corporate ski industry insists it is environmentally friendly and invokes the words and emblems of John Muir and Ansel Adams to promote its products. It plays on the past of this sport of rugged outdoorsmen and -women and endlessly markets images of freedom, nature, and beauty. Yet it creates urban-style problems for mountain valleys. It precipitates a cascade of negative effects, both direct and indirect, on human communities, on air and water quality, on biodiversity and forest health. Those ski-resort corporations that are publicly traded never relent in their quest for a fatter bottom line, and so they strive for growth and more growth in mountain environments that have reached or exceeded the limit of their ability to support both human activity and a diverse and robust natural ecosystem. It is true, as industry officials often proclaim, that the natural environment is the ski industry's greatest asset. But in an ongoing exercise of government and corporate hypocrisy, that asset is being systematically destroyed by those who say they value it.

In 1996, I was hired to write a regular column on ski-area real estate development for *Ski* magazine. That job provided me a window through which I began to see the negative side of the modern ski industry. This book is an attempt to share that understanding, to explain what is happening to skiing, ski towns, and the environment, and to explore how we got here and where we might go. It is also my attempt to help those people—and there are many—who are uneasy with what is happening to the sport, the communities, and the land they love. As any small-town resident knows, it is easy to bury oneself in local problems and lose sight of the larger picture. I have tried here to describe the greater forces at play and the common themes connecting the problems that have beset ski towns in so many places, from Maine to California.

It is the nature of any broad survey to be incomplete. This book is best viewed as a collage assembled from the high points and hot spots of the American skiing scene to portray its current landscape. Despite its flaws, this approach will, I hope, open a public debate about the relationship between the skiing business and the environment and communities upon which it depends.

HAL CLIFFORD
Telluride, Colorado | September 2001

ACKNOWLEDGMENTS

No author labors alone, a truism doubly valid for research-intensive works of nonfiction. A book such as this is brought into being through the patience, forbearance, and tutelage of many people.

John Thornton of the Spieler Agency has worked tirelessly on my behalf. I am grateful to him for his continued faith in me and my work. He is a man of honor, integrity, and good humor. Danny Moses, the editor-in-chief at Sierra Club Books, took a genuine and detailed interest in this project from the beginning. His attitude toward the craft of writing and the encouragement he offered are much appreciated. Copy editor Jacqueline Volin and project manager Scott Norton at the University of California Press added much-needed polish to the text.

Like any journalist, I am deeply indebted to my sources, without whom this would be a thin volume indeed. Dozens of people sat for interviews, which often lasted for hours. Others spent time driving, walking, and skiing with me. To all those whose names appear in the text, my thanks. Many people not included in these pages nevertheless helped me in important ways. Some, for professional reasons, worked on my behalf behind the scenes and prefer anonymity. Additional help came from *New York Times* science writer Sandra Blakeslee, who suggested to me the idea of a quasi-religious war over land use;

freelance reporter Bob Berwyn, who covers Keystone and Breckenridge and who called me out of the blue to offer his help and freely shared his work; Jasper Carlton, executive director of the Biodiversity Legal Foundation; David Dion, who explained life in the Mad River Valley; Eric Friedman, who connected me with Bob Ackland at Mad River Glen; Stacy Gardner, who heads up communications for the National Ski Areas Association and was always quick to send information; Roger Hollowell, who took me to round up stray cattle on the slopes of Buttermilk ski area and graciously spent a day explaining in heartbreaking detail how the success of a resort is killing his small piece of paradise; Doug Kenney, director of Colorado University's Natural Resources Law Center, who was the source for useful writings on the implications of wilderness development, and tourism on public lands; Colin Laird, director of Healthy Mountain Communities, who shared invaluable research on social impacts; Rob Marone, public information officer of the Colorado State Patrol, who researched road accident statistics and put me in touch with patrol officers; Wilderness Society economist Pete Morton, who directed me to excellent analyses of ski-area expansion plans; Jenny Ochtera, sales representative at Sunday River ski area, who walked me through American Skiing Company's sales strategies; Scott Oldakowski and Greg Spearn, who explained much of American Skiing Company's business strategy to me; Alice Pugh of the Leadville Full Circle program, who not only spoke on the record but also devoted time and energy to connecting me with the Latino community there, as did her colleague, Esther Soto; Ed Pitoniak, former editor of *Skiing* magazine and now a vice president at Intrawest, who was forthright about much of what that company is doing, as were his colleagues Gary Raymond and Hugh Smythe; Ed Ryberg of the U.S. Forest Service, who was courteous and helpful in meeting my requests for information, including those I filed under the Freedom of Information Act; the ever efficient Shelli

Schendell at Intrawest's corporate offices, who put me in touch with anyone I wanted to interview and made sure they showed up; Randy Udall, for providing information on the environmental impacts of snowmaking; Michele Varuolo, Les Otten's assistant and chief scheduler; Wendell Wood of the Oregon Natural Resources Council, who provided insight into the impacts of Pelican Butte; and Kristin Yantis and Emily Jacob, who handle public relations for Vail Resorts and arranged for me to meet Vail founder Pete Seibert, who graciously had breakfast with me and looked back on it all.

I owe a special tip of the hat to Jeff Berman, director of Colorado Wild in Durango, and Ted Zukoski at the Land and Water Fund of the Rockies in Boulder for opening their files to me and allowing me to benefit from the vast research they have undertaken. Christy Thomas eased my burden by transcribing a number of interview tapes. Rob Davis, an old friend at the New York Public Library, brought his considerable research skills to bear on my behalf. The staffs and holdings of the Colorado Historical Society, Denver Public Library, Wilkinson Public Library (especially the reference librarians there), Colorado Ski Museum, Vail Public Library, and Pitkin County Public Library were a great help as well. Two online resources, Headwaters News and First Tracks!! Online Ski Magazine, were invaluable in my effort to keep tabs on an industry spread across a continent. I checked them almost every day for two years.

Much of the initial research for this book was undertaken while I was on assignment. I appreciate the ability to kill two birds with one stone while working for others and am grateful to my editors at *Bugle, Business Week, Diversion, High Country News, Mountain Gazette, Mountain Sports and Living, Mountainfreak,* and *National Geographic Adventure* for helping underwrite this effort.

I am particularly indebted to three editors from whom I

learned a great deal. Dave Danforth, the founder of the *Aspen Daily News* (a newspaper with the unforgettable slogan "If you don't want it printed, don't let it happen"), took me under his wing almost two decades ago and taught me not only how to report a story, but also why. While at the *Daily News* I also had the great pleasure of working in close quarters with Andy Bigford, who went on to *Ski* magazine and took me with him. Andy is a journalist's journalist who carries fire in his belly for a good investigative story. In 1996, he hired me as a contributing editor at the magazine, and for three years I reported on ski-resort real estate and development. That job planted the seeds for this book. Under the auspices of *Ski* I gained both understanding of and access to the workings of the modern ski industry. I am grateful for the opportunity.

For six years I was a weekly columnist at the *Aspen Times*. Many of my writings dealt with the ski industry; I thank *Times* editor Andy Stone for the opportunity to work out, in the pages of his fine newspaper, much of my thinking about where the skiing world is going. Andy also graciously agreed to read my completed manuscript, and it benefited from his red pen and sharp mind.

I also am grateful to several insiders in both the federal government and the ski industry who wished not to be named. These people were interested in this book's accuracy and generously read and commented on all or part of the manuscript in draft form, thus helping me to appear wiser than I am. My thanks to all of these people; any errors contained in these pages are my own, not theirs.

I benefited from the hospitality of many people in the course of my research, including Pete and Mary Ellen Gartner in Maine; Lisa Buell and Rick Rouleau in Vermont; Bob and Elizabeth Ward in Utah; and Laura Smith, Lee Ingram, and Keating and Shiva Coffey in Colorado. To all of them, thank you.

I am lucky to come from a family of writers and to be married to one. My colleagues Marty Carlock (my mother) and Mark Clifford (my brother) were steady cheerleaders for this effort. Mary Lou Bendrick (my wife) carried most of the water as my de facto support staff. Her editing, suggestions, love, patience, and understanding have made this book possible.

DOWNHILL SLIDE

CHAPTER 1
From Rope Tows to Real Estate

The last major ski resort to open in the United States during the twentieth century is found at exit 167 off Interstate 70 in Avon, Colorado, a town created in the 1970s. The floor of the Eagle River Valley here is densely covered with high-rise condominiums. You drive south through Avon and cross the Eagle River. A guard checks you through a gate, and you turn south again, driving uphill toward the distant clot of tan buildings wedged into a forested side valley.

You park in an underground garage. If you wish to shop, you may peruse high-end boutiques with names familiar to habitués of New York's Park and Madison Avenues. If you wish to ski, you may ride one of four sets of escalators through the tall buildings to a high-speed chairlift that will whisk you toward the summit. If you wish to dine, perhaps you'll choose to take a horse-drawn sleigh to Beano's Cabin, where rustic Western decor complements your elegant dinner. Here, a brown-skinned young man who does not speak much English fills your water glass while you order the Caviar Beggar's Purse of Caspian Ossetra Wrapped in Crêpes with Crème Fraîche. Welcome to Beaver Creek, the apotheosis of the American corporate ski resort.

From the 11,440-foot ski-area summit you gaze back down the valley, toward the interstate. It's a beautiful view. Perhaps you should buy a little place, a getaway. As you can see from the top of the mountain, there certainly are a lot of homes and condominiums to choose among, miles and miles of them running alongside the highway and the Eagle River. It seems like there are miles and miles of golf courses, too, carpeting the valley floor, their outlines clear despite the January snow.

You push off down Flat Tops, a nice, easy run. Grooming crews drive quarter-million-dollar machines up and down these slopes twenty hours per day, assuring you a corduroy carpet upon which to ski. You turn your skis and turn again, seeking a rhythm, concentrating on the smooth surface ahead of you.

From up here you cannot see the herd of elk milling about near the southern lanes of Interstate 70. The animals are maddened by starvation. The valley where they wintered until the 1970s is the place where you parked your car and rode the escalators. The small, low bowl to the west where they wintered during the 1980s now contains a chairlift, new roads, and multimillion-dollar vacation homes. The valley floor along the river offers no refuge; it has been filled with dogs and golf courses and condominiums and traffic. The elk cannot survive these intrusions. They must find someplace, anyplace, new. A place with forage, without dogs, without traffic or snowmobiles, and most of all, without people.

A single cow elk, and then another, and then a dozen bolt onto I-70's blacktop, their hoofs clattering against the pavement. Tires squeal as drivers struggle to stop. Horns blast. Somebody hits a calf, and it goes down hard. The remaining elk, confused, surge forward. A few turn and leap back down the embankment but now more are coming up, eyes wide with fear, haunches thrusting as they bound and clatter across the tarmac, buck through the dirty snow in the median, and break across the northern lanes. A yearling falls on the slick road surface, its legs splaying out, its feet skittering on the ice. Vehicles are stopped on both sides of the road, drivers gaping, flashers blinking in the afternoon light as scores of elk cross the inter-state and disappear into the piñon and juniper thickets to the north, seeking the last good place.

✸   ✸   ✸

Three corporations whose stock is traded on Wall Street now control many of the largest, best-known ski resorts in North America. These "Big Three"—Vail Resorts Incorporated, Intrawest Corporation, and American Skiing Company—reported in 2000 that among them they had taken in 1.79 billion dollars during the previous fiscal year, earning 298.5 million dollars in before-tax profits.[1] This trio, having sprung on the scene during the 1990s, represents a recent phenomenon in the winter-sports business. They are publicly traded companies that focus almost exclusively on North American ski-resort development and operations. Their ability to do what they do, and to earn the money they earn, is anchored by their exploitation of public lands—principally lands managed by the United States Forest Service. Among them, these three companies, which have interests in twenty-one ski areas in the United States and sell 24 percent of U.S. skiing and snowboarding tickets,* lease forty thousand acres of Forest Service land for their operations.[2] This land lends enormous value to nearby private property where these firms earn significant profits. Without the use of public land, these corporations either would not exist at all or would function on a much smaller scale. With the use of such land, they are operating in a man-

---

* Nobody seems to have come up with an acceptable single term to encompass snowboarding and skiing. For simplicity, in the following pages, when I refer to skiers, skiing, ski resorts, and so on, I generally do so with the intention of including snowboarding as well.

ner that is good for their shareholders but bad for skiing, ski towns, and the natural environment.

* * *

Ski areas, albeit by today's standards primitive ones, which often consisted of little more than a rope tow in a field, sprang up across the country during the first three decades of the twentieth century. The first "destination" ski resort was opened by railroad magnate W. Averell Harriman in Sun Valley, Idaho, in 1935, beginning a resort-building boom that lasted until 1980. Many ski areas stood, and stand, as self-contained and privately held corporations. During the 1960s, 1970s, and 1980s, several corporate conglomerates, including American Cement Company, LTV Corp., Ralston-Purina, and Twentieth-Century Fox, tried their hands at owning all or part of a ski resort, but eventually they sold out. What is new at the dawn of the twenty-first century is the corporation that owns multiple ski resorts and affiliated businesses, to the exclusion of almost all other holdings, and trades its stock in the public markets. This creature is not the ski company of days gone by, and its interests are very different from those of most ski-area owners and operators from previous decades.

In the course of investigating these corporations and their implications, I spent a lot of time studying Colorado. More U.S. skiing happens in that state than any other; about 20 percent of American "skier days" are counted in Colorado each winter. (A skier day, or user day, is the standard unit of measure for the industry; it represents one skier or snowboarder using a ski area's facilities for one day.) Colorado is the only state in which Vail Resorts, Intrawest, and American Skiing—the Big Three—each control a ski resort. Although this book examines events in other parts of the nation, I focus on the industry in

Colorado because I believe it is a harbinger for where the ski business is going.

If the Big Three have their way, where the ski business is going is right into their pockets. Vail Resorts, which controls about 40 percent of Colorado's skier and snowboarder market, summed up its approach to the business this way:

> A key component of the Company's business strategy has been to expand and enhance its core ski operations while at the same time increasing the scope, diversity and quality of the complementary activities and services offered to its skiing and non-skiing guests throughout the year. . . . The Company's business strategy is not only to increase skier days but also to increase Resort Revenue per skier day by capturing a higher percentage of the total spending of its year round destination and day guest by continuing to expand the range and enhance the quality of activities and services offered by the Company.[3]

In other words, Vail Resorts intends to get its corporate fingers into a lot of businesses in its neighborhood.

This statement could have been written just as easily by an executive at Intrawest or American Skiing. As a consequence of this strategy, these corporations are bringing development pressure to bear on a scale never previously experienced by mountain towns such as Steamboat Springs, Colorado; Mammoth Lakes, California; and Warren, Vermont. In so doing, they raise a set of questions that lies at the core of this book. To what use should public lands be put? What should the relationship be between public lands and private profit? Who should benefit? Who should pay the costs? And what should the relationship be between an industrial tourism corporation and the community on which it depends?

At the beginning of the twenty-first century, the residents of many ostensibly bucolic mountain towns find themselves in bitter internecine debates over these questions. While it's probably true that no ski town ever lacked political battles, the fundamental nature of the debates has changed over the last decade, for this simple reason: skiing is no longer an end in itself for those looking to profit from it; instead, skiing has been transformed into a come-hither amenity to sell real estate. This is a fundamental shift away from the roots of the sport and its development, one that is deeply disturbing to many people.

"To the critics of developed recreation and skiing, you're all 'thousand pound gorillas,'" James R. Lyons chided the National Ski Areas Association's national convention in 1999. Lyons, then the under secretary for natural resources and the environment in the Department of Agriculture, was the Clinton administration's point man during the 1990s for the development of the ski industry. The industry's consolidation into large corporations and its aggressive push into real estate developments of unprecedented scale, Lyons said, "is a message of death and destruction for the special places [the ski industry's critics] hold dear."[4]

This is the threat facing modern ski resorts: that they are losing what it was that made them special in the first place, and so becoming more like the rest of America. Such a fate will ultimately undermine the appeal, the quality of life, and the economic success of these places. The primary catalysts for this loss are the Big Three ski-resort development companies. At the beginning of the twenty-first century, their hegemony over mountain towns, and over the sport of skiing, seems almost total—as, at other times, the power of railroads, cattle barons, and timber companies has seemed to other towns. Even in ski towns where they do not own property, American Skiing, Vail Resorts, and Intrawest call the tune by convincing their competitors they must do as the Big Three do or be left behind. Consequently, high-end, high-volume real estate development is not a phenomenon limited to the publicly traded companies; it is being pursued by the privately held ski-resort conglomerates of Booth Creek and Boyne USA, and by every ski-area operator who has a banker offering backing. The question for ski-town residents, and for skiers and snowboarders who visit and love these places, is whether this is an inevitable ordering of the world.

✻ ✻ ✻

Skiing did not start out as a tool to sell real estate, nor as an oligarchic, capital-intensive industry. It was an imported pastime that promised health, moral development, and a superior way of life. The sport came to the United States with Scandinavian immigrants and gained its first toehold in the upper Midwest; the first recorded reference to a modern skier was in 1841, in Beloit, Wisconsin.[5] Skiing then was not about roaring downhill at high speed—indeed, that aspect of the sport did not gain wide credence until the early part of the twentieth century, when a revolution in skiing technique, producing controlled, linked turns, was pioneered in Arlberg, Austria.[6]

For the Scandinavians, skiing—essentially what we would call cross-country skiing today—was both a necessity for winter travel and the embodiment of a moral life. The Swedes and Norwegians who introduced skiing to the United States did not have the word *sport* in their languages. Rather, they referred to the Norwegian *Idraet* or similar Swedish *Idrott* ideal. *Idraet* captured the principle of an outdoor exercise that bred strength, toughness, and manliness. This was an especially important ideal to the Norwegians in the nineteenth century, who at the time were gaining independence from Sweden and saw skiing as a tool for nation building. In skiing they envisioned a pastime that produced a healthy, well-rounded, and moral citizen.[7]

A century later, this principle was still being promoted by

skiing's leading lights. Austrian ski pioneer Otto Schniebs wrote in 1936:

> Whatever degree of skill a skier may possess, he should never forget that his skis are after all only an instrument, a means through which he can enjoy the winter in all its glory and ruggedness, can breathe clean fresh air, can meet human beings in their true character, and can forget all the petty troubles which beset our so-called civilization. These are a few of the reasons why skiing is not merely a sport—it is a way of life.[8]

Between the first skier in Beloit and Schniebs's pre–World War II exhortation, American skiing underwent significant transformation. Scandinavian immigrants had brought skiing not only to the Midwest but also to the mining camps of the Rockies and the Sierra Nevada, where it evolved in isolation. Skis were referred to by miners as Norwegian or Swedish snowshoes, and they were crude at best: simple wooden planks, the tips turned up at the ends, sometimes waxed with a mixture of tar, tallow, and beeswax. Their users steered these boards—sometimes as long as twelve feet—with a stout pole that they straddled or dragged as a rudder. These "snowshoes" allowed some mobility during winter months in the high country, and several individuals were celebrated as cold-season mail carriers who traveled on them through the mountains from mining camp to mining camp.

Skiing as a sport evolved in separate pockets across the country. The first ski club formed in La Porte, California, in 1867, the first ski team in Red Wing, Minnesota, in 1886. Downhill races developed in the Western mining camps during the 1880s—head-to-head events straight down courses on which racers are said to have reached speeds of sixty miles per hour or more.[9] In 1870, a group of Swedes formed the first New England ski club in Maine.[10] The first known ski lift, such as it was, operated on Sundays in Johnsonville, California, during the 1880s, when citizens rode uphill in the ore buckets of the local mine tramway.[11]

The *Idraet* philosophy underpinned the formation of the National Ski Association in 1905 in Ishpeming, Michigan. The association's secretary, Aksel Holter, wrote of "our glorious work for the betterment of mankind, letting the world know we are ever ready to enthuse and assist in the building up of humanity."[12] But as skiing grew in popularity in the Northeast, the ideal of *Idraet* was overtaken there by a new sensibility: Eastern skiers, especially wealthy college students, were taken with the prospect of jumping for distance records and racing downhill on makeshift courses. In the 1920s, "[c]ollege students spent their leisure time learning how to ski. In a society in which time was money, skiing for pleasure in the East became an activity for only the well-to-do."[13]

Interest in skiing surged after the 1932 Winter Olympics in Lake Placid, New York. W. Averell Harriman, owner of the Union Pacific railroad, decided to capitalize on this interest— and generate passengers for his rail line—by creating a lavish ski resort. Harriman's creation would be an end in itself, an attraction that drew visitors from afar and kept them fed, housed, and amused for days or weeks on end. He believed he could expand skiing's appeal beyond its existing markets of die-hard aficionados and wealthy dilettantes. He wanted skiing to be associated with glamour and celebrity, and he wanted to drive that cachet into the consciousness of status-seeking Americans.[14] Harriman employed an Austrian who knew his way around European ski resorts, Count Felix Schaffgotsch, to find the perfect mountain. Schaffgotsch scoured the American West in 1935, reaching the Wood River Valley, near Ketchum, Idaho, at the end of an arduous winter. As soon as he could he cabled Harriman with news of what he had seen, declaring, "I've found it!" What Count Schaffgotsch had found would become the first purpose-built destination ski resort in America: Sun Valley.[15]

Harriman hired a publicist to cast Sun Valley as the St. Moritz of America, and the media obligingly gobbled up the glamorous images emanating from Idaho. Unlike earlier ski entrepreneurs, who for the most part had little interest in growing wealthy off ski lifts, Harriman intended to make his investment pay. He became the first ski-area developer to embrace the idea of the year-round resort, because he wanted a year-round return on his capital. By 1938—three years after the resort opened for skiing—Sun Valley had added warm-weather pleasures to its list of temptations: tennis, golf, fishing, rodeo, hiking, and swimming.[16]

By 1939, skiing in America had become a twenty-million-dollar business.[17] Charged by Sun Valley, Lake Placid, and myriad other ski hills, skiing was primed to explode on the national cultural scene. But World War II interrupted the development of the ski industry, as it did everything else. With the end of the war, a new player, the hard-driving ski-resort visionary, emerged to pick up where skiing's prewar pioneers had left off.

❋ ❋ ❋

As part of the war effort, the U.S. Army had formed the Tenth Mountain Division, an elite corps of fourteen thousand men who were trained to climb and fight in the harshest of mountain conditions. Their training included extensive rock climbing and skiing practice at Camp Hale, near the Continental Divide at the headwaters of the Eagle River in central Colorado (not far from what would become Vail). Soldiers from the Tenth would practice for weeks on end in the high country, skiing, maneuvering, and bivouacking in brutal winter conditions above ten thousand feet. When they had time off, many traveled west through the Sawatch Mountains to Aspen, a forgotten time capsule of a Victorian mining town. There they skied some more on a small ski area on the face of Aspen Mountain, drank in the Hotel Jerome, and talked about what they would do after the war.

The soldiers of the tenth served with great courage in the Italian campaign that rolled the Germans back to their Bavarian redoubts in the final year of the war. More than nine hundred members of the division were killed in action. Those who returned home came back with a passion for life and a belief that they could—and would—do anything they set their minds to. Prior to the war, only about ten thousand Americans were skiers. By the end of it, some two hundred thousand had tried the sport, many as part of their military training.[18] This situation looked like opportunity to the men of the Tenth, many of whom had been counted among the nation's best skiers and rock climbers even before they had joined the division. Approximately two thousand veterans of the Tenth went on to help create the postwar ski industry; ultimately, sixty-two American ski resorts were founded, managed, or had their ski schools run by these men.[19]

For many skiers, the 1950s were the best years of the sport. The ski business was growing rapidly, but ski towns were still small, isolated worlds unto themselves, largely populated by people who loved skiing above all else. For them, skiing as much as possible was the primary objective of daily life. Long before the cultural rebellion of the 1960s, people actively exchanged the American mainstream for the countercultural joys of a winter sport that gave them an enormous sense of freedom and release. The ski towns of America resembled those of Europe: they were relatively stable communities where change was not particularly desirable.[20] As Hal Rothman notes in *Devil's Bargains: Tourism in the Twentieth Century American West,*

> the original ski bums, who came for the pleasures of the [Sun Valley] region, claimed the town as their own. Working in service industries, they skied when they could and stayed on to enjoy the perquisites of a resort

town during the seasons when it was only lightly used. The result was a prototype of a lifestyle peculiar to resort towns, where people took jobs below their social, economic, and skill level to live in the community and enjoy its amenities. Sun Valley developed a personality that would later be mirrored in places such as Aspen, Jackson and dozens of other desirable locations.[21]

Just as the entrepreneurs of the Tenth Mountain Division had expected, skiing was growing. The 1960 Winter Olympics, staged at Squaw Valley, California, gave the sport a boost in the same way the 1932 Olympics had; the number of skiers nationwide jumped from 1.6 million in 1960 to 2.4 million in 1964. Colorado counted 1.1 million skier days in 1964; of these, 393,000 took place in the destination resorts—locales such as Aspen and Steamboat Springs, which catered primarily to overnight guests rather than to day skiers who drove to nearby slopes from Denver and other Front Range cities, then returned home in the evening. By the winter of 1967, the number of destination-resort skier days had risen to 748,000.[22]

Aspen, Winter Park, and Arapahoe Basin in Colorado; Pico and Stowe, Vermont; and Squaw Valley, California, opened for business between 1936 and 1949. As the sport exploded in the 1960s, still more large ski areas opened to accommodate this growth, including Vail, Crested Butte, Steamboat, Powderhorn, Snowmass, and Purgatory.[23] By 1969, the skiing industry grossed more than a billion dollars annually.[24] By 1975, the United States counted 745 ski areas. The sport was fast becoming big business, and as is the case with tourism everywhere, it had become too important to leave to the locals.[25] Corporate conglomerates, smelling real money, muscled in. By 1968, Ralston-Purina owned half of the Keystone, Colorado, ski area, and Leander-McCormick controlled 17 percent of nearby Copper Mountain Resort. LTV Aerospace, a subsidiary of Ling-Temco-Vought (LTV) Corp. of Dallas, purchased Steamboat Springs's Mt.

Werner Resort for four million dollars in 1969.[26] A decade later, Twentieth-Century Fox purchased the Aspen Skiing Corporation.

What these corporations possessed that most ski area entrepreneurs did not was capital, and lots of it. This was money to be used to expand, and so to make more money. Perhaps nobody understood how to do that so well as William Janss. Janss started Snowmass ski area at the same time, and in a similar fashion, as Vail founders Pete Seibert, a veteran of the Tenth Mountain Division, and Earl Eaton, a miner, began work on their resort. Each located a promising mountain valley and began surreptitiously buying land there. With a handful of Denver friends, Seibert and Eaton bought twelve hundred acres of ranch land in the Gore Creek Valley along U.S. Highway 6 under the auspices of the specious Transmontane Rod and Gun Club, an organization that never hunted or fished for anything except land. They got their permit to build a ski area from the U.S. Forest Service in 1959 and fired up the chairlifts in 1963.[27] Janss quietly gathered together thirty-four hundred acres' worth of sheep ranches at the head of the Brush Creek Valley, nine miles west of Aspen. He obtained his construction permit in 1964, sold a portion of his enterprise to American Cement Company, and opened Snowmass Ski Area and Snowmass Village in 1967.[28]

Through his Janss Corporation, Bill Janss already had built Thousand Oaks, California, a postwar planned community for forty-five thousand people near Los Angeles. With his purchase of Sun Valley in 1964 and his creation from whole cloth of Snowmass, Janss brought the sensibilities of high-volume real estate development to the ski-resort world. Nothing had been seen like this before in the ski business, and Janss's approach permanently changed the industry. What he saw in ski slopes was a magnet that would sell second homes—especially condominiums, a new concept in property ownership that made a vacation home affordable for millions of people for the first time.[29]

As Seibert did at Vail, Janss kept a tight rein over land and development. (Seibert handled Vail's planning and development, while Eaton focused on maintaining operations.) Janss even decided who got to open businesses in Snowmass, a resort that was all about controlled experiences.[30] Little was left to chance. As much as possible, visitors to Snowmass would not be surprised—or, if they were, they would be surprised only happily. Snowmass-at-Aspen, as it was sometimes called, had little in common with ski towns like Steamboat Springs, Aspen, and Stowe, which had been towns before they were ski resorts. It had much more in common with a Walt Disney Company theme park. Said John Cooley, Snowmass's marketing manager at the time: "We want the effect to be one of total harmony."[31]

For many of nearby Aspen's residents, it was anything but. "In Snowmass-at-Aspen, everything was coordinated, modulated and adjusted to emulate either the good old days when the rich could escape the riffraff, or some future time when happy endings would be guaranteed," wrote Peggy Clifford in her book *To Aspen and Back*, which chronicles her bittersweet, three-decade love affair with her adopted hometown. "It promised endless fun, comfort, entertainment and surprises that were uniformly pleasant. . . . It was not a town, but merely a good-times machine, and the good times were organized and codified. They were also unreal."[32]

At Sun Valley, Snowmass, and Vail, Janss and Seibert rewrote the rule book on ski-area development. Ski areas now courted anyone from anywhere who wanted to buy a little piece of paradise. For Clifford and other ski bums who had thrived in their isolated aeries during the 1950s and 1960s, mountainside developments of what Janss himself called "cookie-cutter houses" implied the end of their communities.[33] This is not to say that these places became unappealing; indeed, one of the great burdens mountain towns share with all desirable places is that each newcomer loves his or her chosen new home (or second home) just the way it is the day he or she arrives—even if, from the longtime local's point of view, the place has gone to hell.

With the opening of Vail and Snowmass, skiing became an adjunct of real estate development, and this reality has informed much of the ski business ever since. What Intrawest, American Skiing, and Vail Resorts are doing today is no different in tenor than what Bill Janss did at Snowmass, but it is enormously different in scope. Development in the mountains is a forty-year-old story, but development at the levels now practiced by these corporations is unprecedented—and unsustainable. The impacts, too, are unprecedented. The Big Three have carried the Wall Street imperative of continuous growth, of rising returns every quarter, to towns and environments that are ill-prepared to withstand such pressure.

CHAPTER 2

Skiing's Self-Defeating Arms Race

The ski industry is dying. Despite the advent and rapid growth of snowboarding, total skier and snowboarder visits to the slopes did not materially change between 1979 and 1999, and future participation in snow sports is likely to decline significantly. Unless ski areas do a remarkably better job of keeping first-timers interested in the sport, skier days nationwide will plummet. Currently, only 15 percent of beginners go on to become serious skiers or snowboarders, and that's not enough growth to make up for the large numbers of skiers hanging up their boards for good.[1] What happened? Why is a sport that grew so rapidly after World War II and is still America's most popular winter recreation now stagnant and poised at the beginning of a likely long decline?[2]

About thirty-three million Americans consider themselves skiers or snowboarders, but only a third of them actually go out in any given year and slide down a hill.[3] During the last two decades of the twentieth century, the number of U.S. skier days fluctuated between 50.2 million and 54.1 million, with the exception of dips during a couple of low-snow years.[4] The winter of 2000 was a record year, with 57.3 million skier days counted nationwide, but by all accounts that jump was an aberration attributable to good natural snow conditions throughout much of ski country, especially in the Midwest and Northeast, rather than to managerial or strategic brilliance on the part of ski-area operators. Most of the increase—about five million skier visits over the previous year—was recorded during the typically slow months of November and December, when early season snow conditions nationwide were unusually good.[5] Day-skier visits were up, but for many of the biggest resorts, head counts among the more valuable destination skiers declined.[6] Skiing vacations, it seems, do not have the cachet they once did.

Without snowboarding, which came of age in the late 1980s and in the winter of 1999 accounted for 26 percent of lift tickets sold, the number of U.S. skier days might have declined by double digits since the late 1970s.[7] This stagnation occurred during two decades of almost uninterrupted peace that included the longest economic expansion in American history. The business of selling lift tickets, in other words, is a miserable one.

The same two key factors that were responsible for skiing's growth are now contributing to its stall: the Baby Boom and economic progress. Skiing came of age with Baby Boomers, the seventy-eight million Americans born between 1945 and 1964. It's no accident that the last major ski resorts to open in North America—Blackcomb, British Columbia; Deer Valley, Utah; and Beaver Creek, Colorado—all did so in December 1980, when the oldest Boomers were thirty-five. The bulk of skier days traditionally has been provided by people between the ages of thirty-five and forty-two—and twenty years later, the trailing edge of the Baby Boom population bell curve is made up of thirty-five-year-olds.[8] By the time skiers hit age forty-four, their statistical participation in the sport begins to drop dramatically, and it keeps dropping.[9] On average, 10,600 Baby Boomers have passed their forty-fourth birthday every day since 1989. Boomers are growing out of the skiing habit, and ski areas are running out of skiing customers.

Following the Boomers is Generation X: forty-six million

people born between 1966 and 1979. These are the snow-boarders; the median age of riders in 2000 was only twenty-one.[10] But there aren't enough of them to fill up the ski resorts built for their Baby Boom elders. Down the road, the seventy-two million Echo Boomers now coming into their teens and twenties may offer hope to ski-resort executives wishing for long lift lines and busy slopes. But even that prospect may be a chimera, since demographic projections indicate that Echo Boomers and those who follow them are, increasingly, minor-ities: one-third of elementary-school students in 1997 were His-panic (compared to 22 percent in 1974), and the U.S. Census Bureau predicts that by 2050, whites will constitute less than half of the nation's population.[11] This is not good news for those in the snow business; since Tiger Woods arrived to rescue golf from itself, skiing may well be the whitest and least integrated popular sport in America.

Economic progress, ironically, has taken a huge bite out of the ski industry, even though skiing is increasingly a sport of the rich. America is wealthier than ever before. But it is also working harder for that wealth. Between 1973 and 1988, the amount of Americans' free time fell by almost 40 percent—and that was before the unprecedented economic expansion that be-gan in 1991 and brought on the all-day, all-night work life of the New Economy.[12] Today, more than ever before, Americans si-multaneously have less time for leisure and more leisure choices, both in terms of what to do and what they can afford.

It is nothing unusual for an upper-middle-class American (which is to say, someone who might be a skier—almost 70 percent of skiers earn more than fifty-thousand dollars annu-ally)[13] to take a butterfly-watching trip to Borneo, go to cooking school in Florence, spend a weekend at a Napa Valley bed-and-breakfast or catch a Caribbean cruise. At a more quotidian level, these Baby Boomers and Gen-Xers scramble to get their kids to suburban soccer, hockey, and basketball leagues and to take care of their aging parents. Their amusement is likely to be delivered via the Internet or cable television. If they have a spare hour, perhaps they'll browse the local mall's Barnes and Noble bookstore and curl up with a cappuccino in the store's coffee lounge.

"We're competing against work, we're competing against the local athletic club, we're competing against the Internet," says Andy Daly, president of Vail Resorts. I meet him in his corner office in Vail's corporate headquarters, which takes up the ground floor of a conference hotel in Avon, near the banks of the Eagle River on West Benchmark Road. Avon in summer is all clean stucco and flowerpots, although there are some egregious post-Bauhaus condo developments. It's very clean and new feeling, a sort of Stepford wife of a town. Functionally, it serves as the placenta for the rarefied resort of Beaver Creek, supporting it through the umbilicus of the access road.

The feel at the corporate offices is informal. Its portal, a single long, curving corridor leading off the hotel lobby, is guarded by a lone phone receptionist. Adam Aron, the CEO, wanders by in a pressed, deep blue shirt and khakis. A visitor, a former Vail Resorts lawyer, is wearing khakis. Daly is wearing khakis. Khaki shorts wander by. There are also a lot of golf shirts in evidence. Blue jeans are permitted on Fridays.

Daly has a shock of white hair over a slightly ruddy face. His deep, patrician blue eyes don't waver. He speaks calmly, smoothly, and professionally, polished after twenty years of dealing with journalists. A former ski patroller, Daly worked his way up the ranks to become president of Vail Associates in 1989. He weathered the company's bankruptcy and rode out the transition to new owners, reaping an estimated six million dollars in stock options as a reward. Aron, the former head of Norwegian Cruise Lines and once a top executive at United Airlines, was brought in over Daly, but the company veteran remains the public face of what is now Vail Resorts.[14] Nothing ruffles him. His office is spacious, with a bank of windows looking south. Daly sits in a rustic wooden armchair while I take a seat on the couch, both richly upholstered. A coffee-table book about Colorado, another about South Africa, and a copy of *Ski* magazine are among the half-dozen items placed on the table with studied casualness. On the desk behind Daly, a small bronze bull gores a small bronze bear. Family photos are scattered around. Except for the large computer screen on the desk, on which a document titled "Goals & Objectives" is displayed, the place almost could be a den.

"We compete against the other ski resorts, but we really also compete against Las Vegas, against the warm-weather resorts, the cruise lines," Daly says. He fiddles with a button on his dark green, patterned shirt when he is thinking hard. "We compete for people's leisure time, and people are working more instead of less. We're competing, more than anything, for leisure."[15]

It doesn't help the business of this sport that skiing is hard to do, despite the innovations the 1990s brought, such as hourglass-shaped skis that make learning quicker and easier. Anybody who skis understands that the learning process can be very slow, especially for an adult beginner. All sports that are difficult are suffering from a decline in core participation.[16] In today's instant-gratification world, a sport that requires years of practice simply to acquire basic proficiency is not as appealing as it once was. As if all that weren't enough, going skiing is not an easy proposition. As Skip King, chief spokesman for American Skiing Company, put it:

> This sport is a pain in the ass until you've actually got your skis on the snow. You've got to travel, you've got heavy gear. If you have kids, you've got to corral them and bring them along, and they're probably small enough they're going to whine if they have to carry their own skis, so

you're going to carry them. You're going to pack them into a car and then you've got to schlep across a parking lot, into a crowded base lodge, and stand in line for tickets. It's a tribute to the sport that people will put up with all that crap.[17]

It is a testament to the sheer joy of skiing and snowboarding that the sport hasn't declined significantly. But the lack of growth over two decades, and the prospect of decline in the future, have brought some hard realities to bear. The most basic is that if a ski area is going to increase its skier visits, it is going to do so at the expense of other ski areas. Through the 1990s, the big have gotten bigger at the expense of the small. At Intrawest's ski resorts, for example, visits rose 10 percent per year from 1992 through 1998, even as the industry as a whole declined 3.6 percent for the same period.[18]

This pattern is not unusual in a consolidating industry, which is what the ski business has been for two decades. Consolidation is typical in a stagnant or overbuilt market, a market wherein the deep-pocket players are the ones most likely to survive. They're the companies able to ride out downturns, to accept losses for a while, and to make the capital investments necessary to gain market share, a strategy that, according to management textbooks, should lead to profitability as the industry reconfigures itself to the realities of a changed marketplace. American automakers, steel mills, and even beer brewers went through this process in the twentieth century. In the ski business, consolidation also has meant raising the standard of the products and services offered to skiers—a by-product of resorts trying to steal customers from one another. This is good for skiers in the short run, but it has been bad for skiing in the long run and is a significant reason why the sport is not growing, because it has resulted in rising prices.

Adam Aron was very proud to note in 1997 that Vail Resorts was growing "50 percent faster than the rest of Colorado" and "at a rate thirteen times that of industry growth." He attributed this to the high quality of guest experiences at Vail, Beaver Creek, Keystone, and Breckenridge, the company's four ski resorts. "With a high-quality position," he said, "you can successfully drive price." He added, tellingly, "We have seen for over a dozen years now that our company has been able to successfully increase price every single year."[19]

Aron and his counterparts at other destination ski resorts are quick to argue that with rising prices comes rising value. Les Otten, the founder of American Skiing Company, gets almost indignant when the question of value is raised.

"You can buy or make yourself a pair of wood hickory skis with long thongs and bear trap bindings, and you can get a pair of old leather mountainering boots and strap yourself to them, get some skins and find a log-cut on a side of a mountain in New England, and you can go up to the top and you can ski down, get maybe two runs a day. Pack your lunch and that's skiing pretty inexpensively," Otten begins on a rainy February Sunday in his office at the base of Sunday River ski area in western Maine.[20]

Otten looks tired. He resembles a young Donald Sutherland, with a trademark swept-back shock of black-and-silver hair. Around fifty, he looks youthful and trim, except for the bags under his eyes. He works on his IBM Thinkpad and PalmPilot while we speak, but he is distracted beyond that. In the months prior to our meeting, which took place in February 2000, his company went through a brutal financial restructuring and he had seen its stock beaten down to a few dollars per share. Behind his desk hangs a framed copy of a quote from Teddy Roosevelt: "The credit belongs to the man who is actually in the arena, whose face is marred by dust and sweat and blood, who knows the great enthusiasms, the great devotions, and spends himself in a worthy cause; who at best, if he wins, knows the thrills of high achievement, and, if he fails, at least fails daring greatly, so that his place shall never be with those cold and timid souls who know neither victory nor defeat." It is a telling choice of decoration, and it will turn out to be a prescient one. Within a year of our meeting, Otten will lose his job as the chief executive of the company he founded.

Otten's office is small and simple. It does not look like that of a man worth hundreds of millions of dollars. The whole administrative suite, in the upstairs of the Sunday River base lodge, is classic 1970s ski-area vernacular: a bit rickety, the doors cheap and hollow, everything a little shaky and beaten from people walking around in ski boots.

"But," Otten continues, "if you want a molded ski with an edge and a nice side cut and a good camber that's going to last four or five years, fifteen, twenty, thirty days a year of skiing, with nice graphite poles that are easy on the wrist to make sure you don't get carpal tunnel syndrome from planting your pole; and if you want to wear clothing that won't restrict your movement, that will keep you warm, you're going to be putting on a couple of hundred dollars' worth of Gore-Tex.

"Then you're going to say, 'I want to ride up to the mountain, and I want to ride in relative safety, and I'd like to ride up there relatively quickly so it doesn't take me fifteen minutes of sitting on a chair freezing to death until I get to the top. I want load-sensing devices on every tower so that if the cable shifts just a quarter of an inch the lift will shut down before it can derail. I want a braking system on the lift that's the same braking system that's used on a locomotive to bring it to a stop—and by the way, I'd like padded seats, and if it's possible for me to be in an enclosed cabin, then I'd like that too, and then when I get to the top of the mountain I'd like to make sure that if I happen to be cold there's a place where I can go inside and get warm and have something to eat without having to traipse back through a lift system halfway across the mountain—I'd like to have that. And then when I finally put my skis on and I start heading down the hill I'd like to make sure that I have an immaculately groomed surface, I'd like to have some nice soft bumps where they've made some new snow if it's New England, or out West where it's been powder. I'd like to be greeted nicely, I'd like the person who's speaking to me to have a total understanding of the sport that I'm in. I'd like them to be able to be helpful. I'd even like them to valet my car and help me carry my kids into the day-care center.'

"That isn't going to happen for nineteen dollars a day," Otten concluded. "It's not going to happen."

Most major ski areas today are delivering the Mercedes-Benz-style experience Otten describes, compared to the Chevrolet-style experience that typified skiing in the early 1970s. Ironically, this is the third reason skiing is dying: many skiers and snowboarders do not want, or at least cannot afford, that experience. Otten and his cohorts are building magnificent temples to skiing, but new skiers by and large are not coming.

Skiing is sold as it always has been sold, as a product. In the language of marketers, skiing is product driven, not customer driven. That is, ski areas generally promote what they have—a mountain, new lifts, snowmaking—rather than finding out what customers want and then creating a product to deliver it. This is not absolutely true, of course. Many ski areas survey customers, listen to their concerns, and try to provide for them, whether it's tissue boxes in the lift lines or better grooming. Nevertheless, during the last two decades the race has been on to create the best, flashiest product to attract skiers, and nobody has set the pace more aggressively than the Big Three ski conglomerates. While this struggle has succeeded in drawing skiers to one resort or another, it has not increased the total number of skiers, and that fact has led to some in-house soul searching.

"Do we in the ski industry really have a clue as to what the customer wants in the way of pass prices, freebies, specials, deals, packages, snow reports, events?" asked Ken Hulick, a marketing consultant in Durango, Colorado, in *Ski Area Management* magazine. "Has anyone asked the customer lately what type of package they want? The ski industry is very low on the scale of marketing research; of understanding customers; and of pricing to customers' desires."[21]

The truth is, high prices are a significant reason why more people don't ski or snowboard.*

"We found that price has really motivated people to go skiing, and we found that as prices came down it really expanded the market," says Jim Spring, president of Leisure Trends Group, a sports-industry analysis and polling organization. Spring, who is middle-aged, wry, frank, and beefy, learned to ski in New England. Now, he keeps his finger on the pulse of skiing from an office on the plains east of Boulder, Colorado. "If you ask most people who ski or ride, one of the biggest barriers or obstacles is price—what it costs. Every time a price goes up, I think there's some increment of the population that says, 'Gee, now you've gone through a threshold, I can no longer afford to participate in your sport.'"[22]

Yet prices do keep going up, and they do so because Aron, Otten, Intrawest CEO Joe Houssian, and executives at com-

---

* Many observers argue that the price of a single-day lift ticket is watched too closely and unfairly attacked, since lift tickets generally constitute only a small percentage of the total cost of a ski vacation. However, lift ticket prices, fairly or otherwise, do serve as a de facto benchmark against which many other prices are set in a resort. So although on the one hand, consumers may read too much into ticket prices, on the other, the ticket prices give a potential visitor a good indicator of what he or she can expect from the whole resort.

peting resorts have engaged in what can only be called an arms race on the slopes.

* * *

It began in the Northeast with Otten, who in 1980 purchased Sunday River Skiway from Sherburne Corp. and began investing in snowmaking. Sunday River was the first ski area in what would become Otten's American Skiing Company empire. Here, in western Maine, he recognized that the great uncertainty in skiing was snow. A skier who commits for a week of vacation, only to find the snow quality is poor or—as is often the case in New England—nonexistent, will be disappointed and may not return. To take this uncertainty out of the vacation-planning equation, Otten began investing money in snowmaking. His strategy worked. In 1980, Sunday River counted 40,000 skier days. By 1998, Sunday River possessed 1,300 snow guns that could make snow on 92 percent of the resort's 654 acres of trails, consuming up to 9,000 gallons of water per minute doing so.[23] In large part because of this investment, in 1999 the ski area counted 512,000 skier days.[24]

"We were smoking people," says American Skiing's Skip King. King resembles a shorter, wider version of the author Stephen King. His office, a tiny space, is a total disaster. Precarious stacks of paper, some more than a foot high, cover the built-in desks that run along two walls and under the single window that looks out over a bleak patch of rainy woods. King is obsessed by weather forecasts. On a huge Dell computer monitor a polar view of the globe rotates, simulating a fourteen-day forecast. He is studying it intently when I arrive. "Killington [in Vermont] was terrified of Sunday River," King continues as he recounts American Skiing's history. "They weren't keeping up, they weren't investing in lifts, and their business was going down the road to Okemo, which was operating under the same sort of idea as Sunday River: trails people want to ski, fast lifts to get them up the mountain, and snow quality. Those three components are the components upon which everything else rests."[25]

Snowmaking isn't cheap. An air compressor to run a bank of snow guns costs $250,000; snow guns themselves go for $300 to $1,500 apiece. Quieter, fan-driven snowmaking machines cost $10,000 each. And the annual electric bill to run a snowmaking system will easily top $1 million.[26] Between 1997 and 2000, American Skiing invested $172 million in on-mountain improvements, including snowmaking and lifts. At the end of that time the company was making snow on three thousand acres of ski trails at its various resorts—almost five square miles.[27]

Today American Skiing Company has recipes for nine grades of snow and guarantees the result. If visitors don't like the quality of the company's trademarked Signature Snow after taking their first run, they get a voucher worth their ticket price. It's a great strategy to help convince skiers that their vacation won't be wasted. However, it also means enormous operating costs for ski areas that embrace extensive snowmaking, guaranteed or not.

"Once you put snowmaking on line, you then have such a huge marketing demand to create skier days," says Bob Ackland. Ackland was vice president of finance for two years in the late 1990s at Sugarbush, a ski area in Vermont's Mad River Valley that was purchased by American Skiing Company in 1996. In early 2000 he had just settled in as the general manager at the fiercely independent Mad River Glen ski area a few miles up the road. Of medium height, Ackland is a little heavy around the middle, and when I meet him he's hobbling around with a broken leg he received the first day of the ski season. He's dressed in Vermont casual: corduroy trousers, rumpled shirt. I sit next to his desk in a seat constructed out of varnished rawhide and bent wood. A few photographs of racing yachts are propped beneath the windows that look out over Mad River Glen's base area. Before he got into the skiing business, Ackland built boats. He is honest, forthright, thoughtful, and slightly contemptuous of his old employer, American Skiing Company.

"It's just mind-boggling what snowmaking costs," he continues, "and you need a hell of a lot of skiers to cover it. It's about $1,000 per acre per inch, operating cost. I had no idea. I knew it was expensive, but there [at Sugarbush] I was looking at [monthly] electric bills of $300,000, $400,000."[28]

Once a resort makes snow—or even if it doesn't—skiers expect it to be groomed. Snow grooming machines cost around $200,000 apiece new, and a decent-size ski mountain needs a half-dozen. Then there's lifts.

The earliest lifts were simple rope tows, often powered by an automobile up on blocks. The first chairlift was constructed in 1939 from salvaged mine cables and towers at the now-defunct Pioneer Ski Area near Gunnison, Colorado. Most skiers, however, learned the sport in subsequent decades on rope tows, platters, J-bars, and T-bars (T-bars were invented in 1940 in Pico, Vermont).[29]

The fixed-grip double chair (it seated two skiers) soon became the standard for uphill transportation. In 1985, Vail upped the ante with the installation of the first detachable quad chairlift, the Vistabahn, capable of carrying four skiers at a time at much greater uphill speeds,[30] because the cable on such a lift travels much faster than on older, fixed-grip lifts. The chairs grab on to the cable with spring-loaded grips; they are derailed from the moving cable to allow for loading and unloading at slow speeds. The same technology is used for gondolas. Such modern lifts are expensive machines to make, to install, and to run. In 2000 a typical detachable quad chairlift made by

POMA of America cost about $2.85 million to install, plus another 15 percent in site-preparation costs. The electric bill to run it amounts to around $14,000 a month. An eight-place gondola that rises twenty-two hundred feet sold for about $6 million and uses more than $20,000 worth of electricity per month.[31]

With the advent of Vail's Vistabahn, the arms race was on. In 1986, Colorado ski resorts invested $77 million in capital improvements, and the pace of investment has not slowed much since then.[32] In 1998, Vail Resorts alone spent $65 million on resort capital improvements, and in some years, Intrawest's operations division has invested $200 million on the company's slopes.[33] In the 1990s, United States ski resorts invested up to $100 million annually in lifts alone.[34]

These expenditures obliged resorts that compete with the Big Three to run faster to keep up in the struggle for a piece of the skier-day pie. Between 1996 and 1998, Jackson Hole resort invested $25 million.[35] In 1998, Deer Valley ski area announced $18 million in improvements.[36] The following year, Colorado resorts announced a record $233 million in investments—triple the record investment made twelve years earlier.[37] In the Lake Tahoe region, several resorts announced 1999 capital spending plans totaling $500 million.[38]

This is an enormous rate of capital investment in a market that is not growing, and it has helped box the ski industry into a high-cost corner. "I have never heard a person say that they did not go to XYZ ski resort because they didn't have a new lift this year," says Jim Spring of Leisure Trends Group. "But if you turn that around, almost every resort, every year, wants to build or replace a lift. So their costs to create this infrastructure are enormous, and yet there's not one of them who can draw a straight line between that investment in infrastructure and an increase in skier days."[39] Those costs are passed on in the form of lift ticket prices, which generally now run from fifty dollars to the mid-sixty-dollar range for a single-day ticket at a major resort.

* * *

Between 1975 and 2000, the number of ski areas in the United States declined from 745 to 509.[40] Most of those that folded were the small mom-and-pop operations where many Baby Boomers first tried the sport.[41] There was a rope tow, maybe a couple of T-bars, J-bars, or chairlifts. The total vertical rise might have been a few hundred feet, and there were only a handful of runs to choose from. A lift ticket cost a few dollars a day, and if you skied with any regularity, the folks running the lifts got to know you.

This was the farm league of skiing, but these were ski hills that would not or could not keep up with the capital investment frenzy. Not all such ski areas have closed, but many have, and their loss exacerbates the problem of enticing people to ski. Cheap skiing options are going away, and it's hard to convince somebody to try a sport when the price of a lift ticket, equipment rental, and lessons can easily run $150 per day at a large resort. Commercial skiing always has been a pastime of the upper-middle and upper classes, but with the rising prices that have accompanied the on-mountain arms race, skiing for the less-than-wealthy is truly becoming a thing of the past. In 1984, more than 80 percent of alpine skiers earned less than $50,000 annually; in 1999, more than 70 percent earned *more* than $50,000. The percentage of skiers earning between $15,000 and $35,000 dropped by about two-thirds in noninflation-adjusted numbers.[42] Forty percent of today's skiers earn more than $75,000; 50 percent of the visitors to Vail and Beaver Creek earn more than $100,000; and the household median income of U.S. skiers in 2001 was $91,400.[43] Inflation aside, this is a significant upshifting of the ski industry into the realm of luxury sport (or, as one skier ruefully described it to me, "snow polo"). These are nice demographics for the moment for big ski resorts, but this change means there is a much smaller pool of potential skiers who feel they can afford to ski or snowboard.

This situation is not the result of dark machinations by faceless resort executives. Skiers and snowboarders voted with their feet by frequenting those resorts that have made big-dollar investments. Now, however, ski-resort operators are in a trap. They have created an expectation among skiers and boarders of constantly new, constantly fresh product, be it lifts, grooming, snowmaking, or terrain. So Vail Resorts, for instance, wants to expand into the Jones Gulch area at Keystone, adding 125 acres of trails to the 1,861-acre ski area—even though Keystone has fewer skiers per acre than any ski hill in Colorado's White River National Forest.[44] The Jones Gulch proposal came as Vail was going through a brutal public battle with environmentalists, federal officials, and the town of Vail to add 4,100 acres of new terrain to Vail Mountain. The expansion area, Blue Sky Basin, opened in 1999, yet the ski area's capacity remains capped at 19,900 skiers per day. Evidently, the new terrain at Vail is not a response to an inability to accommodate the crowds.

In a 1997 white paper submitted by eleven Colorado ski resorts to the U.S. Forest Service, the assertion was made that "to meet public need, resorts will require more intermediate, advanced and expert skiable terrain and additional specialized terrain for a variety of new winter and summer activities."[45] The Forest Service seems to agree; during the 1990s, when growth in Colorado skier days averaged 2 percent annually, skiable terrain grew at 7 percent annually and doubled over the course of the decade.[46] In the year 2000, yet another thirty-five hundred acres of expansions at Colorado resorts—almost the equivalent of another Snowmass ski area—were planned or under way.[47]

But the ski industry is making a shell-game argument, asserting that more public land must be used to meet an alleged public need for more skiing. The truth is in the numbers. Skiing is flat and likely to decline; there is no public need for more skiing nationally, or for more skiing in Colorado. These expansions are not driven by growth in new skiers; they simply shuffle the same skiers around.

As publicly owned corporations, Vail Resorts, Intrawest, and American Skiing have a responsibility to keep showing improvements to the bottom line, and at least for a while those improvements may be found via expansions that poach skier days from competitors. But this strategy comes at a real cost, and the endgame is in sight. At Mammoth Mountain, California, Intrawest is investing five hundred million dollars in controversial on-mountain improvements and base-village construction. The strategy there is to bring the resort, which currently sees about 940,000 skier days annually, back to its historic high levels of 1.4 million. But where will these skiers come from? They'll be Los Angelenos who now fly to Salt Lake City and Vail to ski, according to Intrawest. In other words, they won't be new skiers.[48] Arguments likely will be made at Mammoth about how improvements are needed on lands of the Inyo National Forest to accommodate this "new" demand. There may be a demand on the part of ski-area operators to develop more public lands to lure skiers from competing resorts, but that's a very different proposition from accommodating new skier demand. Vail Resorts executives make the same arguments in justifying the "need" to expand Breckenridge in order to compete with Utah's resorts, which were upgraded for the 2002 Winter Olympics. One does not have to be a hard-core environmental activist to question the wisdom of letting corporations develop public land in order to service their debt and boost shareholders' profits without materially advancing the public good.

It's unrealistic to think that skiers and boarders wouldn't

have expected improvements over the last twenty years at ski areas, since improvement is one of the things capitalism does best. What is significant about the industry's recent strategy is that it has saddled ski operators with a heavy capital investment and little likelihood that they can grow sufficiently in terms of overall skier days to pay for it. Facing this reality, ski-resort operators—especially the Big Three, but also Winter Park, Snowmass, and Crested Butte, Colorado; Jackson Hole, Wyoming; Big Mountain, Montana; Stowe, Vermont; and others who compete with them—have turned to other ways of making money. Throughout the 1990s, there was a growing recognition that if ski areas are going to grow and be profitable, they are going to have to do so via some other revenue stream than lift ticket sales. Reading the demographic tea leaves, two potential profit centers became apparent: selling real estate to Baby Boomers, and attracting nonskiers to ski resorts.

CHAPTER 3

Wall Street Comes to the Mountain

Like so many famously attractive places—Key West, Greenwich Village, Santa Monica—ski towns had a golden moment. They were magical, vibrant, and full of creative souls. From 1945 until about 1980, ski-resort towns were escapist enclaves, places where Americans slipped out of the mainstream culture. They were hard to get to, and once you got there it was hard to earn a living. People who came found themselves deeply underemployed, a phenomenon encapsulated in the apocryphal story, heard in almost every ski resort, of someone with a doctorate who was washing dishes in a local restaurant.

That was the trade-off to choosing life in a ski town: Those who did so actively stepped off the career track. They made significant compromises in terms of income, living situations, intellectual challenge, career choices, health care, schools, and all the other things that are supposed to matter. Scratch anyone who lived in a ski town for long during that time and you'll find someone who worked as a lift attendant, ski patroller, carpenter, cook, cocktail waitress, raft guide—or all of the above. The whole point of mountain-town life was that it was different from life in the rest of America. Ski towns gave people who loved the mountains a place to live, a way to survive, and the opportunity to spend as much time as possible playing in the out-of-doors. That, after all, was the whole point. That was what mattered in a ski town, not the trappings of the mainstream.

A few other sports—surfing, big-wall rock climbing—can, like skiing, spawn a way of life for devotees. Skiing, however, accommodated the largest group of people who wanted to drop out for a while, or forever. From the 1950s until well into the 1980s, the skiing way of life was a reality for tens of thousands of people. The life was a large part of the romance of the sport, for there was an intriguingly egalitarian potential to it. Skiers could pack up their Econoline van or Volkswagen microbus and drive to the mountains. They could find a way to make a little money. But where they came from, what they did for a living, who their parents were, where they went to school—none of that mattered. What mattered was skiing, and the social hierarchy that developed each season was predicated on their abilities on the mountain. The skiing life was the American myth of the new beginning in as real and distilled a form as could be found during the latter twentieth century.

Skiing's golden age peaked at different times for different towns. It was epitomized by a sense of freedom, a shared camaraderie in the face of hard times, and a deep understanding that the ski life was about something very different from what was going on in the rest of America. As one journalist wrote in 1970 about Crested Butte:

> Go into a home and admire an antique piece. You might hear that a tourist had offered $1,000 for it. A week later you might get it as a gift. In Crested Butte you're still liable to get a loaf of home-baked bread from a neighbor the day you move in. It's a place where you can leave your home unlocked and keys in the car. The young people migrating to town soon discovered this spirit. They found not only the uncrowded skiing and relaxed atmosphere of a small town, but acceptance, a place to utilize their talents, and, if they chose, the warmth and security of a large family.[1]

Ski towns during the 1950s, 1960s, and 1970s resembled the boom towns of the 1870s and 1880s. Not because they were booming—many weren't—but because of the similar social bond that was created. When a town like Park City or Steamboat Springs sprang up, it did so for a reason. In Park City's case, that reason was the nearby silver mines; for Steamboat, it was a ranchers' town. Everybody who lived and worked there had in common that community's reason for being. It didn't matter where you came from—indeed, almost everyone came from somewhere else. What mattered was that you were there for what the place offered, and you pulled your weight in terms of taking advantage of that offering and creating a community. The result was a tightly knit group of people.

Ski towns were the same way. Even into the late 1970s, downtown Aspen shop owners would close up for the morning if more than six inches of new snow had fallen overnight. They'd hang a sign in the window saying, "Powder Day," and head up the slopes. By and large, they were there to ski first, to make money second. That shared set of priorities—and the shared disinterest in what mainstream America was offering—drew many ski-town denizens. "I came here because of the influence of the [Vietnam] war," Rick Silverman, who moved to Telluride, Colorado, in 1971, told me. "I was really interested in the idea of building new communities."

Silverman, now in his mid-fifties, with unruly, shoulder-length hair and a thick, auburn beard, holds a doctorate in political science. Passing through Telluride on a motorcycle trip, he found himself enchanted and soon returned to stay. Like so many others, his working career in Telluride was one of mountain subsistence, doing anything he could to pay the bills while reveling in the magic of the place.

By the late 1960s, the word was getting out about such hideaways. Skiing was becoming big business, and with that growth came media coverage. Bill Janss and Pete Seibert had demonstrated the way to make money, real money, in the ski business: by building and selling condominiums to the masses. Perhaps one wouldn't have to give up so much to live in a ski town after all. Corporations were buying in. For an increasing portion of residents, especially new arrivals riding the corporate coattails, making money became as important as skiing, even more important, and resort economies grew. More people wanted to taste the magic of these towns. More money, consequently, could be made accommodating them. Development was no longer a way to enjoy the mountains; it became an end in itself. And it brought an end to the ski towns' golden moment. Today, executives at the Big Three companies insist that what they are doing is good—good for the town, good for the environment, good for everyone. They promise to bring more business to town, to fill up the "shoulder seasons" of spring and fall, to turn the place into a four-season resort, and to help everybody make more money. This, in the worldview of these companies' executives, should be understood implicitly as a good thing.

* * *

Today's dominant ski conglomerates—Vail Resorts, Intrawest, and American Skiing—were assembled during the 1990s. So was Booth Creek Ski Holdings, a privately held firm that issues public debt and behaves in a manner similar to the Big Three. (Although this book focuses on the effects the Big Three have had on the ski industry, Booth Creek is a significant mid-level player.) Together, these four accounted for 28 percent of U.S. skier days during the 1999 winter. All except Booth Creek are publicly traded on the stock exchanges, and all four bring Wall Street's imperatives to mountain towns. They are the end result of the mass-market commercialization of ski towns, a result predicated on the dubious premise that to prosper in the modern ski industry, one must get big or get out.

Each of the four conglomerates has been shaped by the individuals who built them. American Skiing Company founder Les Otten got his start when he bought Sunday River Skiway in 1980. He began his now-famous and widely emulated strategy of investing in snowmaking, and the resort flourished. In 1995, Otten went on a buying spree, picking up eight New England ski areas: Attitash, Waterville Valley, and Mt. Cranmore in New Hampshire; Killington, Mount Snow, Sugarbush, and Haystack in Vermont; and Sugarloaf in Maine.[2]

By 1996, American Skiing dominated the markets of the Northeast—but it was deeply vulnerable to weather and regional economic downturns like the one that hit New England in the late 1980s. Otten needed geographic diversification, so he purchased Wolf Mountain, a sleepy resort adjacent to Park City in Utah's Wasatch Front, immediately east of Salt Lake City. He renamed his acquisition the Canyons and sketched grandiose plans to make it the largest ski area in North America. In 1997, the firm bought both Steamboat ski area, in northern Colorado, and Heavenly, at South Lake Tahoe, from Kamori International Corp., a Japanese firm that had done little to improve them. That autumn, American Skiing Company went public on the New York Stock Exchange, raising 236 million dollars.[3]

Intrawest CEO Joe Houssian came into the business not as a skier, but as an urban real estate developer of office buildings and so-called festival markets, patterned after Boston's Fanueil Hall and Seattle's Pike Place Market—experience that would inform his resort strategy. In 1986, the Aspen Skiing Company wanted to sell Blackcomb Mountain, a ski area that had opened six years earlier beside Whistler Mountain in British Columbia's Garibaldi Mountains. The 1982 recession had bankrupted the public-private partnership in charge of developing Whistler Village, a nascent base village situated between Whistler and Blackcomb, ninety minutes northeast of Vancouver, and the Aspen Skiing Company wanted out. (Blackcomb's development was separate from the partnership's work on Whistler Village, and the Aspen firm was not part of the bankruptcy.) Houssian saw the potential for real estate development associated with the struggling resort. He wanted in.

Houssian understood the impending demand for vacation real estate as Baby Boomers aged. By 1991, he had shifted Intrawest out of urban real estate and begun a decade-long resort-buying spree. Intrawest purchased Mt. Tremblant and Mt. Ste. Marie, Quebec; Panorama and Blue Mountain in Ontario; Whistler, next to Blackcomb (including much of Whistler Village); Stratton Mountain in southern Vermont; Copper Mountain, Colorado; Snowshoe, West Virginia; Mammoth Mountain, California; and Mountain Creek, New Jersey.

Houssian also made plans to build a ski village at Squaw Valley and partnered with Vail Resorts to build a forty-five-hundred-unit residential development at the base of Keystone, Colorado. In April 1997, Intrawest began trading on the New York and Vancouver stock exchanges. Its first offering of four million shares raised ninety-three million dollars.[4] In 2001 Intrawest teamed up with the Aspen Skiing Company to build a village at the base of Snowmass ski area.

Houssian branched into warm-weather destinations with the purchase of golf resorts in Florida and Arizona, and he launched a residential project in Las Vegas. The company got into Europe with a large stake in Compagnie des Alpes, a French mountain-resort operator. It bought the Breeze and Max ski-shop chains, and 45 percent of the company that owns Canadian Mountain Holidays, Canada's largest heli-skiing and helicopter-hiking company. It was all part of a strategy to help Intrawest rake in a larger portion of the visitor's dollar. With its careful understanding of the Baby Boomer demographic, Intrawest had positioned itself by the end of the twentieth century as a vacation brand, capable of satisfying the cold-weather and warm-weather whims of its customers.

George Gillett, founder of Booth Creek Ski Holdings, is an empire builder who threw together disparate businesses during the 1980s—principally meatpacking companies and television stations—with the help of Drexel Burnham Lambert, the infamous Beverly Hills junk-bond deal maker led by Michael Milken, a man who epitomized the avarice of the 1980s and eventually went to jail for fraud. With Milken's help, Gillett put together a billion-dollar empire and bought Vail Associates in 1985. Six years later, unable to service bonds that had interest rates as high as 17 percent, he declared bankruptcy. His friends at Drexel Burnham Lambert, however, did not abandon him. Leon Black, who had been hired by Milken, bought Vail out of bankruptcy, paid Gillett an annual salary of 1.5 million dollars to run the resort, and gave him stock options that eventually yielded 32 million dollars. With that nest egg, Gillett was back in business. He formed Booth Creek Ski Holdings in 1996 and acquired eleven ski resorts during the next two years.[5]

Gillett snapped up second-tier properties. These included Loon Mountain, Waterville Valley, and Mt. Cranmore in New Hampshire (the latter two spun off by American Skiing Company as part of an antitrust settlement with the U.S. Department of Justice); Northstar-at-Tahoe, Sierra-at-Tahoe, and Big Bear Mountain in California; the Summit at Snoqualmie, near Seattle; and Grand Targhee in eastern Idaho.[6]

Gillett's buying binge made Booth Creek the fourth-largest ski-area operator in the country, with 2.3 million skier visits in 1999, not counting Grand Targhee. In early 2000, Gillett stepped down from the job of running Booth Creek and bought Grand Targhee for eleven million dollars from the company he had founded.[7]

Leon Black, Gillett's old and generous friend, has been equally aggressive about muscling in to the ski industry. After purchasing Vail Associates (which encompassed Vail Mountain and Beaver Creek Resort) out of Gillett's bankruptcy, Black bought nearby Keystone and Breckenridge resorts from Ralston-Purina. In early 1997, what was now Vail Resorts hit the stock market with an initial public offering that raised 266 million dollars.[8] Vail Resorts also acquired Arapahoe Basin as part of the Ralston-Purina package; the U.S. Department of Justice obliged the company to sell this 490-acre ski area at the head of Keystone's Snake River Valley to avoid antitrust problems. But the company still held four of the largest resorts in Colorado, all within fifty miles of one another and a hundred miles or fewer from Denver. By 2000, Vail Resorts controlled 42 percent of Colorado's ski market and 8.8 percent of the U.S. market.[9]

✸ ✸ ✸

The ski industry consolidated during the 1990s because the market was flat and because the industry was expensive to run, costly to expand, and was now competing against other industries that sold "consumable experiences": theme parks and cruise lines. Unlike the post–World War II pioneers who commercialized skiing for the American public, these four major companies are not, at bottom, in the skiing business. Their quest for profit is not tempered by a love of the sport, nor is the joy found in mountain life their reason for doing business in the mountains. They are in the money-making business, yet paradoxically, there's little money to be made selling lift tickets. One only has to see it raining at the bottom of Sugarbush in February to appreciate how risky the ski industry is. When ski areas were small and low-tech, that risk was acceptable. If a small ski area didn't open until Christmas or closed before the end of March, it wasn't a big deal; there wasn't a lot at stake. Now, with hundreds of millions of dollars invested, high carrying costs on loans, and unceasing demand from Wall Street for rising rates of return, a great deal is on the table. For managers of these firms, minimizing the risks of weather and the vagaries of a flat and fickle market is a critical part of their job descriptions and corporate strategies.

To pay their debts, expand their companies, and keep stock-holders happy, the boards and executives of these firms have looked beyond the sport itself. That search has led them to move aggressively into real estate development and the conversion of ski areas into high-volume, industrial-scale, four-season resorts. They reduce risk by making skiing and snowboarding them-selves a relatively smaller portion of the corporate financial picture. "The U.S. continues to lead the world in investment in resort real estate," wrote *Ski Area Management* magazine in 2000, "and the trend to use winter sports almost as a loss leader to bring in revenue from base operations continues to be the more dominant financial model."[10]

It's a good strategy for the stockholders and bondholders, perhaps, but not so good for the communities that find the biggest company in town expanding its reach into retail stores, restaurants, property management, travel services, and other ostensibly local businesses.

From the companies' perspective, it made sense to tap into investors' understanding of the Baby Boomer demographic and consumer trends by issuing public debt and seeking equity financing amid the go-go stock markets of the 1990s. After all, the four major ski-area operators are trying to position them-selves to satisfy Boomers' demands; for many Americans, es-pecially wealthy Baby Boomers, the business of acquiring second homes and purchasing "consumable experiences" is the latest consumer fad. In a 1997 survey, six of ten Americans said they'd like to own a vacation home, making a second home the nation's most sought after status symbol.[11] One marketing di-rector at Intrawest noted that if Boomers buy vacation homes at the rate their parents did—seven per hundred—the number of second-home owners could rise 40 percent between 1997 and 2007, thanks to the population slug of Baby Boomers moving into their late forties and early fifties—their peak earnings years and, statistically, the age at which many people buy second homes.[12] Baby Boomers are not only earning top dollar at the turn of the millennium; they're also on the receiving end of an enormous intergenerational transfer of wealth. The average Boomer will inherit ninety thousand dollars from his or her World War II–generation parents. Put all that together and, demographers predicted, vacation-home purchases will jump from the 3.3 million homes bought in 1997 to 5 million in 2013, when the youngest Boomers will be forty-nine. From that date, with the passing of the Baby Boom generation out of its peak buying years, the second-home boom is expected to start a long decline.[13]

During the quarter-century that runs from the late 1980s until 2013, however, ski-resort developers, led by the Big Three, have a product to sell, and sell it they will. At a greater scale than ever before, ski areas have become amenities to drive real estate sales. As Intrawest CEO Houssian candidly admitted, "We don't consider ourselves in the ski business."[14] In his 1996 annual report to shareholders, Houssian defined the company as "a marriage of snow and steel, land and lumber, membership and service to create a company that redefines the mountain resort industry."[15]

Executives at the Big Three tend to shy away from blunt characterizations like Houssian's, preferring to maintain the marketing and advertising fiction that the purity and glory of skiing lies at the heart of their endeavors. But Vail Resorts made the relationship between skiing and real estate abundantly clear in its 1997 annual report: "To facilitate real estate development, VRDC [Vail Resorts Development Company, the firm's real estate arm] invests significant capital for on-mountain improvements, such as ski lifts, trails and snowmaking. These improvements enhance the value of the Company's real estate holdings." The report goes on to note that the installation of a chairlift into the Bachelor Gulch area of Beaver Creek "allowed VRDC to contract to sell 101 ski-in/ski-out,* single-family home sites adjacent to the Bachelor Gulch ski terrain for an average of $750,000 per home site."[16] Former Vail Resorts president Harry Frampton, now a real estate mogul whose company, Slifer, Smith and Frampton, is half-owned by Vail Resorts, reportedly has said that he is not concerned about whether or not his clients ski.[17]

Ironically, given that their business has less than ever to do with the passion of skiing, Intrawest executives in particular have the fervor of true believers. They seem convinced that what they are doing is good and right and that they are serving a profound need. "The type of real estate development we do creates a new attraction that goes beyond the skiing side of the business, and we think that has been a major success of our resorts," says Gary Raymond, Intrawest's vice president in charge of acquisitions and real estate. "We believe people are choosing our resorts for a lot more than the skiing. A huge part of the resort experience is coming out of the ambiance, the bars and restaurants. I think our villages are substantially changing the experiences when people come to a resort."[18]

From Intrawest's point of view, this "new attraction" fills an important need. "The direction is toward family and reconnecting with friends," says Michael Coyle, Intrawest's vice president for marketing. People want a place to gather, he says, and the dynamic ski villages built by Intrawest and its cohorts are providing that. "This big bunch of people is saying, 'I've got to make time for family and friends; I've got to make time for myself.' We [Intrawest] are booming because people do not consider this a luxury anymore; they consider our product a necessity."[19]

---

* "Ski-in/ski-out" is a real estate term for "beside the slopes."

For their part, American Skiing Company executives insist their primary interest is in running good ski areas, but even here, skiing's fit with real estate is a tight one. At each of American Skiing's resorts, the company has built or planned to build a "Grand Summit Hotel." Innovative when they were launched in the early 1990s, these 150-unit condominium hotels are sold in a quarter-share fractional-ownership format to six hundred buyers. An owner buys one-fourth of a condo and may use or rent it for thirteen weeks annually. This arrangement is similar to time-share ownership, except that under fractional ownership the buyers own tangible property, rather than an intangible right to occupy a unit for a certain increment of time. The net result is to make vacation property more affordable. At the company's new Jordan Grand Hotel at Sunday River, for example, a quarter-share of a studio can be purchased for a relatively affordable $24,900—far less than an entire condominium or house.[20] Fractional ownership gives a regular visitor a place to stay without the hassles of upkeep and maintenance— selling points for buyers who want mountain property but don't wish to spend their vacation taking care of it. These condos also provide owners with potential rental income. That income is split roughly fifty-fifty between the owners and American Skiing but is offset for each quarter owner by the company's management and utilities fee of several hundred dollars a month.

"The initial sale of quarter share units typically generates a high profit margin," declared American Skiing's 1998 annual report, "and the Company derives a continuing revenue stream from operating the hotel's retail, restaurant and conference facilities and from renting quarter share interval interests when [the units are] not in use by their owners."[21]

Les Otten's fractional-ownership strategy has been widely emulated throughout the ski-resort industry; shares as small as one-twelfth are being sold in some places. Despite this innovation, American Skiing has been, financially, the shakiest of the Big Three. Highly leveraged and battered by two bad snow years, the company was teetering on disaster's brink in 1998. American Skiing reportedly faced $400 million in debt; Oak Hill Capital Partners, an investment firm controlled by Texas billionaire Robert Bass, bailed the company out by providing $150 million in cash in exchange for 48.5 percent ownership.[22] The cash infusion helped, but not enough. By the end of July 2000, American Skiing showed long-term debt and redeemable preferred stock obligations of $627 million against $236 million in shareholder equity.[23] Some of the company's debt at that time bore exorbitant annual interest rates ranging from 17 to 25 percent, indicating a strong belief on the part of lenders that American Skiing Company might default on its loans. In the summer of 2000, majority control of American Skiing shifted from Otten to Oak Hill. Bass, according to a spokesman, saw potential in the company's resorts under construction, calling them "real growth opportunities."[24]

American Skiing had slid into a debt-workout situation, with the shots being called by a new owner likely to tighten the screws and get serious about straightening out the balance sheet. The value in that workout, given the demographic realities of the ski industry, almost certainly lay in American Skiing's real estate. Base villages, each comprising approximately twelve hundred residential units and 140,000 square feet of retail space, were planned and had been at least partially approved at the Canyons, Heavenly, Killington, and Sunday River.[25]

After Otten lost control, the slide continued. In December 2000, under intense financial pressure, American Skiing announced it would cease to exist under its own name. Citing demographic, industry, and meteorological realities, Otten announced the merger of his company with Meristar Hotels and Resorts, which runs 231 hotels and eleven golf courses across the United States. The merger was designed to help American Skiing restructure its debt and cut costs. It also got American

Skiing a $25 million loan from Meristar to complete the Heavenly Grand Summit Hotel in California. The planned merger appeared to have pushed the wolf back from American Skiing's door, but executives made it clear they were going to have to sell real estate aggressively to succeed.[26]

Three months later, however, the merger was off and Otten was out of a job. Two months after that, in May 2001, American Skiing announced it was cutting 14 percent of its full-time staff; would sell Steamboat ski area; would try to restructure $73 million worth of debt; and would shift its focus away from on-the-hill ski-area improvements and toward developing and selling real estate.[27] The conversion of Les Otten's dream from a skiing company to yet one more condominium sales office was effectively complete.

❋ ❋ ❋

Despite American Skiing's difficulties, the potential to make a lot of money from real estate development at these resorts is very real. At the Canyons, American Skiing had its greatest success with the Sundial Lodge, its first condominium hotel there. On August 4, 1998, the company created a feeding frenzy to sell the project. Borrowing a page from a sales technique Intrawest established, American Skiing created enough buzz to cause would-be buyers and real estate agents to stand in line for eight hours or longer for the right to purchase one of the 150 condominiums—units that existed only on paper. At the end of the day, the company had taken in $42.6 million, selling all the condos for prices ranging from $149,000 to $498,000.[28] That worked out to $450 to $480 per square foot, comparable to prices at the very high end nearby resort of Deer Valley.[29]

Intrawest's real estate sales performance has been even more impressive. During four consecutive weekends in 1998, the company sold 376 yet-to-be-built condominiums for $94 million at Stratton, Snowshoe, Copper, and Mammoth.[30] In April 1999, 139 condos-on-paper at Squaw Valley were sold in six hours for $73 million.[31] In August of that year, the company took in $25 million in only forty-five minutes at Keystone, selling twenty-six single-family home sites for prices from $279,900 to $624,900, and twenty-three condos for an average price of $635,000.[32]

This land rush also has helped bring about the resurgence of time-shares at ski resorts. Once the purview of the silk-shirt-and-gold-chain crowd of hustlers, the time-share industry reinvented itself in the 1990s. Unlike fractional ownership, time-share ownership does not convey a legal interest in real estate. A time-share buyer purchases only the right to occupy a property for a fixed time period each year. Major hotel chains, including Hyatt, Four Seasons, and Radisson, have jumped into the time-share business. They see a significant play in the ski-resort industry, and with good reason: sales of new U.S. time-shares jumped from $1.5 billion in 1992 to an estimated $4 billion in 2000.[33] Some of the hottest time-share property is at ski areas; in 1998, Marriott partnered with American Skiing to develop time-share hotels at five resorts. At Beaver Creek, the Hyatt Corporation sold the right to one week per year for an average price of $60,000. That's equal to a whole-ownership sales price of $3.1 million for each of the condos in the Hyatt Mountain Lodge.[34]

This is very profitable soil for developers to farm. In fiscal 1999, Intrawest made an operating profit of $59.6 million on $341.5 million in real estate sales—a margin of 17.5 percent. That margin was expected to rise to around 22 percent in future years.[35] Despite these healthy returns, the real estate component of the "New Ski Villages" being built by the Big Three does not stand alone. Resort executives tout the synergy of creating lively base areas full of people who will not only buy real estate, but also go on to spend money in other ways: skiing, shopping, dining, getting massages, renting videos, taking balloon rides, playing golf. The whole idea behind the New Ski Villages—an architectural and commercial concept adopted and spun to near-perfection by Intrawest—is not to make a single killing on real estate, but to keep making a killing.[36]

✳ ✳ ✳

Historically, on-mountain operations were divorced from what happened at the base of the ski hill. Those running the lifts had little or no interest in base area development. If a ski area was close to a town such as Aspen, the town provided the after-hours pizzazz. If it was farther out, such as Stowe, strip development along the access road sprang up. The exceptions were at Vail, Sun Valley, and Snowmass, where Bill Janss and Pete Seibert tried to control and profit from both the mountain and its base area. Their development model, invented in the 1960s and predicated on controlling and marrying base real estate and mountain operations, is for all intents and purposes the model now embraced by the Big Three. It has been updated and meticulously refined, and it is being implemented by corporations that can bring hundreds of millions of dollars to bear on design and construction, but the Big Three, with their New Ski Villages, are essentially reminting Seibert's and Janss's ideas of using ski-area amenities and strict development control to create valuable base real estate, marketed to as large a population of potential buyers as possible.

Making this strategy work means building, or rebuilding, base villages. The New Ski Villages are designed to be pedestrian friendly, human scale, lively, and inviting, full of retail energy and visitors of many ages, and free from motorized vehicles. If you think that description sounds like a giant retail mall, you wouldn't be far off; one of the buzz-phrases often used to describe the village formula is "entertainment retail," which—like many malls—predicates itself on positioning shopping as a form of entertainment. For many Americans, it is. According to the *Wall Street Journal*, the average American spent six hours shopping per week in the late 1980s, and only one in four mall shoppers was searching for a particular item.[37]

The inspiration for New Ski Villages comes largely from small European villages, but there aren't many American ski towns built like Lech or Zermatt. Unlike the Europeans, Americans created their mountain resorts in the era of the automobile, and it shows. So the reinvention of ski resorts is an enormously capital-intensive process. Intrawest, Vail, American Skiing, and Booth Creek, plus the privately held firm Hines Interests (which is developing villages at Winter Park and Aspen Highlands, both in Colorado, and at Montana's Big Mountain), plan to ante up more than $5 billion by 2008 redeveloping thirty U.S. and Canadian ski resorts.[38] With their leverage and market-leading positions, the Big Three have set the rules for how the resort game is being played. In a response that typifies the industry's follow-the-leader mentality, the Kircher family, which owns Boyne Mountain, Michigan, and several other small ski areas, announced in 2000 it will build a $150 million, four-season resort at Boyne.[39] And in Colorado, ten ski areas—including relatively tiny ones such as Wolf Creek—plan to invest $3 billion in development and redevelopment.[40]

Of course, village developers expect to earn their investment back in spades. The extension of the real estate–based ski area strategy to its absurd—albeit most profitable—extreme can be found at the Yellowstone Club, in southwestern Montana, open only to members and their guests. Here Tim Blixseth, a logging magnate who owns Big Sky Timber, is developing a five-thousand-acre ski area on eighteen-thousand acres of land near the resort of Big Sky. The new ski area is bigger than Snowmass, but Blixseth plans to sell a mere four hundred memberships. These people will pay $1.5 million simply to join the Yellowstone Club, and another million, on average, to buy a home site. Total estimated take for Blixseth: a cool $1 billion. That's not bad, considering his firm paid a reported $26 million for the entire property in 1991. Blixseth plans to invest $75 million in developing the resort—money he is reported to have cleared from other lands he logged and then swapped back to the federal government. Bottom line: with $26 million out of pocket, $1 billion is likely to come back.[41] At those rates of return, lift-ticket sales become irrelevant.

* * *

The Yellowstone Club is its own, insular world. Many other resorts where New Ski Villages are being built, from Stowe to Breckenridge to Mammoth, are closely affiliated with existing communities. It is impossible for a real estate feeding frenzy of this magnitude, and development of these boomtown proportions, to take place without the impacts being felt by everyone and everything in the neighborhood. Making money from this phenomenon is good for ski corporations. But what does it mean for their host towns?

Snow is a commodity, just like timber or oil or gas. Snow-dependent towns find their economies are commodity-dependent, and thus vulnerable to the vagaries of weather and the market. If the snow falls early and pictures of it show up on the Weather Channel, Monday Night Football, or national television news programs, more people book their vacations and the town prospers. If it doesn't snow significantly until December or later, as happened in Colorado in 1998 and 1999, skier numbers drop (despite extensive investments in snowmaking), and local merchants take a hit. In such a situation, ski-area host towns are doubly vulnerable—not only to the weather, but also to being deeply influenced by a corporation that might better survive these uncertainties.

"The community is to a large degree powerless as to what

the large corporation wants to do," says Les Otten. "There's a huge responsibility that comes with being the biggest business in town. Everything that you do affects everybody. It is not a democracy. People can't vote to remove us."[42]

Nevertheless, ski town residents can and do register their feelings. After American Skiing purchased Steamboat ski area from Kamori International in 1997, many residents had high hopes that the new owners would rejuvenate the thirty-eight-year-old northern Colorado resort, which had languished for a decade.[43] But Otten and his team overpromised and underdelivered, flooding the real estate market with new condominiums, preparing to compete with local businesses, and laying off veteran employees. Residents responded angrily, and bumper stickers declaring "More Snow, Less Otten" began appearing. When Otten lost his job in March 2001, a local restaurant held a party under the moniker "Otten to Be Forgotten." The ski area was put up for sale, and it was expected to go for 40 million dollars less than the company had paid four years earlier. The Steamboat Grand Resort Hotel and Conference Center, a condominium hotel the company built at a cost of 80 million dollars, also went on the block. In the wake of American Skiing's disastrous entry into the Colorado ski market, Steamboat Springs residents and resort executives did agree on one thing: American Skiing's strategies did not mesh with the goals or self-image of a town that has fielded more than fifty Olympic skiers and calls itself Ski Town USA.[44]

"Small communities have a profound and pervasive dependence upon 'uncle,' and I don't mean Uncle Sam," says Michael Kinsley, a community development consultant with the nonprofit resource policy think tank Rocky Mountain Institute in Old Snowmass, Colorado. "I mean Uncle Somebody-That's-Going-to-Come-In, and that will be our economic base, whether it's the government or the mine or the mill or whatever. One of the manifestations of this dependency is an incapacity to build internally, an incapacity for a community to get its act together for itself, and that's pervasive. It is so profoundly disempowering."[45]

In Steamboat Springs, Vail, and Breckenridge; in Bethel, Maine; in Mammoth Lakes and Winter Park, the big ski operators are the "uncle," the company in a company town. True, the economies of these towns are much more diverse than they were a century ago, when the company may truly have been all there was. But one need only imagine the effect of the ski area vanishing to understand that these investor-owned corporations remain by far the biggest player at local tables. As skiing has become more capital intensive, ski towns have become ever more dependent for their livelihoods on outside corporations and their publicly raised capital. No local entrepreneur can raise the sums of money necessary to compete at the top levels in today's ski industry.

✳ ✳ ✳

Although ski resorts resemble theme parks and cruise lines more than ever before, they are different in one key component: they develop public land in their search for profit. Without this key asset, ski areas have little to sell, especially in the West, where federal public lands make up a far greater portion of the landscape than in the East. Just as it once gave railroads alternating square-mile sections of land to promote westward expansion, the federal government today facilitates corporate mountain recreation through industry-friendly leases. At the Colorado Ski Museum in Vail, the U.S. Forest Service promotes itself in a diorama as "World Leaders in Skiing" and features its SKI US logo, shaped like a federal badge. The statistics here inform visitors that in 2000 there were 27 ski areas in Colorado, and 146 in the United States as a whole, situated on federal land. Among themselves, the Big Three ski operators lease more than forty thousand acres of Forest Service property.[46] Relative to the total holdings of the U.S. Forest Service (about 191 million acres nationwide), this is a minuscule portion of the public estate; ski areas nationwide lease less than one-tenth of 1 percent of Forest Service land.[47] Nevertheless, without that portion, these ski resorts would not exist in anything like their present configurations. Resort executives often argue that their effect on public land is tiny, because ski areas occupy so little of it. But that argument is disingenuous; there is a significant difference between the land actually occupied by ski areas and the land that is affected by them.

Resort development creates what economists call "positive externalities"—that is, ski lifts and ski trails on public land make the private property near them very, very valuable. This is a critical concept; it's the bedrock on which the major ski resorts' business plans are constructed. It's why Vail Resorts could sell Bachelor Gulch home sites for $750,000 apiece. If those were not slope-side properties, they would be worth significantly less. This reality—that on-mountain development drives off-mountain real estate prices and creates the initial attraction around which the New Ski Villages are constructed—is embedded in the business strategy not only of the Big Three and Booth Creek, but also of every ski resort now trying to build a base village.[48]

The ski-resort development phenomenon is structured by both industry and the government to profit the shareholders of public and private companies through the development of public lands. This business model would look familiar to an eastern capitalist investing in western development in the decades after the Civil War. Although they are dressed more presentably, and they are arguably not as rapacious as the railroad, logging, and mining companies of a century ago, Intrawest, American Skiing, and Vail Resorts at their core are predicated on exploiting the public estate for the private gain of distant shareholders—just as their Gilded Age predecessors were.

Resort executives strenuously deny such characterizations. "A hundred years ago, when people came into a valley and cut down all the trees and mined all the minerals and then got out of town is quite different than our business," says Intrawest CEO Joe Houssian. "We're in the environment business, we're in the nature business. We can't come into a town, into a mountain valley and change it. That is what attracts people to the place to start with, so we can't leave it in a worse condition than when we found it. Our objective is to put it in a better condition and to provide to the community things they would not otherwise have had—churches and schools."[49]

That sounds well and good, and it's important not to tar one company with the behavior of another. But a look at how Vail Resorts treated the small community of Minturn, Colorado, demonstrates that when push comes to shove, big ski-area developers are very willing indeed to behave like the corporate Goliaths that ran the show in much of the American West in the late nineteenth and early twentieth centuries.

✳ ✳ ✳

Minturn, a quiet former railroad town of about two thousand people, sits beside the abandoned Denver and Rio Grande tracks along the Eagle River. Minturn is sandwiched between Vail and Beaver Creek, a mile south of Interstate 70. It has a lot of potential land for development—room for a residential population of seven thousand. Until recently it had water rights to seven cubic feet per second (cfs) from the Eagle River, enough to support that level of development. But Vail Resorts, which is developing thirsty golf courses and subdivisions downstream, wanted that water, and it challenged the town's well-established water rights in court.

Colorado water law is perhaps the most complex in the world; by some estimates, roughly half the world's water lawyers live in Colorado. (Samuel Clemens, traveling the West, supposedly said that in this region, "Whisky is for drinking, and water is for fighting.") What Vail's attack meant for Minturn was an intolerably expensive legal battle. The town budget in 1998 was only $801,000, and almost one-fifth of that had to be dedicated to legal fees for the fight with Vail Resorts. The cost for the community was brutal: Minturn could not afford to keep paying its fire chief, police chief, public works director, town clerk, or other employees. It sold its town hall to a private developer. It began accepting private donations for its legal fund. After a year battling Vail Resorts, facing bankruptcy without ever having had even a first court hearing on the merits of the case, Minturn folded its hand and agreed to let Vail Resorts have the water. "This is about development and snowmaking, and they can't do either without water," said Minturn town manager Alan Lanning shortly afterward. "We've nearly exhausted our reserves. I don't feel we have a lot of choice here." Vail executives denied the assertion that the water was needed for snowmaking and development—but it's hard to imagine why else the company would go after the town so aggressively.[50]

Profit making from public resources, often at the expense of others, is a good deal for corporate stockholders. It is a venerable tradition that dates from the nineteenth century. American mining companies, for instance, pay no royalty at all to the federal government for hard-rock minerals such as gold and silver that are removed from public lands, courtesy of the 1872 Mining Act, which is still the law. For decades during the twentieth century, the U.S. Forest Service lost money in its dealings with private business. It subsidized the logging industry by selling public timber for too little and footing the bill for the construction of roads to drag that timber to market. Cattle ranchers—many of them operating on behalf of large corporations—still graze livestock on the public domain at a cost of less than two dollars per month for each cow and calf pair, and the cattle trample stream banks, foul rivers, overgraze forage, and displace native wildlife.

The cost to the nation of corporate feeding at the public trough in the ski-resort world is more subtle, at least insofar as human communities are concerned. What is almost universally left unsaid by resort executives is that there is a real cost to converting a ski town into a year-round, full-to-the-gills resort. The town's atmosphere and fabric are transformed. Life in the ski town starts to look a lot more like the daily rat race anywhere else.

It may be romantic to believe that the changes brought to ski towns by the Big Three and their imitators are not good. But that is not necessarily reason to dismiss this belief. The whole premise behind skiing, and the appeal of the sport, always has been based on its romance. Skiing traditionally was about freedom to be in the mountains in winter, to enjoy nature on its terms—it was about *Idraet*. This ideal infected ski towns. The past always looks better from a distance, and the argument that those were the good old days does not paint a complete picture. But it is a legitimate argument, one that acknowledges there was a golden moment for most ski resorts. Nevertheless, the assertion that the way things used to be was better is quickly dismissed by pro-development corporations as uninformed opposition to progress, or a selfish desire to keep others from enjoying what the obstructionists already have. What those who promote development fail to understand, or willfully ignore, is that it was precisely that act—keeping others out, by choice, by geography, or by the nature of the local economy—that made so many ski towns special. A place is not an enclave, not an escape, not a magical part of the cultural margin if it is easy to get to and if its economy and values mirror those of society at large.

During the 1950s, 1960s, and 1970s, most of the world was not kept out of ski towns; it simply did not want to come in.

What the New Ski Villages and their developers do is make it easier for everyone to come, to go, to profit. They have significantly lowered the barriers for visitors and new residents. These places are easier to get to, more familiarly pleasant to stay in. The economy gets bigger, and it becomes possible to make a decent living—quite often working for the New Ski Village developer. The trade-offs of living in the mountains as compared to urban areas become less distinct, and the possibility to ameliorate these trade-offs grows with population and tax receipts. Medical clinics are built, schools are improved, roads are widened, high-speed Internet access becomes available. Some of this is funded by developers as part of the cost of development; some of it comes from the increased populations now living in and near the ski towns. Everything grows.

✳ ✳ ✳

The corporate realities of the modern ski industry compel ski resorts to compete for the mass market. By definition, that means appealing to large volumes of people who will enjoy what are essentially standardized experiences—rather than the unique and distinctive experiences that made each ski town attractive in the first place. Scott Oldakowski, vice president for real estate and marketing at American Skiing, describes the company's approach to how it is providing its product this way:

> I would draw a parallel to Disney. There's a certain expectation you would have that's been set by Disney when you get to their resort. When you get there, the experience is always the same, although the experience feels new to you individually. We've gone out and said, "This is how a skier would like to be treated, this is how they'd like to find things and discover things and experience things." We can create what we feel is a collective expectation of a staged experience when they go on vacation at this particular location at this particular resort.[51]

At the Canyons in Utah, for instance, skiers won't only be presented with what Utah is—they'll be presented with what American Skiing thinks that skiers think Utah should be.

American Skiing spokesman Skip King makes a similar argument. The McDonald's Corporation is successful, King said, because it standardizes everything. American Skiing is trying to standardize its snowmaking, for instance, so that all its snow is of consistently good quality. King reaches for another corporate analogy when he describes his company's Holiday Inn approach to standardization, breaking its various business operations down to core, measurable performances that combine to create an easily replicated, standardized visitor experience.[52]

Doing this makes sense for American Skiing and other corporations in the ski industry. But how is it fundamentally any different from what is done by Disney, Carnival Cruise Lines, McDonald's, or Holiday Inn, where you can expect every experience, meal, or room to be the same? Should it come as any surprise that the Disney Corporation reportedly pondered purchasing Intrawest in 2000?[53] Or that the National Ski Areas Association annual convention in 2000 was held in Orlando, Florida, to study theme park operations?[54] To a man and woman, everyone involved in developing the New Ski Villages will deny they are killing the goose that laid the golden egg—an oft-voiced fear regularly raised in the face of new development. They say their whole approach is to preserve and nurture that goose—call it nature, a sense of specialness, community, the beauty of the mountains—because it is what makes their particular ski town attractive. Yet this insistence verges on the absurd when the very essence of what industrial-volume tourism corporations do is to standardize visitor experiences in towns that were attractive precisely because they weren't standardized at all.

It is true that bringing more business, and more money, into ski-town economies often has an economic benefit for the people who live there. But if they have to work all year because they can no longer afford to take a couple of months off; if they have to commute an hour each way because housing near the ski slopes is too expensive; if they have to risk their lives on icy roads just to get to their jobs; if they hardly have time to ski anymore; if all these things are true, are they really better off?

The modern ski business as practiced by the Big Three brings urbanization and all its problems and imperatives to places that historically have been wholly nonurban—and that some residents wish would remain that way. The realities of modern life are being shoved into mountain enclaves that were not part of the American economic mainstream until the last two decades of the twentieth century. The Big Three ski companies did not start this process, but they are pursuing it more aggressively, and more effectively, than anyone ever has before.

CHAPTER 4

What Is Land For?
A Theological Schism

In June 1996, Wayne Ethridge came to understand in his gut the true cost of ski-area development. Driving at night, Ethridge came across an elk calf frothing at the mouth as it desperately tried to get through a half-mile-long wooden plank fence lining a dirt road that is a short cut between Snowmass Village and Aspen.

The fence belonged to Peter Guber, a Hollywood producer who, during the 1980s, purchased eight hundred acres of prime elk calving ground in a low saddle at the edge of the Maroon Bells–Snowmass Wilderness area. The decorative fence Guber built cuts across the traditional narrow migratory route for a herd of what was then three hundred elk that summered in the wilderness area and wintered on public and private land farther down the Roaring Fork Valley. Local residents had long criticized the fence as a serious barrier to an elk herd already being pressed hard by Snowmass ski area on one side and Buttermilk ski area on the other. Government officials did little more than wring their hands. In October 1995, Aspen environmental activist Dan Kitchen kicked several boards out of the fence in the presence of a newspaper photographer to make his point that elk were dying while bureaucrats fiddled. He went to jail as a vandal for a few days; the fence stayed up.

Ethridge—a former Pitkin County commissioner who

struggled vainly in the 1980s and early 1990s against resort sprawl—wrote in a letter to the editor of the *Aspen Times* about how he tried with a friend to help the calf, which only terrified the animal further. Eventually it scrambled over the fence. "Since its mother was nowhere to be seen," Ethridge wrote, "we could only hope that it would find her before it was discovered by predators."

Can the Aspen Skiing Company, the privately held firm that runs Aspen, Snowmass, Buttermilk, and Aspen Highlands resorts, be held directly responsible for the fate of that elk calf? No. But there is a chain of connectivity between development of the ski resort—and even more directly between the associated development of surrounding private lands that takes advantage of the "positive externality" (that is, rising real estate values) created by ski area development—and an elk calf trapped by a decorative fence.

Peter Guber almost certainly bought his mountain retreat because of the natural beauty and wildlife that came with it, as well as the great skiing nearby. He wasn't present that June night to see the results of his aesthetic choices. Few such people are. But across the West, elk are being squeezed out not so much by ski areas themselves as by the people, traffic, dogs, and developments the ski lifts bring in their wake.

What's happening to elk happens to other species around resorts, too—just less visibly. A growing understanding of these kinds of environmental costs has led many mountain town residents into deep opposition to the modern ski industry. Their profound beliefs about the land—often more of a gut feeling than an articulated philosophy—are informed by the ethics of John Muir, Henry David Thoreau, Aldo Leopold, and David Brower. They resent in their hearts the venerable corporate strategy of squeezing shareholder profits from public lands at the expense of the natural environment.

The most expensive and widely publicized act of environmental vandalism ever committed in the United States was perpetrated against the ski industry on Vail Mountain. Throughout the late 1990s, a bitter political battle raged as Vail Resorts ground through the approval process to expand its flagship ski area. Already 4,644 acres in size, the ski area would nearly double with the addition of 4,100 acres via an expansion called Category III that pushed into the timbered terrain south of Vail's Back Bowls. Included in that land were seven hundred acres of old-growth forest and what many conservationists and biologists considered to be among the very best habitat in Colorado for the shadowy and rare Canada lynx, an elusive feline predator. On the night of October 18, 1998, just after construction on the expansion had begun, somebody set fires that destroyed Vail Mountain's Two Elks Restaurant, its ski patrol headquarters, and four of its ski lift buildings. The damage was estimated at twelve million dollars. An underground group calling itself Earth Liberation Front put out an e-mail press release declaring, "Putting profits ahead of Colorado's wildlife will not be tolerated. This action is just a warning. We will be back if this greedy corporation continues to trespass into wild and unroaded areas."[1] More than two years later, despite FBI and grand jury investigations, nobody had been charged with the Vail arson.

※ ※ ※

In his 1971 book *Encounters with the Archdruid*, the journalist John McPhee described how David Brower, longtime executive director of the Sierra Club, preached a form of religion through his environmentalism. The creed that Brower espoused is a relatively new idea in the western world. It is the philosophy that drove the Vail arsonists to do what they did,[2] and it is one-half of a bitter, essentially theological schism in the collective American consciousness about what land—in particular public land—should be used for. Is nature a warehouse or a temple?

(Albeit perhaps a temple with a gym attached.) The answer depends on whom you ask, and those on opposite sides of the fence share little common ground. This philosophical divide runs as deeply through ski towns as anywhere in America; the resulting cultural battle is joined most closely by ski-resort developers and those who oppose them.

For most of the last two thousand years, European cultures, including those that settled North America, have followed religious doctrines, and their attendant philosophies, which maintain that nature is to be used for human benefit. The most widely accepted origins of this concept, at least as far as the United States is concerned, lie in the first pages of the Bible:

> And God blessed them, and God said unto them, Be fruitful, and multiply, and replenish the earth, and subdue it: and have dominion over the fish of the sea, and over the fowl of the air, and over every living thing that moveth upon the earth.[3]

The idea of "dominion" has generally been understood to mean control over, use of, and superiority to the rest of the natural world. In the developing United States of the nineteenth century, this worldview was elevated to its apogee through the popular apprehension and application of the concept of manifest destiny, a phrase coined by John L. O'Sullivan, editor of the *New York Post*. Writing in the August 1845 issue of *United States Magazine and Democratic Review*, O'Sullivan declared, "It is our manifest destiny to overspread the whole of the continent which Providence has given us for the development of the great experiment entrusted to us." The "great experiment" was America's approach to democracy, a democracy rooted in land ownership. Thomas Jefferson hoped the citizenry would be composed of "yeoman farmers," each working his own small plot of territory. Jefferson is believed by some scholars to have referred to philosopher John Locke's "life, liberty, and property" when he drew up the immortal phrase "life, liberty, and the pursuit of happiness" as the trio of "unalienable rights" cited in the Declaration of Independence. The similarity of phrase suggests that, in the minds of many early Americans, property and happiness sprang from the same wellhead. For many Americans today, this idea still holds true.

The founding fathers' philosophical support for widespread ownership and use of land was one of the underpinnings of American society that made the new nation so different from Europe. There, land generally was held by an elite and worked by a mass of landless laborers. America truly was different from the rest of the world in this regard. To nineteenth-century Americans living east of the Mississippi, the territories of the American West were represented as boundless, fertile, and ripe. These lands cried out for settlement, which Americans believed to be the Christian, civilizing (in other words, good) thing to do. The fact that Mexico, Russia, England, and native tribes had claims to or inhabited the lands in question was of little concern to American settlers or to the American federal government. The principle of manifest destiny was that God and progress (often commingled in the popular culture) were on the side of the settlers. Typically, empires on the move claim God as their ally and as a justification for their acts; the moral foundation for U.S. expansion into what was to become the American West was no different.

Horace Greeley, editor of the *New York Tribune*, famously advised, "Go West, young man, and grow up with the country." The West, like America itself, was and remains a nearly mythical region where people could reinvent themselves—a concept that was in itself profoundly and uniquely American. In the nineteenth century, the West was a territory where settlers could stake out a piece of land as their own. The federal government actively promoted this process with the Graduation Act of 1854, which reduced the sale price of public land to twenty-five cents per acre; with the Homestead Act of 1862, which allowed settlers to claim land they farmed; and with the 1872 Mining Act, which promoted exploitation and settlement of mineralized areas.[4] The land in question was not simply there for the taking, according to those who promoted such settlement; it was a bountiful, munificent, modern incarnation of Eden that would shower its blessings on settlers.

This gauzy conception of the West was advanced by many boosters during the mid- and late nineteenth century. William Gilpin, the first territorial governor of Colorado, may have been more overwrought and more willing than any other man to overlook the facts on the ground in his tireless promotion of settlement and human development.[5] The land breathlessly described and ceaselessly championed by Gilpin and others, for whom facts were of little use, did sound like a veritable Eden—and Eden, of course, was a place God had created for man. But beginning around the mid-nineteenth century—about the same time as the idea of manifest destiny seized the public imagination—an alternative American vision of the relationship between man and nature began to be advanced by Ralph Waldo Emerson, Henry David Thoreau, and John Muir. This conception was best summarized by Thoreau's phrase "In wildness is the preservation of the world."

Thoreau in particular developed the idea that the natural world was a wonderful and valuable thing in and of itself, that it did not need to be improved upon by man and indeed was the manifestation of God. "Nature is full of genius," he wrote, "full of the divinity; so that not a snowflake escapes its fashioning hand."[6] Thoreau, placing himself diametrically opposite Jefferson's Lockean definition of happiness, argued that man cheapened himself by striving for material riches: "A man is rich in proportion to the number of things he can afford to let alone."[7]

Thoreau died young, at the age of forty-five in 1862, never having been much of a literary success during his life. Like so many men before their time, he is posthumously celebrated, his works still in print worldwide 150 years after he wrote them. His ideas were enlarged upon, and much more widely disseminated, by John Muir, the founder of the Sierra Club, who was born when Thoreau was a young man and died in 1914. Muir made the beauties of California's Sierra Nevada famous, campaigned to protect what became Yosemite National Park, and fought ceaselessly to save the great redwoods. Building on Thoreau's thinking, Muir often wrote of trees as sentient, animate beings. For example, in an essay published posthumously, he wrote:

> We are often told that the world is going from bad to worse, sacrificing everything to Mammon. But this righteous uprising in defense of God's trees in the midst of exciting politics and wars is telling a different story, and every Sequoia, I fancy, has heard the good news and is waving its branches for joy. The wrongs done to trees, wrongs of every sort, are done in the darkness of ignorance and unbelief, for when light comes the heart of the people is always right.[8]

He went on to refer to a dead redwood that

> still stands erect and holds forth its majestic arms as if alive and saying, "Forgive them; they know not what they do." Now some millmen want to cut all the Calaveras trees into lumber and money. But we have found a better use for them. No doubt these trees would make good lumber after passing through a sawmill, as George Washington after passing through the hands of a French cook would have made good food. But both for Washington and the tree that bears his name higher uses have been found.

This is an extraordinary, head-on attack on the premise that nature's bounty should be employed only for economic purposes. Muir appropriates Christian symbolism in his assertion of a philosophy that is directly opposed to the idea of man's dominion over the natural world. In Muir's essay the reader can hear echoes of Jonathan Swift's seminal satire *A Modest Proposal*, an ironic economic treatise that suggested the starving children of Ireland could profitably be butchered to feed the English gentry, thus ameliorating Irish poverty.[9] Muir's writings often reflected his own satirical exasperation at Americans' insistence on viewing the natural wonders of the land simply as so much bounty for the taking.

Thoreau and Muir believed nature was an unadulterated good, that it was more than a rude and savage place that required taming and control at the hand of man in order to yield its riches. Theirs was not a new concept to Native Americans or to indigenous peoples who lived, and continue to live, in a traditional subsistence manner around the earth. But it was surely strange new ground for Americans who tied their national identity so deeply to the Judeo-Christian philosophy of dominion over nature and to the national might and greatness waiting to be tapped in America's imperial inland territories.

✳ ✳ ✳

The idea that nature should be valued in its own right gained currency slowly during the twentieth century. The most significant early result of this nascent philosophy was the creation of a system of national parks intended to preserve the crown jewels of America's natural beauty from human depredations. The first park, Yellowstone, was brought into being by Congress in 1872. Such preserves were an American invention; no other nation had ever thought to set aside portions of its territory for their natural beauty and to make these places available to average citizens for pleasure and admiration. It was a popular idea; 130 years after Yellowstone, 341 national parks and monuments have been created in the United States.[10]

Muir was a great champion of national park designation.

His ideas were advanced in a different direction after his death by a movement that craved not simply parks but wilderness. In 1919, a U.S. Forest Service architect named Arthur H. Carhart was sent to Trappers Lake in northern Colorado to plan for the development of private cabins around the water's edge. Carhart returned with the plans, but he also brought a radical idea back to his office at the Forest Service: the lake should not be developed at all. He became one of the first agitators for protecting portions of the public estate as wilderness.[11] Trappers Lake was included in the Flattops Primitive Area in 1932 and is often cited as the home of the idea of wilderness. Others in the agency, including Bob Marshall and Aldo Leopold, were pushing in similar directions around the same time.

"We abuse land because we regard it as a commodity belonging to us," Leopold wrote in *A Sand County Almanac*, a slim 1949 text that many conservationists regard as the *Walden* of the twentieth century. "When we see land as a community to which we belong, we may begin to use it with love and respect." He laid out plainly an alternative set of values, values quite apart from those that had informed the development of the nation for two centuries: "We face the question of whether a still higher 'standard of living' is worth its cost in things natural, wild and free. For us of the minority, the opportunity to see geese is more important than television, and the chance to find a pasqueflower is a right as inalienable as free speech."[12]

Through efforts spearheaded by the Wilderness Society (founded in 1935) in the 1950s and 1960s, that "right" was formally recognized in another extraordinary American innovation: wilderness protection. The 1964 Wilderness Act, passed after eight years of congressional wrangling and signed by President Lyndon Johnson, made a remarkable statement in light of the nation's heritage of manifest destiny: "In contrast with those areas where man and his own works dominate the landscape, [wilderness] is hereby recognized as an area where the earth and its community of life are untrammeled by man, where man himself is a visitor who does not remain."[13]

Rather than being the end of the question, however, the Wilderness Act became the beginning of a movement and set the stage for contemporary clashes over, among other things, ski-resort development. Outside the national park system, wilderness is the only designation that can prevent despoliation of public land. And there is a great deal of land in the public domain, especially in the West. Today, the Bureau of Land Management, created within the Department of the Interior in 1946 in a merger of the General Land Office with the Federal Grazing Service,[14] controls 264 million acres; the U.S. Forest Service, part of the Department of Agriculture, holds 191 million acres. For the most part, the BLM oversees the lowlands and deserts, the Forest Service the higher country. It's a lot of terrain, and for the latter half of the twentieth century most of it was managed by those agencies as a supply depot. By and large, officials at the BLM and Forest Service believed their job was to encourage and facilitate logging, mining, and grazing. Despite changing times and ethics, many still believe that.

Nevertheless, the idea of wilderness as proposed by Thoreau and Muir and advanced by Leopold and Carhart gained a firm toehold in the American consciousness. Its defenders became, if not legion, at least vocal and effective. They challenged the historic American approach to public lands ingrained in the bureaucracies of federal land agencies. They turned the nineteenth-century logic of dominion, of the inherent good of human progress, on its head. "Instead of mountain men," wrote Edward Abbey, perhaps the most vehement and widely published defender of wilderness in the 1970s and 1980s, "we are cursed with a plague of diggers, drillers, borers, grubbers; of asphalt-spreaders, dam-builders, overgrazers, clearcutters, and strip-miners whose object seems to be to make our mountains match our men—making molehills out of mountains for a race of rodents—for the rat race."[15]

Abbey became most famous for his 1975 book *The Monkey Wrench Gang*, a novel in which an unlikely quartet of activists attempts to wreak havoc on everything from billboards to dams across the American Southwest. Soon *monkeywrenching* had entered the popular lexicon. In 1981 a group of environmental activists inspired by Abbey formed Earth First!, committed to defending the earth from human depredations. Its symbol was a raised green fist; its slogan, "No compromise in defense of Mother Earth." Today, the Earth First! ethic has spread broadly. Tree-sitters camp for months in old-growth forest to thwart loggers, public officials are smeared with buffalo entrails and rotten salmon by critics of their environmental policies, and lawyers nationwide fight to defend the habitats of endangered animals and plants. And they have achieved some measurable successes. By 2000, wilderness advocates had convinced Congress to increase the 9.1-million-acre wilderness designation of 1964 to 96.4 million acres.[16]

✳ ✳ ✳

For the skiing world, the Vail arson was the exclamation point marking the final rupture in a deep, truly unbridgeable gap within American society regarding man's relationship to nature. The vast majority of Americans still believe in the Judeo-Christian ethic of dominion. But many question how far that ethic can reasonably be extended, and a significant portion of the population thinks it isn't necessarily an appropriate, valid, or ultimately wise approach to the natural world. The schism plays out in many arenas, from the question of whether global warming is scientific fact to the morality of genetic engineering to debates over establishing new wilderness areas.

The division is especially visible in battles that pit wilderness advocates against adherents of the so-called Wise Use movement, whose creed is the modern extension of manifest destiny. Wise Users, whose organizations often are funded in part by corporate contributors who support their agenda, have a deep antipathy for wilderness designations, endangered species protection, and other limitations set on behalf of nature. They believe public lands exist to provide livelihoods (often via resource extraction) and recreation for local residents and that the rest of the country—particularly as represented by the federal government—shouldn't tell them what to do or how to do it. This is the approach to public-lands management that held sway for much of the twentieth century, and Wise Users see no reason to abandon it. Some of their professed beliefs—for instance, that endangered species should be allowed to go extinct because they can't evolve fast enough—brush against the lunatic fringe. But the deepest roots of the Wise Use movement and its strategies tap into the Judeo-Christian philosophy of dominion. Wise Users embody the distillation of that belief system.

On the other side of the debate is a more diffuse group of Americans who see nature as a shrine. Like Muir, Thoreau, and Abbey, they believe humans must change their ways. The use of nature for profit, for growth and more growth, is to them an obscenity. To people on this side of the divide, using land— especially public land—for corporate profit is a cardinal sin.

"We are all the poorer because some of the last, best lynx habitat in the state [of Colorado] is now a rich skier's playground [in Vail's Category III expansion area]," says Sloan Shoemaker, conservation director for the nonprofit Aspen Wilderness Workshop. "Even the value of knowing they were out there was immeasurable."[17]

Shoemaker, a lanky, fit, and articulate man who possesses a smile like Bobby Kennedy's, spends a lot of time in his home office in Basalt, Colorado, fighting the constant pressure for ski-area growth. His battleground is the White River National Forest, which hosts more skiers than any other forest in the country. "Public lands weren't set aside in order to continue to provide a growth possibility for industry," he says. "Public lands are the last place where the ecological processes and evolutionary processes that created these lands may be allowed to continue. We have so altered every other square foot of land in North America that, really, public lands are the only places where large-scale fires may happen, where natural succession can continue to happen, where insects and disease can continue to shape how ecosystems function and work, and where the evolutionary processes of natural selection can continue."

Like the late David Brower, who was a skier and a Tenth Mountain Division veteran, many early skiers considered themselves environmentalists, and many of the early environmentalists were skiers, just as they were hikers and climbers. The appreciation of beauty in nature, beauty quite apart from nature's potential utility, has always been an inherent part of skiing's history. For the Swedes and Norwegians who brought skiing as *Idraet* to the United States, the sport depended on wild nature. It was a way to get out and enjoy the winter world. It seemed reasonable to early wilderness activists and environmentalists to reach out to recreationists such as skiers for political purposes. After all, who better to help fight for protection of wild places than those who had visited them and come to understand them?

Activists who would rather not see prime public lands developed or despoiled made a conscious decision four decades ago to embrace outdoor recreationists, to draw them in as allies. In the late 1950s, Brower learned the hard way the consequences of not involving more people in the fight to preserve America's wild places. In his preface to Eliot Porter's book *The Place No One Knew: Glen Canyon on the Colorado,* Brower describes how he and the rest of America's environmental community did not oppose the U.S. Bureau of Reclamation's plans to drown Glen Canyon beneath Lake Powell because neither he, nor almost anyone else, had visited the canyon in time to intervene effectively.[18] Perhaps the most sylvan and beautiful locale on the Colorado River, Glen Canyon was a deep and mysterious gorge where the Colorado River cut through the lonely, forbidding, and almost unknown red-rock deserts of southern Utah. Those few travelers who did traverse the gorge before its inundation remain almost universally enraptured with its beauty and mournful of its loss.

Brower learned that lesson well, and in the years since the loss of Glen Canyon the Sierra Club and many other environmental organizations became adept at taking their arguments to the American public, building large memberships, and buying expensive national advertisements to promote their conservation agendas in the political mainstream. The strategy worked, as the nation's record of wilderness preservation and the growing list of national parks and monuments can attest. What the conservation and preservation community did not count on, however, was how recreationists would become partners not only of preservation on the one hand, but also of development on the other—and perhaps nowhere so prominently as in skiing.

The scope of today's ski-town developments—which are, after all, at least nominally predicated on recreation—is mindboggling. In Mammoth, California, a town of 5,500 residents on the Eastern Sierra Front, Intrawest is investing $500 million in real estate, golf courses, and on-mountain upgrades of lifts and restaurants; total planned investment, including that of other parties, approaches $900 million, equal to $164,000 for every current resident.[19] At the Canyons Ski Resort, near Park City, Utah, the American Skiing Company is proceeding with its ambitions to build the largest ski resort in the United States, planning five million square feet of new construction in retail space, hotels, and residences.[20] Vail Resorts and Intrawest Corporation, which jointly own land at the base of Keystone ski area known as Keystone Village, plan by 2012 to have constructed 4,500 residential units and 382,000 square feet of commercial space in an alpine valley 10,000 feet high.[21]

National environmental groups have been slow to grapple with the implications of this new, virulent ski-resort development, perhaps in part because many members of those groups are skiers, just as they are mountain bikers, hikers, kayakers, rock climbers, and peak baggers. As logging and grazing on public lands diminish, recreation is growing to the point where it is becoming the most significant human impact on our lands. Even though many Americans have come around to Muir's and Thoreau's views of nature, our collective behavior still treats nature as a commodity—a place to be mined, if not for resources then for experiences. It is precisely this attitude that has given rise to the corporate ski development of today. It is easy for an environmental group to point to someone else—a logging company, a mining firm, or a ski resort—and charge that they are the problem. It is much harder to look in the mirror and say, We are the problem. This may be why the executive director of the Sierra Club admitted in 1998 that the group did not yet have a "fully realized strategy" for dealing with the implications of such industrial recreation.[22]

Those implications are huge. The United States Environmental Protection Agency recognized this when its staff at the Region VIII office in Denver provided comments to Colorado's White River National Forest on a revised forest management plan:

> No other land management prescription on the Forest directly results in more stream-water depletion, wetland impacts, air pollution, permanent vegetation change, or permanent habitat loss [than ski areas]. In the last planning cycle, more wetland impacts and stream depletions resulted from ski area expansion and improvement than from all other Forest management activities combined, including many direct and indirect impacts that are permanent (irreversible and irretrievable).[23]

* * *

Developments on public lands "are subsidizing the rich to get richer," says Joan May, executive director of the Sheep Mountain Alliance, a bare-bones environmental group of a few hundred members based in Telluride, Colorado. In the land-use wars over ski area development, May and her group stand clearly on the Thoreau-Brower side of the divide. "Why are we doing that? It's public land for everybody. Why are we using it to make wealthy people wealthier?"

Phil Miller, a fifty-year veteran of the ski business, agrees. "The early years that I was in it, a ski area, there really wasn't anything wrong with it," he says. "The most significant thing is this obscene wealth that's descended on us. Before this big boom we just didn't have this wealth and all these people who have these extravagant lifestyles. I think it's really bad that ski areas have become kind of like the golf course—it's nice to have the ski-in, ski-out place, or live next to the ninth hole."[24]

Phil and Linda Miller moved to Telluride in the 1970s. I sit with Joan May and them in the Millers' home on Columbia Avenue, a tall, narrow, brick Victorian house with aspen trees out front and a view to the south toward the ski slopes. Phil, although a little stooped now, is thin and fit, given to riding his mountain bike around town in the summers and cross-country skiing in the winters. Linda is vivacious, full of smiles, and quick to laugh, with sparkling blue eyes.

After spending almost three years as a combat infantryman in the Pacific during World War II, Phil returned to the West to begin a three-decade career with the U.S. Forest Service. During the 1950s, he was a Forest Service snow ranger at Winter Park ski area. He took a couple of years off to be a ski bum, patrolling the mountain and teaching the sport. He met Linda in Winter Park and went back to work for the Forest Service. When he retired in 1979, they settled in this eighty-year-old house in

Telluride and Phil started teaching skiing again. But in the years since, he has become a powerful opponent of the Telluride ski area, particularly its expansion plans. In 2000, after an acrimonious legal battle with the Millers and their allies, the Forest Service approved Telluride's plans to add 733 acres of new terrain to its existing 1,050 acres. It was a decision that deeply saddens the Millers.

"What they tell you is they want to have this ski area here, Telluride, be competitive," Phil says. "But what does that mean? Is it competitive against ski areas on the White River [forest], on another national forest? Here you've got one national forest competing against another. This is driven by profit, and then profit becomes paramount and the environment becomes secondary. The human species is just a weed species. It's an opportunistic invader."

Those are fighting words to Wise Users, resort developers, and ski-area executives who deeply believe in the Judeo-Christian approach to land use. They may mouth platitudes about limits and environmental protection, but they fundamentally believe that growth is an inherent good and that what they are doing brings the greatest good to the greatest number of people. In their minds, their work is a worthy enterprise.

"For some people who want to live in a very small place with no people around and one ski lift and one local grocery store, probably what we do isn't good," Joe Houssian told me a few months before I met with the Millers. Houssian, a soft-spoken, tan man with deep brown eyes and a frizz of curly white hair, met me at his home in Whistler, British Columbia. The sprawling building on the hillside had just been completed. Teenagers romped in the high-ceilinged great room; Houssian and I retired to a small den, crowded with overstuffed couches, recessed lights, and dark paneling. The chief executive of Intrawest spoke like someone who is accustomed to being listened to. "But," he continued, "I think for the large majority of the population, they would like to see a mountain valley stay pristine but at the same time provide services. For the visitors who come to the valley, services like restaurants, chairlifts, and all of the things that really are attractive. For those who live in the valley, they're interested in those, but they're also interested in schools and recreational centers and hiking trails and biking facilities and churches. And those things can only come from economic development. I think we have the best of all worlds here. We will grow our resorts within an environmental set of principles and maintain the pristine nature of these valleys while at the same time providing new facilities."[25]

This can sound like Orwellian doublespeak—how can a valley be both "pristine" and "provide services"?—and opponents of the ski industry hear it that way. A less sinister interpretation gleans from this sort of statement the philosophical underpinnings that have carried America's development for so long. Houssian's view of what is "good" is not only similar to the nineteenth-century expansionist William Gilpin's; it represents the thinking of most of the ski industry and the western world:

---

* The one notable exception is the Aspen Skiing Company, whose management and owners were, in the late 1990s, at least trying to grapple with the question of "how much is enough." While the firm still may be criticized with reason, the Aspen Skiing Company is leaps and bounds ahead of the rest of the ski industry in its attempts to reconcile capitalism with environmental and social constraints. It is worth noting, however, that the Aspen Skiing Company is owned by the Crown family of Chicago, a major shareholder in General Dynamics, and it is not the family's primary business. Although the company is profitable, according to CEO Pat O'Donnell, it is not *very* profitable. It is a common belief in Aspen that the Crowns retain their control of the Aspen Skiing Company because they like the place and fear another ski-resort operator would diminish the town or the resort. So although the Aspen Skiing Company can be lauded for its attempts to be more environmentally conscientious, this "benevolent monarchy" model of ownership cannot be held up as a particularly apropos strategy for other resort operators to follow.

growth is good.* In the end, neither the Mays and Millers nor the Houssians truly can understand the other side, because the conflict is one of belief systems. Like opposing sects in a religious war, neither can accept the other's point of view, because to do so would necessitate repudiating one's own beliefs.

Despite Houssian's rational-sounding approach, the net effect of his strategy is a creeping—indeed, galloping—suburbanization and urbanization of mountain valleys that can ill sustain such development, a form of progress that is viscerally opposed by counterculture refugees who came to ski towns to get away from all that. Ski industry execs by and large cannot comprehend the validity of an opposition that is based on having tried to opt out. When Rick Silverman and the Millers arrived in Telluride twenty or thirty years ago, they were trying to opt out of the same system that Houssian and the corporate ski industry represent and promulgate. Silverman and his ilk don't want what these corporations have to offer, yet they can't seem to escape it. Opponents of ski-area development, although by no means of one mind or one voice, have different answers from land developers to the question What is land for? Often, when "progress" comes rolling down the road, they pack up and move on, looking for the next undiscovered place. But some stay and fight. Among them is Andrea Mead Lawrence.

Lawrence is a square-jawed, handsome woman with pragmatically short white hair, flashing blue eyes, and a razor-sharp mind honed by sixteen years of service as a county supervisor in Mono County, California, home to Mammoth Mountain ski area. Lawrence was born in 1932 near Rutland, Vermont. When she was in nursery school, her parents opened Pico Peak ski area, which still operates today (ironically, now as part of the American Skiing Company's empire). "My family just skied," she remembers. "You walked, and you paddled about on skis, and you never thought about it."[26]

She lost her father to a boating accident when she was ten. A few months later, her mother was asked to captain the Eastern Girls' Ski Team, which was how Lawrence gained the opportunity to forerun a slalom course, preceding the racers. "I characterize it as a psychic click," she says of that experience. "You know when something happens inside and you know this is where you're supposed to be? I knew that." Five years later, at the age of fifteen, she became the youngest member of the U.S. Olympic ski team that competed in the 1948 games. She was on the 1952 team, and the 1956 team, too. She skied slalom, giant slalom, and downhill and won two gold medals in 1952. In 1955, six weeks after giving birth to her third child, she began training for the 1956 events; that year, she finished fourth in the giant slalom, just missing a third medal.

Lawrence was introduced to backpacking in the Sierra Nevada by an acquaintance in 1966. She has lived in Mammoth Lakes ever since and is convinced that what Intrawest plans to do there will be a debacle. "What underlies where I'm coming from on what we're doing to mountain communities is I'm indigenous to mountains," she says. "I'm one of those indigenous people." Lawrence stands in the path of what she calls "the juggernaut." Intrawest plans two thousand new homes and condos and eight thousand lodging beds in three clusters of development at the base of the ski area, which lies west of and slightly uphill from the town of Mammoth Lakes. The company hopes to upgrade the sleepy local airstrip to attract direct Boeing 757 service from Dallas and Los Angeles to the open, lightly populated desert valley running along the Eastern Front of the Sierra Nevada.

"It's mindless," she declares. "It is unthinking and it is uncaring and it is absolutely detached from any other value other than their bottom line. They answer to their stockholders and Wall Street. They do not answer to the town of Mammoth Lakes or the town of Keystone, or the town of Stratton,

Vermont, or any of these other places where they are. They are purely driven by dollars. They bulldoze everything out of the way."

Mammoth Lakes is a beautiful place, tucked in the trees on the edge of the Owens River Valley. The escarpments of the Eastern Sierra, which form the western rim of the Great Basin Desert, rise above the town, and the John Muir and Ansel Adams Wilderness Areas wrap around it. The town itself covers four square miles of ponderosa pine and rabbitbrush in a small alcove in the Sierra Nevada range. There is none of the typical resort-related sprawl along U.S. 395, the two-lane highway running up the Owens Valley, because decades ago, the Los Angeles Department of Water and Power bought ranches on the valley floor in order to gain their water rights—a story of raw urban power being exerted against the colonies of the rural West that has been told many times over. Los Angeles' water grab effectively destroyed the ranching communities in the Owens Valley and had the unintended consequence of leaving behind a wide-open and striking landscape. Mono Lake, famed for its exposed tufa towers and for its defenders' fight against Los Angeles, which was prowling for yet more water, is twenty-six miles north; the town of Bishop lies thirty-nine miles to the south; little interrupts the grand spaces in between. The place is a contrast of huge sky, sere desert, and soaring peaks. Ironically, it almost certainly would have been overdeveloped, as the nearby Carson Valley in Nevada has been, if Los Angeles had not precluded that possibility by snapping up most of the region's water—drying out Owens Lake in the process—and shipping it hundreds of miles south. Now another great outside power, Intrawest, proposes to change the landscape again.

"The fundamental objective is to transform Mammoth into the number-one mountain resort community in North America," says Dana Severy, an Intrawest vice president and the man running the company's show in Mammoth Lakes. "We are building the infrastructure to allow destination visitors to come and enjoy the resort, and that has positive economic benefits throughout the town."[27] Growth, in other words, is good.

If you are speculating in real estate in Mammoth Lakes, Intrawest's presence has been very beneficial, as prices skyrocketed during the late 1990s. If you're trying to find a place to live and you make the going wage of six dollars an hour, it's another story. And if you run a business in downtown Mammoth Lakes, a diffuse community that spreads through the ponderosa pines, you have to wonder seriously about your ability to compete with the new, shiny developments that will be full of new, shiny shops at the ski area.

"It's not about cutting the pie, it's about growing the pie," says Severy. "It's about bringing a lot of people to the resort so there is going to be enough business to go around."

His patter sounds convincing, but the reality remains that skiing is a zero-sum sport. With flat total skier numbers, where are Mammoth's new skiers—as many as a million new skier days annually, if Severy has his way—going to come from? Severy quite readily notes that although Mammoth's skier days are down, many of its former visitors didn't quit the sport. They chose instead to fly from Los Angeles (Mammoth's traditional market) to Vail or Utah or Whistler. So if he can lure them back to Mammoth, what happens to the ski resorts in those places? Most likely, their promoters will argue they must build more and shinier attractions to bring the people back. In this arms race, among the people who will pay the price are those who live in Mammoth Lakes.

A dozen of these people, all longtime Mammoth Lakes residents, gather in the living room of Lawrence's condominium. They eat pizza and drink wine and talk about their fears. "This will be the Colorado-ization of California," says John Walter. People are afraid, he says, to speak out against Intrawest. They behave as residents of colonized Western towns have for a century, obeisant to the outside power and money that can make or break them. Intrawest can succeed because the town is afraid of the bust and longs for the boom. "We have a lot of environmentalists here," says Walter. "If it's an issue of putting together more wilderness study areas, we can put a hundred people in a room to speak, and we did. If it's an Intrawest issue, we'd be lucky to get ten people to stand up in public."

The proposed development, says Pat Eckart, "displaces people, changes the culture. The record shows there will be displacement. How much there will be, no one knows." Eckart expresses a belief shared by everyone in the room that the town's government has, perhaps, been seduced by Intrawest psychologically, if not literally. Local officials will be wined and dined and charmed into giving the company what it wants. The people around the pizza box point to the Salt Lake City Olympic Committee, which bribed officials of foreign countries in order to win support for its successful bid for the 2002 Winter Games, and say that they expect the same thing is happening in their town. They don't think town officials have secret Swiss bank accounts, and they can't prove anything, but they still believe their town is being sold out from under them for what Eckart calls "a box of cigars and a bottle of booze."

Nobody has specifics, but everybody feels frustrated, angry, and powerless. This feeling isn't limited to Lawrence's living room. Diana Draper, proprietor of the small hotel where I stayed, also believes the town council is in the developer's pocket. Why? "Money," she says, looking disgusted and rubbing her fingers together.

There's plenty of money in the air. Rick Davis, a real estate broker at the local Coldwell Banker office and Intrawest's director of sales for the base village at Squaw Valley, 130 miles northwest at Lake Tahoe, takes me on a tour of some of Intrawest's new properties in Mammoth Lakes. Davis has small dark glasses, graying hair, a cell phone in a holster on his right hip. He wears loafers and khaki pants; he's tan, green-eyed, earnest, and personable. We drive across town in his polished black GMC Yukon Denali sport utility vehicle, a truck as big and comfortable as a living room, and he takes me through the numbers. If Lawrence is in the Thoreau-Muir camp, Davis is of the Church of Manifest Destiny.

Juniper Springs Lodge, constructed by Intrawest in 1999, has 174 condos going for $300,000 to $400,000, Davis says. The seventy-seven condominiums at the Sunstone building sold out in two-and-a-half hours in a Los Angeles sales event the previous spring. A new gondola to Juniper Springs (one of the three development pods) will be installed in the summer, along with the new golf course. Real estate values town-wide rose 3 percent per month from September 1998 to June 1999. Happy days are here again.

We stop at the Timbers, thirty-two Intrawest town homes that are a hive of construction activity. Fifteen already have sold at prices of $700,000 to $900,000. The Timbers supposedly reflects a southern-California-Craftsman bungalow design, but the town houses have none of the elegance and lightness that mark the real thing. These are big, blocky buildings that look as if they have been inflated. The siding is concrete, textured to resemble wood and painted a dull beige.

"It's indestructible," Davis says proudly.

The interior has a charmless, high-ceilinged elegance, like that of an upscale hotel suite. There's no apparent Craftsman influence except for a flat, pyramidal cap on a stairway newel. If you want to buy a furnished town home, you can get everything you need, right down to the napkins, for an additional fee starting at $65,000, Davis tells me. "The sky's the limit," he says, taking me into the newly built wine closet—an option that sells for an extra $31,969, including three hundred pre-selected bottles of wine: just one more way to buy your way to good taste.

Out on the nearby, soon-to-open golf course, the mechanical golf-ball washers on the tees are built into four-foot-tall, carved wooden bears. "It gives the place character," Davis says. "We're hoping in a few years when this is done we'll be competing with the Vails and Aspens and Beaver Creeks. We have all that nature offers. We just need the man-made stuff."

CHAPTER 5

Selling the New Resort

What is for sale at Mammoth Lakes, as well as in the villages at Copper Mountain, Sunday River, Big Mountain, Keystone, Jackson Hole, and all the rest, is a lifestyle—something that is a marketing concept, a blow-up sex doll simulacrum of a life, not a way of life nor a life itself. The energy and resources put into this sales effort are enormous, and nobody does it so well, nor so smoothly, as Intrawest.

Rick Davis, the Mammoth Lakes real estate broker, ushers me in to what Intrawest calls the Discovery Center, a revamped one-story building that eventually will be torn down to make way for the planned North Village. The Discovery Center cost Intrawest $250,000. A miniature model of the resort as Intrawest envisions it ran another $70,000. Tiny Mercedes-Benz sport utility vehicles sit on this model in the tiny driveways of tiny homes representing the Timbers.

"I wouldn't say the Discovery Center is a tourist attraction," Davis says, "but hopefully the locals are saying, 'You've got to go through the Discovery Center.' "

In fact, some of the locals I've met refuse to set foot in the place. These centers—there is one for every Intrawest village project—are designed to convey a warm, comfortable, yet exciting feeling about what the company has planned. The one here includes carefully assembled displays of the complementary interior finishes and appliances a buyer may select for his or her condo or town home, each assembled in a package that leaves only a few thematic choices. Buyers implicitly are assured that although they may not have the time, expertise, or taste to select their interiors, Intrawest experts have made sure that whatever design package they choose will be an artful manifestation of their discernment, values, and style.

Davis seats me in a small, plush screening room where I am to watch the centerpiece of the sales job, a twelve-minute video. "Enjoy," Davis says before turning out the lights. "You'll come out inspired."

Actually, I come out slightly nauseated. The film is extraordinarily well done, a piece of late-twentieth-century agitprop composed of beautiful video and still images. There are scenes of earnest planners and designers in apparently important meetings, interviews with Mammoth Mountain ski-area founder Dave McCoy, footage of happy families and active athletes in every season, all of it lubricated with hip music and breathless voice-over. What is breathtaking is not the planned real estate development, but the audacity of Intrawest's marketing strategy. The company has chosen to liken McCoy and Intrawest to two of the greatest conservationists of the Sierra Nevada, John Muir and photographer Ansel Adams. When I mentioned this later to a resident of Mammoth Lakes, she asked acidly, "Did they mention Jesus and Mohammed too?"

The film describes Intrawest as a group of "envisioners and storytellers" who are building "Project Sierra" here on the Inyo National Forest—*Inyo* being a name, we are told in an apparent nod to political correctness, that is the local Indian term for "dwelling place of the Great Spirit." Evidently, the Native Americans have been enlisted in the sales job as well.

"John Muir's nineteenth-century writings can still help guide the development of a twenty-first-century resort," says the narrator. I wonder what Muir, an ascetic who hiked for days with no more to eat than tea, bread, and cheese, would have to say about marble kitchen counters, wood-patterned concrete siding, and a thirty-thousand-dollar prestocked wine closet. "We envision the town of Mammoth Lakes taking its rightful place as the gateway to the Eastern Sierra," the narrator says, adding later, "The qualities of this community are as important as the mountains themselves." The first phrase has the familiar ring of manifest destiny about it; the second is laughable in light of the bitter opposition many residents feel toward Intrawest and its plans.

The winter footage in the film isn't about skiing per se, but something Intrawest calls "snowplay." Then, piling hubris upon hubris, the film ends with a quote from Isaac Newton: "If we have seen further than others, it's because we have stood on the shoulders of giants." Intrawest, in other words, intends to claim Muir and Adams—and maybe Newton and the local Indians too—as the moral foundation for enormously profitable commercial development here. What is being marketed at the Discovery Center is a feel-good sensibility that boils down to this: Buy our property and you will be part of a good and wonderful undertaking that environmental giants smile upon. It's a marvelously subtle way to assuage Baby Boomer guilt about consumption and its negative effects on the natural environment. The message here implies that the buyer will purchase a life, but in truth all that's for sale is a lifestyle: a pretty stage set to entice visitors and buyers, and a nice second home.

✳ ✳ ✳

Skiing used to be the warp and woof that knit America's cultural escapees into their newfound mountain refuges. Of course, there are still ski bums today. There are still college students who come to the mountains for adventure, live close to the bone, and ski 120 days per season. But they don't set the tone for ski towns anymore. They have been overshadowed by the potential to make money, an activity that takes place around the edges of skiing itself even as it simultaneously marginalizes the sport from the ski town that nurtured it. The principal gestalt in ski towns is no longer about living in a world described by snow and a shared sense of specialness; now, the ski town and the ski bum are the come-on, the carnival barker for those who are serious about making money. Ski and snowboard magazines are full of pictures of skiers getting big air, and many ski-town real estate ads feature photos of hardy skiers hiking to remote ridges or dropping into steep, powdery chutes. But it's all a marketing chimera, of course. Money is the man behind the curtain.

Today, people who operate small ski areas for the love of the sport are considered to be anachronisms, likely to be the subject of loving, sepia-toned profiles in newspapers and magazines. The Big Three corporations setting the pace in the industry are all about number crunching. You're interested in the romance of the sport? Sure, let me transfer you to the marketing department. The men (and it is almost exclusively men) who make the decisions that matter are on the hunt for more ski areas to buy as they fight for market share.

"Generally, we're looking for resorts that have scale," explains Gary Raymond, Intrawest's soft-spoken, elegant, and dapper vice president for acquisitions and real estate. He meets me for breakfast over starched linen at a waterfront hotel next door to Intrawest's glass-tower offices in Vancouver. "[We seek] resorts that are close enough to a regional market to have a [customer] base and to have the physical attributes and the market attributes to allow it to have four seasons. For our formula, sufficient land [must be available] at the base of the mountain to be able to dramatically change the experience to a village-type concept, and grow the resort through the village-type concept. Accessibility is an important issue. We'd like to always be within a couple hours of a major airport. I almost think in terms of being a regional resort with long-term destination capability."[1]

A ski resort probably has to have at least three hundred thousand annual skier days to interest one of the Big Three, according to Jerry Jones, a Vail-based ski-area broker. Other estimates put the number closer to five hundred thousand.[2] The initial wave of resort consolidation peaked in the late 1990s as the conglomerates snatched the low-hanging fruit in the industry. Several of the remaining independent destinations, including Crested Butte, Purgatory (now Durango Mountain Resort), Stowe, Jackson Hole, and Telluride, have significant sex appeal for the biggest players, but they haven't quite made the grade. They are hampered by a missing component in Raymond's catechism: each resort is far from a big city, or lacks an airport capable of moving large volumes of people, or both.

A big city can't be created, but the problem of air access can, with enough money, be solved. "We learned that it is absolutely necessary to figure out how you get more people to your resort more often," says David Greenfield, Intrawest's youthful president for mountain resort development.[3] The best example of how this has been done is found at Eagle County Airport, thirty-five miles west of Vail. In 1990, Eagle was a typically somnolent mountain airfield. Airlines scheduled commercial service representing about twenty thousand passenger seats into Eagle—the equivalent of a couple of thirty-seat commuter planes daily from Denver. Seven years later, thanks to the investment of more than eleven million dollars by the Federal Aviation Administration and lobbying of airlines by Vail officials, that service level had jumped to three hundred thousand commercial seats.[4] That winter, American Airlines, Continental, Delta, Northwest, and United all flew 757 jets into Eagle, offering direct flights from New York, Newark, Washington, Atlanta, Miami, Chicago, Minneapolis, Detroit, Dallas/ Fort Worth, Houston, Denver, and Los Angeles. The proportion of visitors to Vail arriving through the airport rose from 9 percent in 1990 to 42 percent in 1996–97.[5] The net effect of the improvements at Eagle County Airport was to make Vail much more accessible much more quickly to a much larger group of potential customers. That is precisely what Vail resort executives want, and it is one of the biggest steps resort developers take in the process of urbanizing and mainstreaming mountain valleys.

During the spring and summer of 2000, Mammoth residents, elected officials, the Federal Aviation Administration, and Intrawest wrestled with a complex deal that illustrates the high stakes of the modern ski-resort poker game. The FAA put $30 million on the table to upgrade the Mammoth/Yosemite Airport, a small strip a few miles outside Mammoth Lakes that had experienced only intermittent commercial service up to that point. American Airlines said if the airport were upgraded, it would provide direct 757 service from Dallas and Chicago, and eventually from Los Angeles and San Francisco, for five years beginning in 2001. But it would do so only if the operators of Mammoth Mountain ski area, in which Intrawest holds a majority stake, guaranteed the airline a subsidy of up to $40,000 per flight, covering American's costs and profit. That's the equivalent of guaranteeing to fill 55 percent of the seats of every 188-seat airplane. Mammoth ski area needed to borrow $10 million from Wells Fargo Bank to make this guarantee to American. To get the loan, Mammoth Mountain and Intrawest had to show Wells Fargo that the town government of Mammoth Lakes had approved its aggressive development proposals at the new North Village—development that would make it more likely that enough new business will come to Mammoth to enable Intrawest to pay off the bank's loan. In other words, to get the visitors to fill the beds that were not yet built, the town had to approve the beds that were not yet built to get the visitors. It all had a certain *Through the Looking Glass* feel.

The town, meanwhile, also had to come up with an estimated $6 million to $9 million to pay for a new airport terminal, and $3 million in matching funds to qualify for the $30 million FAA grant. "There is little doubt," declared the *Mammoth Times*, "that Mammoth cannot build a successful commercial airport without the $30 million [in] FAA grant money."[6] The complexity of the deal neatly illustrates how incestuously the town, resort developer, and federal government interact in order to construct the mutual back-scratching apparatus of a big-league resort. If things go the way these parties hope, by 2005, American Airlines will bring 570 757-sized aircraft into Mammoth/Yosemite Airport during the sixteen-week winter season—about five round-trip flights per day. Even if those planes are only 55 percent full on average, that amounts to almost fifty-nine thousand airborne visitors over the course of the winter. Whatever else it means, such a high-volume, high-speed travel option is certain to radically change Mammoth Lakes, in much the same way Eagle County Airport's improvements helped spur the Vail region's 1990s boom.

A similar scenario would change Klamath Falls, too. Developers of the proposed Pelican Butte ski area in southern Oregon believe that obtaining expanded commercial air service into Klamath Falls is critical to their plans to build their new resort, which would be capable of handling six thousand skiers daily.[7] Residents of Aspen, understanding too late that easy access almost guarantees the ascendancy of resort interests over community interests, fought bitterly and successfully in the mid-1990s to defeat a plan to upgrade Sardy Field—already served by eighty-two-passenger BAe-146 jets—to handle 757 jetliner traffic. By the same token, many Telluride citizens believe the 1985 opening of their airport to commercial traffic was the beginning of the end of their small, close-knit community.

‚ ‚ ‚

Difficulty of access is one of the last defenses ski towns have against gentrification and homogenization. Making a place easier to get to means that a larger potential pool of real estate buyers can reasonably think about owning property at the ski resort in question. It's a lot easier for a buyer in Chicago to justify a town home at the Timbers if he or she knows there are direct daily flights from O'Hare International Airport to the outskirts of Mammoth Lakes. Suddenly, getting from the Loop to North Village is a straightforward weekend commute. That, of course, is precisely what resort developers and real estate agents want. Greater demand chasing limited supply results in higher prices, which is a great thing if you're in the business of selling real estate.

It is a disaster, however, if you're in the business of trying to live or work in that real estate. "In a highly inflationary condition, those who have the means of production do well, and those who don't, don't," says Rocky Mountain Institute's Michael Kinsley. A former Pitkin County, Colorado, commissioner whose craggy face brings to mind Robert Redford, Kinsley jokes that he has to find a different term than *means of production,* for he fears being branded a Marxist—something he patently is not. "Specifically, if you own a building in Aspen, you're in fat city," he continues. "If you're trying to rent there, you're always falling behind. You are always on a spiral of impossibility. The more a place succeeds, the more those who don't own the land and buildings fall behind."[8] Kinsley's spiral of impossibility, a visual aid he uses in presentations to communities around the world, is a series of nodes on a circle that reads like this: at the top node, "I can't make the rent"; the next node, "I've got to get more people in the door"; next, "Let's expand the community"; next, "The community expands"; next, "More people are coming in the door and I'm getting more revenue"; next, "The landlord raises the rent"; back to "I can't make the rent."

This spiral accelerates the gentrification of ski towns. Gentrification is not, however, entirely the result of the efforts of Vail Resorts, Intrawest, American Skiing Company, and their imitators. It is facilitated not only by those who bought the town, but also by those who sold it. Individual property owners, many of whom may have lived through hard times and seen enormous increases in the value of their homes or businesses, often are all too happy to cash out and head for warmer or cheaper climes. The cumulative effect of these choices doesn't physically destroy a town, but it does deeply erode a community. Like Kinsley's spiral of impossibility, this process, too, feeds on itself: As a town becomes known as a resort, prices rise, which leads some people to sell their property to outsiders drawn by the resort, making it more cosmopolitan and boosting the resort's image, thus causing prices to rise, and so on. The only way such a cycle could be short-circuited is if essentially everyone in town decided they preferred to stay where they were and live as they had chosen, rather than individually cash in and get out. Needless to say, that sort of collectivism is not part of the American ethic or capitalist practice.

Resort development companies have their own culpability with regard to gentrification. For instance, improved air access feeds the spiral of impossibility, displacing locally owned business that can't pay rising rents. But why are the rents so high, if local businesses can't pay them? Wouldn't the market dictate that landlords could charge only as much as the merchants could pay? Yes, but there is a threshold of success past which the market for commercial real estate is not limited to local shop owners and restaurateurs. It becomes national, even international. Aspen and Vail are prime examples of towns where the name carries significant cachet for the merchants that retail there. It is not unusual to see something along the lines of "Paris

New York London Aspen Hong Kong" stenciled on a boutique window. More than three dozen high-end chain stores operated in Aspen at the turn of the millennium, including Fendi, Chanel, DKNY, and Ralph Lauren. For these corporations, cost is no object. Indeed, they don't particularly need to sell any products whatsoever from their ski-town stores. They will pay a rental rate that is untenable for a local business because what these corporations are buying is placement, and placement gives their product an affiliation with the resort, which gives it a certain cachet that justifies a premium price. This is a self-fulfilling phenomenon that grows truer as skiing increasingly becomes a sport of the wealthy. If the visitor goes home and buys these firms' products in the local mall, the companies' investment in Aspen, Vail, et al. is worthwhile.

In Vail, annual downtown retail rents now reach $125 per square foot—typical of very high end rates in major urban centers.[9] Local businesses, unable to compete with chains that will pay almost any price, bail out. During the 1980s, several local landmarks and watering holes vanished from downtown Vail, at the same time that much of the working population was fleeing for more affordable housing down the Eagle River Valley. The Deli, Donovan's Copper Bar, Garton's Saloon, and the Casino all left because the people who frequented them were leaving. Vail was hollowing itself out as more and more local businesses and workers moved out of the village proper to someplace downvalley where they could afford to live and work.[10]

Vail, like Aspen, has become a shell of its former self, a parody of the distinctiveness that made each of these ski towns appealing and attractive to begin with. By 1995, thirty-nine of the forty-eight people working in Vail's police and fire departments could not afford to live in town.[11] Today, more than 70 percent of the homes within the town of Vail—a municipality that runs for ten miles along Gore Creek—are second homes, empty for much of the year. Only 38 percent of Vail employees live within town limits.[12]

"One of our shop owners said this past winter has been the first one she's had when she didn't have an employee living in a tent," said Vail senior housing policy planner Andy Knudtsen in the summer of 1998. "They would have a membership in the local athletic club, sleep out in the woods, and shower in town."[13] Vail's town council belatedly tried to solve this problem with a proposal to build new housing for 1,680 people. But wealthy homeowners rose up in outrage over the idea that mere workers might live next to their trophy homes— an uprising that killed the housing plan and caused Vail mayor Rob Ford to quit in disgust in 1999.[14]

This is what gentrification is. Typically, the term is applied to run-down urban areas that become hip and interesting and are then taken over by those who want that sense of coolness, that *je ne sais quoi*, to rub off on them. Mountain towns, their beautiful surroundings notwithstanding, suffer the same pressures. People who are doing culturally interesting and innovative things usually are marginalized, either by society or by their own choice, and for forty years, ski towns thrived at the margins. America has a long history of art and culture that was created or embraced on the edge, then swept up by the mainstream— jazz and blues, rap, hip-hop, microbrewed beer, meditation, yoga, mountain biking, organic food, even casual Fridays and ear studs for men. Inevitably, the physical outposts where interesting things happen, from Key West to Santa Fe, Greenwich Village to Venice Beach, are subject to gentrification as Americans swarm over and suffocate them with money. "How many stop to think about what gentrification literally means?" asks Harvard sociologist Juliet Schor. "Namely, creating a gentry—asserting upper-class credentials through ostentation and superfluity."[15]

While the investment of money and energy into marginal areas can be positive, it also is negative, as many observers have pointed out. Most obviously, it displaces many of the people who were making the place interesting to begin with and haven't figured out how to cash in on the boom or don't want to—people who put art, music, poetry, community theater, or 120 days of skiing ahead of getting ahead. Some make money from the changes; some move on. None of this is new, or news. What's noteworthy is the conceit behind the process that gentrifies ski towns, that cleans up Aspen and Jackson Hole and Taos and leaves them as the equivalent of high-end, open-air shopping malls. The conceit is that money can get for you what you gave up. The implicit message in the marketing of the modern skiing lifestyle, and especially of the real estate associated with it, is that although the buyer chose at a young age not to drop out and live an alternative life on the edge, but instead to stay on track with his or her nose to the grindstone—that despite this fact, with enough money, the buyer supposedly can go and purchase the alternative life he or she did not choose.

Stated like that, such an assertion seems patently false. We all understand intellectually that we have one life, and the life we live shapes who we are. Nevertheless, there is a deep emotional imperative to have it all in America, an imperative that is driven by our consumer culture and that is embraced perhaps most deeply by Baby Boomers. So the message in the marketing is this: Buy it, and you can be like this. Never mind that you are a corporate manager with two kids in college, out of shape, and have no understanding of avalanche behavior, ice-screw placement, or riparian ecology; you can be the skier hiking the ridge to the secret powder stash on a snowy morning; you can be the nervy ice climber scaling the frozen cliff; you can be the knowledgeable trout fisherman with a deep understanding of the local river. Pay enough, and you can be the relaxed, creative man or woman who lives in a world where how you ski matters more than anything, and you can possess the bliss that comes with such a life.

Almost all of this message is communicated subliminally. Buying real estate—especially vacation real estate—is a highly emotional undertaking; subliminal messages are powerful in this arena. In Intrawest's sales video for Creekside, a five-hundred-bed redevelopment of Whistler Mountain's original base area (southwest of the current Whistler Village), the marketing is premised on 1970s flower-power culture. The seventy-thousand-dollar sales-pitch film is built around period footage of skiers in the 1960s and 1970s and a theme of a Volkswagen van being driven to the ski area. The Discovery Center at Creekside even includes such a van—sliced lengthwise, the driver's side carefully repainted and bolted against an interior wall—to take us all back to that ostensibly happier, freer time. The implicit sales pitch is the same: spend enough money and this lost youth, whether it was yours or not, will be yours in a new Intrawest development. In an age when the songs of the Beatles, Pink Floyd, and the Rolling Stones have been conscripted into selling consumer products, such a cynical marketing ploy reflects, perhaps, only the tenor of the times.

This is an endless consumerism that, like all other consumerisms, must promise but cannot—indeed, must not—truly deliver. If it did, consumers would acquire the nirvana they are promised and would not need to buy again. Wanting is at the core of selling. That endless, unfulfilled hunger that so many people believe will be filled by purchasing something plays very neatly into the modern resort's strategy of selling a lifestyle—because they are implicitly selling you a new life, the one you didn't choose. They are telling you that you can have it all.

❋ ❋ ❋

In Telluride, the international gold-mining company Newmont Mining is moving—via its subsidiary Idarado Corporation—into the resort real estate business. As part of a complex annexation and zoning agreement regarding thousands of acres of inactive mining claims owned by the company, Idarado officials asked Telluride's town council in 2000 to vote to annex into the town about four hundred acres of company property at the head of Telluride's box canyon, and then to approve the construction of several dozen trophy homes there. Associated with this subdivision, Idarado proposed to build eight high-altitude luxury "cabins" in the basins above Telluride, where it holds more mining claims. These luxury cabins would be reserved for the use of homeowners and their guests who had bought in to Idarado's newly annexed subdivision. In conversations with town officials, Idarado executives made clear that their marketing strategy was to sell the subdivision home sites (each of which they wanted zoned for a twelve-thousand-square-foot "house") to people who want "adventure without risk." The cabins would be positioned in the real estate pitch to provide the promise of just that.[16]

"Adventure without risk" is a marvelously nonsensical turn of phrase, but it goes directly to the heart of ski town gentrification. Idarado expects its buyers to want to be in Telluride, to want some of the skill and attitude of Telluride's residents to rub off on them. The subliminal message is that if Idarado's home buyers brush up against the authentic culture of backcountry skiers and ice climbers that is so prominent in Telluride, some of that cachet will be transferred. (This proposition was deliciously complicated by Idarado's desire for private roads around these new homes, which would exclude those very same Telluride residents.) But that is like buying in to Greenwich Village and hoping the artists' sensibilities and talents will rub off. It won't make you cool and groovy, and most insidiously, it will change the nature of the place in question.

This problem could be called the tarantula-in-the-bananas syndrome. "The modern escapist brings with him most things, material and otherwise, from which he thought he was trying to escape" declared the *Skier's Gazette* in 1970.[17] Twenty or forty years ago, people who moved to mountain towns were generally from the mold of Linda Miller and Rick Silverman; they were actively choosing to give something up for the skiing life. But beginning in the 1980s, the barriers to life in the mountains began to be eroded. Highways and airports were improved, so it was easier to get in and out, which meant it was easier to live there part time. The prospect of making a real living in a legitimate career improved. High-volume tourism meant more money, which attracted more people, and those people wanted more things, and the spiral of impossibility began. So now there are stretch limos and twenty-four-hour room service in Aspen, home security companies in Vail, massages and manicures at every resort.

More insidious than such luxury services is the creeping development of more mundane stores and services—the Wal-Marts and Wendy's franchises that are finding a toehold. "The people who come here now, they want things we never dreamed about wanting," says Linda Miller. "For instance, it's really a treat to go down [sixty-five miles] to Montrose to go grocery shop [at a chain grocery store]. But now people are talking about, 'Oh, we need a big grocery here, and we need this here.' Now you get the feeling they want everything right here. Not the innovative things, they want the mainstream things." Not having "mainstream things" was part of what made life in these ski towns hard and obtusely appealing. There was a certain pride that came with making a life in a hard place. Driving for higher tourist volumes, ski-resort operators make life easier—and make ski-town life more like life elsewhere.

Through all of this, skiing itself is being marginalized. The Big Three and those competitors who follow their strategy are trying to make skiing a less significant part of their bottom line. They sell the four-season resort concept, and they use the environment and its pleasures to market their real estate. Skiing is no longer the point of a ski resort in the eyes of these companies.

Resort executives tend to disagree with this assessment, since it cuts across the grain of the image they are trying to portray. But even in their disagreement they prove the point. "If you can get into the situation where you've got more than just skiing as an amenity, whether it be golf or that it be swimming or that it be tennis, those are becoming almost as important if not more important," says Intrawest's David Greenfield. "Those are the things people are relating to." The net effect is the same; if enough lifestyle immigrants displace those who actually live the mountain life, a ski town isn't what it was before, and its gestalt isn't, either. The result is a class divide between those who live the ski life and the lifestyle immigrants. As a resort becomes more successful, the authentic is displaced by the wannabe.

✳ ✳ ✳

Ski towns during the decades following World War II were some of the most egalitarian places in the nation. Old-timers in places like Mammoth, Jackson Hole, Aspen, and Stowe tell wistful stories about how everybody skied together and drank together, that the millionaires hung out with the ski bums. There's a certain rose-colored hindsight to all this, but there's a kernel of truth to it, too. A common goal and shared adversity almost always produce a tight-knit community. The introduction of significant profit potential to ski towns has torn that fabric. Where once it was possible to live, work, and ski in the same place, now those elements are being separated. An increasing portion of the working population lives somewhere else and commutes, while the houses in town have been snapped up by nonresidents who visit occasionally to play, but not to work. On

Phil and Linda Miller's Telluride street, seven of the ten nearest houses are usually empty, tended by commuting caretakers. In Aspen, so many homes are empty that several home security businesses thrive there—even as thousands of workers vie for price-subsidized employee housing.* Telluride's Grey Head development, a former ranch several miles outside of town that has been subdivided for trophy homes, advertises its "network of private hiking trails" in its real estate promotions. Such an amenity may appeal to the urban refugee who wants a pretty place to escape to for the occasional weekend, but it is diametrically opposed to the sensibility of shared interests, shared concerns, and shared pleasures that made a place like Telluride so interesting and appealing. A private hiking trail is the opposite of the ski town in which you left your front door unlocked and your keys in your car. It is the sine qua non of banana-borne cultural tarantulas, yet it is promoted without irony.

The haves-versus-have-nots reality has bitterly split ski towns and, in combination with the theological schism over land use, has deeply faulted the socioeconomic and political landscape in many mountain communities. This is not to say that money is inherently a problem in ski towns, any more than it is elsewhere. The problem is the introduction of the opportunity to make a lot of it, and the unequal distribution of that opportunity in a community that used to be able to share what it cared about most. Those who own property, or profit from its sale and development—and that includes not only real estate

---

* When I sold my price-restricted, two-bedroom Aspen condominium in 1998 (we were moving away), fifty-two couples qualified under the local housing authority rules to bid on it, and every one bid the maximum allowable price. Only one couple, of course, was able to buy it (they were chosen by lottery), leaving more than a hundred people still scrambling for affordable housing.

agents but also lawyers, accountants, architects, engineers, gardeners, interior designers, carpenters, tilers, concrete companies, plumbers, home furnishings retailers, caretakers, charter pilots, security firms, window glaziers, and more—stand to do well by an increasing volume of sales and development in a ski town.

Those who do not own property for income or speculation purposes, however, stand to do worse. The assertion that "growth is good for everybody," so often made by pro-development forces where development is barreling down the road, is simply not true. It is good for those who are positioned to get a piece of the action. It is bad for those who benefit from, or can survive in, the status quo. The latter group generally includes hourly employees, ski bums, artists, those on fixed incomes (often including a town's old-timers), businesses and residents who rent their property, and so on. If you don't have capital, you probably won't benefit from more capitalization in your resort town. As the saying goes, them that has, gets.

So ski towns change. They change at a faster rate, and with more far-reaching consequences, than they would have in the absence of publicly traded resort corporations driving that change. Some people benefit, but those who do are those who value expansion. The pioneers who made these places interesting often lose out. And the uniqueness that made such places attractive to begin with is packaged, marketed, and ultimately eradicated.

CHAPTER 6

Potemkin Villages
and Emerald Cities

On the plaza of Keystone Resort's River Run Village, in front of Starbucks, a fire pit blazes with light and warmth on a cold January weeknight. A man with heavy wrinkles around his eyes and a long white beard stands beside it, talking to a dozen adults and preteens. He wears a thick Indian blanket made of red wool, a coyote skin cap, fur boots, and fur gloves. This faux mountain man is regaling his audience with the lore and legends of the Snake River Valley.

Beside him, the fire roars steadily. Or, rather, it hisses. The four-foot "logs" that are stacked in a rough pyramid in the pit are made not of wood but of blackened iron. The metal ends are marked with fake tree rings, the logs welded into their unvaryingly casual heap. The flames licking around them are fueled by natural gas. There are practical reasons why a gas fire is preferable to a wood-fueled one. The gas flame burns cleaner, reducing the air pollution in a high, cold valley subject to smog-trapping thermal inversions. There are no ashes or wood chips to clean up, and one can ignite the blaze with a switch. There's no need to harvest the multiple cords of wood that would be necessary to fuel such a fire each winter and drag them from the surrounding lodgepole pine forests, a process that requires noisy chain saws and trucks. Exposing visitors, even summer visitors, to the messy reality of cutting firewood isn't something resort executives want to do. After all, the ski industry devotes so much energy to insulating the sport's customers from the impacts of their pastime. The gas that fuels this fire comes from hundreds of miles away—from the arid tablelands of northwestern Colorado or the plains of eastern Wyoming—and that's the way resort planners want it. The fact that natural-gas drilling is a highly disruptive industrial process that can ruin water tables, pollute homeowners' drinking wells, destroy property values, and devastate wildlife habitat is well hidden from the bundled visitors listening to the mountain man's stories.

The fire is warm enough. And while nobody here this evening believes the mountain man is the real thing, the deception runs much deeper than is obvious in this little circle of light. The mountain man is paid by a commercial association that taxes the surrounding merchants to the tune of a million dollars or more annually (the association goes by the pointedly quaint moniker Keystone Neighbourhood Company). At the end of his shift, he will walk out to the sprawling parking lot east of this so-called village, get in his car, and drive a dozen miles down U.S. Highway 6 to Dillon, a real if ugly accretion of condominiums, strip malls, and fast-food restaurants sprawling around Interstate 70's exit 205. He'll probably kick back with a beer and watch SportsNight on cable. While the fakery of the mountain man and his fire are evident to all but the smallest children, the real and much more effective sleight-of-hand involves the whole place, the "village" that is not a village at all. It is a carefully planned, highly managed, centrally controlled commercial construction designed to manipulate visitors for the sole purpose of relieving them of a maximum amount of their funds, then funneling as much of that money as possible into the pockets of Vail Resorts and Intrawest, partners in the village's development.

I leave the mountain man and retreat to my lodgings. My

room is comfortable, but not too comfortable. The developers don't want me to snuggle in here; they want me out in the village, spending money. I reside for the evening in a one-bedroom condominium, which in Intrawest's development schemes typically run as large as 590 square feet. Studios run up to 480 square feet, two-bedroom condos up to 850.[1] Not only does Intrawest want me to spend my evening, and my savings, in nearby establishments; if I happen to own this condominium, Intrawest also wants me to be only moderately rich. The truly wealthy don't buy small condominiums like these; they buy big condos that cost a million dollars or more. That's a nice one-time windfall for the condo's developer, but such expensive units are rarely made available for rental. They stay empty most of the year and are known in the industry as "cold beds." If nobody stays in them, nobody can leave them to spend money in shops and restaurants. The size of these smaller condos is a function of price; they need to be just nice enough, just big enough, and just expensive enough to attract buyers who are well off, but who still won't turn their noses up at the prospect of rental income.

The resort developer's objective is to create and manage "hot beds"—units that are rented out with a high occupancy rate, that function like a hotel room. If the developer does things right, each condo in a village provides both a onetime profit at its point of sale and an ongoing annuity. Management companies (which in the New Ski Villages are owned by the village's corporate developers) usually split rental income about fifty-fifty with owners. Plus, of course, there's all the money to be made everywhere else in the village from the people sleeping in those rented beds. So the developer profits three times: from the sale of a unit, from its rental, and from the income earned in other village concessions frequented by renters. Hot beds help indirectly, too, in that success breeds success: people like to stay in a place that's bustling.

The inside of my River Run condominium is as pleasantly bland as the tasteful spaces outside: maple veneer and blued steel around a glassed-in gas fireplace; distressed pine coffee table and chairs; heavy pine trim around the doors and windows; pine sideboard, bed, and tables; and a color palette that's a study in beige. A few tasteful black-and-white period skiing photographs grace the otherwise empty walls. It's all very nice, yet in combination with the blandly fake village outside, the whole place makes me long for something, anything, authentic: a child's paper drawing taped to the door of the condo's empty refrigerator; a dead weed poking up through the heated paving bricks in the plazas; a Chicano low rider driving past the gas campfire; even dog shit in a snowbank.

But I won't find any dog shit, because there aren't any dogs here—a sure sign that nobody actually lives in this, the modern Potemkin village. Everyone involved in their development, operation, and promotion calls these creations "villages," but saying it doesn't make it so. Sure, the place is bustling, the beds are hot. But nobody here knows anybody else—what sort of a village is that?

✳ ✳ ✳

New Ski Villages such as River Run are considered by the industry to be a better mousetrap, an innovation that will save and revive the ski business by paradoxically making skiing responsible for a smaller portion of the profits.[2] They lie at the center of the strategies being embraced by Vail Resorts, American Skiing, Booth Creek, Hines, and many smaller operators, including the Aspen Skiing Company, Jackson Hole Resort, Winter Sports, Inc.'s Big Mountain, Grand Targhee Resort, Telluride Ski and Golf Company, Stowe Resort, Durango Mountain Resort, Boyne Mountain Resort, and Crested Butte Mountain Resort. Yet no developer executes the New Ski Village concept so well, so effectively, or so completely as its innovator and pace-setter, Intrawest.

Intrawest had enormous early success with villages at Whistler, British Columbia, and Mt. Tremblant, Quebec. Both ski resorts took off in the 1980s and early 1990s in conjunction with the development of their base villages. Those developments were the brainchild of the grandfather of the New Ski Village, Eldon Beck. Beck is the principal of his eponymous Richmond, California, landscape architecture firm. He first learned his craft when he helped convert the original Vail Village core to a pedestrian-friendly hamlet in the 1970s. He and Vail's first town manager, Terry Minger, then moved up to Whistler, where they shaped that nascent development. Beck went on to create the village at Mt. Tremblant, which he considers his greatest success. Intrawest—and the industry—committed themselves to the village concept after they saw the bottom line at Whistler and Tremblant, which had become cash cows and top-rated resorts in skier surveys. Beck went on to work at Keystone and Copper Mountain in Colorado; Northstar, Mammoth, and Squaw Valley in California; and Vermont's Stratton.

Beck does not design the buildings in New Ski Villages. He designs the villages themselves, sculpting their spaces, views, and forms to make them attractive places. He determines the placement, height, and mass of a village's buildings, then leaves the details to others—in the case of Intrawest's only Colorado resort, Copper Mountain, the cleanup hitter designing the actual building is OZ Architecture, based in Denver. This firm's name is just right, for the result of Beck, Intrawest, and OZ's collaboration is fantasy world not far removed from the one at the end of the Yellow Brick Road.

Throughout most of the twentieth century, the vast majority of ski-resort developers failed to connect the ski-area base to the ski slopes as well as they could have. This failing usually was a function of the financial limitations of a developer who couldn't control sufficient land. Pete Seibert tried to do it at Vail, as did Bill Janss at Snowmass, and each achieved limited success. Development such as Beaver Creek and the original Copper Mountain attempted to follow in their footsteps, but often the result was disappointing. At Copper Mountain, for instance, the base area was dominated by a muddy parking lot when Intrawest purchased it. And many ski areas—Aspen Highlands, Crested Butte, Sugarbush—simply are too far from the nearby town.

Intrawest enlisted Beck to solve that separation problem by building fake villages right at the bottom of the ski lifts, and the corporation put its financial muscle behind his ideas. During his formative years as an architect, Beck traveled extensively in Europe, Australia, and Mexico, developing themes that he has brought into play in the New Ski Villages. Much of what Beck does is import the best elements of Old World villages, then tweak them to their specific resort locales. His other major influence: Mother Nature. "I spend a lot of time backpacking," Beck told me, "looking at natural systems as another basis for how I design."

One of his favorite templates is a creek. In designing a pedestrian passage through a village, he will create "eddies"— spaces out of the flow where people can pause, window shop, or have a cup of coffee, while leaving the center of the "stream" open for walking. Usually such eddies are slightly elevated— perhaps eighteen inches above the main walkway's pavement— to create a sense of separation yet still allow immediacy and interaction. His stream-based walkways blend with what Beck calls "entertainment retail" design. "The most important level of the village is the pedestrian level, and we should do everything we can to keep people's eyes down at that level," he says, noting that he specifies hanging store signs, low street lights, and small canopy trees wherever he can.

Beck's vision can be summed up in a few elements common to all of his villages and emulated, generally with less success, by Intrawest's competitors:

- The pedestrian system is the structure of the village. Wherever possible, people and cars are separated.
- Diversity in terms of architectural detailing and retail content is everything. "Diversity is strength; uniformity is the death knell of a village," Beck says, pointing to Tremblant as his greatest success in this regard.
- The villages are carefully oriented to their sites, so that visitors are given glimpses of the best mountain views. The visitor walking through River Run at Keystone, or Vail Village, or the base of Mt. Tremblant, is supposed to feel connected to the landscape around him or her. The resort is not an agglomeration of condominiums plopped heedlessly onto a landscape, but a set of buildings designed to relate to one another and to the land around them.

At Squaw Valley, Beck is designing a fourteen-acre site that will be home to seven hundred condominiums when it is complete. "It's going to be absolutely the most European village of all, in that it will have many narrow lanes," he says. "All of these lanes will focus on views of the mountains. There will be real drama; it will be an intense experience."

That's the goal—an experience. "Visitors want an experience that is not typical of their daily lives," Beck says. "They really want to go to a place that is different and is memorable. If we bring to the mountains the trappings of an urban or suburban area, I think we've really blown it."[3]

✳ ✳ ✳

Many ski-resort developers, Beck included, have been influenced by Aspen, which for years was the archetype of an interesting town combined with a ski area to create a vibrant, organic, four-season resort. It was a place that looked, felt, and functioned differently from the rest of the world, and it embodied many of the elements that resort developers have tried to capture in the second half of the twentieth century.

Aspen's modern roots go back to 1945, when the Chicago industrialist Walter Paepcke decided the town should be home to what became the Aspen Institute. Paepcke wanted to create a resort that was a refuge for the harried modern American, a place that would lift individuals onto a higher plane, feeding their spirits, minds, and bodies. The Aspen Institute was his flagship, a place where America's businessmen could meet with the world's great thinkers. The years that followed saw the creation of the Aspen Music Festival, the Aspen Center for Physics, and similar intellectual and cultural centers. Paepcke's Aspen Skiing Corporation, which developed Aspen Mountain, would serve to feed the body, while the beauty of the surrounding mountains would elevate the spirit.

Paepcke's vision of a resort that fully rejuvenated the whole man was a great success—so much so that by the late 1960s and early 1970s, major battles were being fought over the future of the town. (One reason Seibert and Janss wanted to control their own developments so tightly was that they wished to avoid the messy politics on display in Aspen.) In an effort to limit resort development, which many Aspen locals felt threatened the town, elected officials began instituting growth controls in the 1970s, putting a tight cap on construction in town and in the surrounding Pitkin County. The effects were twofold: real estate prices began an inexorable climb (since supply had been limited, but not demand); and locals who could no longer afford to live in Aspen began moving down the Roaring Fork Valley and commuting to work. By the end of the 1990s, Aspen's problems—a community dominated by absentee homeowners, a downtown full of expensive boutiques, an unhappy workforce of commuters—looked similar to those of many other resorts, but they had been arrived at by a very different route. For decades, Aspen was on the leading edge of high-end ski-resort development. That position meant there were few or no examples the town's leaders could learn from. Aspen's demise as a small, intimate ski town came not because a major ski corporation had cashed in on consumer demand for second homes and mountain resort life; rather, Aspen demonstrated just how much demand there was for such things. Aspen's experience was the proof that gave impetus to the New Ski Village developments, which sprang up in the 1990s to profit from that demand.

✳ ✳ ✳

Eldon Beck is Intrawest's public face, the avuncular, visionary front man for what's happening at these massive new resorts, featured in laudatory articles and even in the company's 1999 annual report. But the wizard behind the curtain is Lorne Bassel, Intrawest's senior vice president for resort development. Young, athletic, and earnest, with dark eyes and a steady gaze, Bassel describes himself as the villages' producer. "All the village is a stage," declares a PowerPoint presentation Bassel makes to prospective tenants "and all the tenants in it are the players!!" Bassel runs the show—for it is a show—at Copper Mountain and Keystone; Mountain Creek in New Jersey; Blue Mountain, Ontario; and Les Arcs, France. In the past he has been responsible for Intrawest's villages at Tremblant, Quebec; Stratton, Vermont; and Snowshoe, West Virginia. The degree of almost fanatical control Bassel and his staff exert over Intrawest's villages—who gets to do business there, what business they do, under what terms it will be done, what public face they will present, and even what hours they will be open—is extraordinary.

At Keystone, Intrawest operates a joint venture with Vail Resorts, and Bassel is disappointed with the results of River Run, a village he can't fully control. But at nearby Copper Mountain, Intrawest alone owns the ski area and the base village (with the exception of some existing 1970s-era condominiums), and so Intrawest pulls the strings. With Beck's help, the corporation is redeveloping Copper Mountain to produce a signature base village.

Imagine visiting the Village at Copper Mountain. You are walking through the pedestrian zone when you come upon a chocolate shop. What serendipity! You and your kids watch the woman working in the window, making the chocolate in a huge copper bowl. The kids can't stand it any longer—they drag you inside, where you buy chocolate treats for the whole family. Back out on the street, you probably think you've had a nice, spontaneous, European-style experience.

What you don't know is this: The location of that chocolate shop was determined long before ground was broken on any of Intrawest's buildings at Copper Mountain. Its site was dictated by a careful analysis of the angle of the sun at varying times of day and times of year; analysis of traffic patterns for different demographic slices of the expected-visitor pie through the village at various times of day (especially families with children); and an understanding of which activities and other businesses would lie in the shop's immediate vicinity, with an eye toward mutual compatibility and the creation of a particular retail "neighborhood" with a very specific feel.

Although the woman working in the window owns the business, she didn't just wander in and lease the space. She answered a casting call for chocolatiers. She had to audition with Intrawest, not only demonstrating financial and professional capability but also proving to corporate executives that her chocolate shop would mesh with Copper Mountain's corporately determined theme of "high alpine, high energy." She pays a portion of the ten or twenty dollars she liberated from your wallet to a village corporation, in the form of a tax that makes sure you and your kids stay entertained by musicians, jugglers, and faux mountain men in the public spaces. She pays part of her profit to Intrawest. Before she even signed a lease with Intrawest, the company already had determined how big her chocolate shop was going to be—based on calculations about what sort of people will come to Copper Mountain, and how many will want to buy chocolate—what hours it will be open, and what color it will be painted, both inside and out. The developer built the shell of her shop with a thorough understanding of how Intrawest wanted the interior to be laid out, so that utility hookups such as sinks and electrical outlets were already positioned. The sign and interior decor were approved by an Intrawest executive, who also signed off on the menu and price list. The shop owner is expected to earn (and reveal) a minimum gross annual income, and if she does not do so, or if she otherwise displeases the management at Copper Mountain by failing to meet various "standards," she can have her lease revoked in favor of someone else who can run a chocolate shop more to Intrawest's liking.

The centralized, command-and-control economy thrives at the cutting edge of the North American ski industry.

All of Lorne Bassel's efforts at Copper Mountain, as at other Intrawest resorts, are directed toward creating a village that is an ongoing revenue generator for Intrawest. His goal: 15 percent annual return on investment, minimum. (Intrawest plans to invest a half billion dollars in Copper Mountain, both on the ski area and in the base village. Much of it will be recouped through real estate sales.) There's nothing wrong with this; corporations, after all, exist to make money. But there is a significant element of legerdemain. Visitors to Copper Mountain probably believe that they have come to a nice resort where they spend their money with a variety of shopkeepers, restaurant owners, hoteliers, and street vendors, each of whom is an independent businessman or -woman. While these people are indeed independent, their freedom to do as they please is controlled by Intrawest's very short leash. The truth is, a portion of almost every dollar the visitors spend at Copper Mountain goes into Intrawest's pockets, and the "independent operators" that Intrawest characterizes as "mom and pops" cannot choose their offerings or decorative themes without the approval of company executives. They work hard and they are sincere, but Intrawest's tenants serve as human window dressing that disguises a corporate strategy committed to harvesting an ever larger portion of visitor dollars for Intrawest shareholders.

The company's control starts with the village plan, and the plan starts with a matrix. First, Intrawest examines the demographic components of its visitors: Kids, Students, Independents, Families, and Gold Coasters. Within these groups there are day visitors, destination visitors, and residents. Almost all of Intrawest's efforts are dedicated to attracting and retaining destination visitors, who are a relative gold mine, spending roughly three times as much as day visitors. At Mt. Tremblant in 2000, the average destination visitor spent seventy-seven dollars daily on retail items, food, and beverages, in addition to lift tickets and lodging.[4]

For each demographic group, Intrawest analyzes how individuals are likely to spend—or can be coaxed to spend—their time. "The reality is that at ski resorts, one of two guests staying at the resort is skiing, and those guests are skiing only about four hours a day," Bassel says. "That means that on average your guests are skiing about two hours a day. What are you going to do with them for the other twenty-two hours? What's the experience that's going to make them come back or not come back? We realize, and we've seen this from the data, the places where we have strong villages, people stay longer, which is very important for our villages. One of our financial goals, beyond anything else, is to get [visitors] to want to stay longer. If they stay a day longer, everything else takes care of itself."

The Intrawest matrix then breaks the day into periods: early morning, morning, lunch, après-ski, evening, and night. Bassel and his team—an Intrawest working group known as The Village People—calculate how to cater to each visitor component during each time period, with the goal of getting every visitor to spend money around the clock, and with a particular goal of finding and exploiting marginal expenditures—that is, getting each visitor to spend above and beyond normal daily needs.

Some of the results of this analysis are obvious. At après-ski, for example, a large portion of almost all the demographic groups wants to hit a bar at the base of the mountain and grab a beer. But that's about the only time of day when the needs of the various demographics coincide so tightly. For dinner options, a well-designed village will include brew-pubs and high-end restaurants—but The Village People's analysis indicates they also should provide a kid-friendly place that can get a family in and out in forty minutes at 6 P.M. Miss that understanding, Bassel says, and you miss a chance to provide an "experience."

"We want to keep busy twenty-four hours a day," Bassel says. "What if I can come out of a bar at two o'clock in the morning and there's a place that sells slices of pizza? Holy cow, you've just extended my time clock and added to my experience. That's very different from having a Swiss *raclette* restaurant open—I won't go there. But if you can understand how I behave and provide that . . . " He shrugs, his sentence unfinished. Give him what he wants, Bassel says, and he'll spend more money on that "experience," even if it is as banal as buying a slice of pizza.

Bassel uses the word *experience* a lot. So do other people who work at Intrawest. Their company, they say, is about providing experiences; in our modern world of material surfeit, we all understand (don't we?) that what we crave now are experiences. And the ski industry markets experiences. When it sells you something, it is selling an experience. But it doesn't talk about selling; it talks about "providing an experience." In Intrawest's lexicon, the word *experience* is code for "an opportunity to get the visitor to spend money." It is true that skiing and vacations are about having experiences; what's extraordinary is the comprehensive, entangling net of commerce Intrawest has woven around every possible experience to be found within its resorts. The Village People are committed to finding new ways to get you to reach for your wallet. Although a multitude of advertising signs hangs outside the shops and restaurants in an Intrawest village, and many different people run these enterprises, Intrawest pulls the strings at every one. For starters, the firm's Operations Group retains about 20 percent of the commercial space. Typically, it will run the big base-area restaurant—at Copper Mountain, it's a food court and bar called Jake's—and the sporting goods store where visitors get skis tuned, rent mountain bikes, or sign up for a guided hike. The Operations Group may also run several other restaurants (this includes the demographic-analysis-driven mid-price pizza-and-pasta place at Copper Mountain called Beachside Pizza) and other shops. The remaining 80 percent of retail space is rented out to other operators—cast members, as Bassel sees them—on strict terms.

Not only are tenants obliged to pay taxes to the village merchants' association (about six dollars annually per square foot of retail space at Copper), which is responsible for arranging "animation" such as the jugglers and storytellers; tenants also pay their prorated share of property taxes and utility bills. This arrangement is not unusual in resort leases. Nor, even, is it unusual that these ostensibly independent businesses must share their profits with their landlord. These lease terms are common in ski resorts nationwide, yet they are not too far removed from the now reviled practices of sharecropping in the American South, or tenant farming in medieval Europe: the tenant does the work, the landlord skims the cream. This income stream, combined with rent, provides Bassel with his 15 percent annual return on investment.[5]

Intrawest's goal is to neither overbuild nor underbuild for the market, but to match rental accommodations to retail and restaurant space so that everybody catering to visitors, from coffee shops to rock climbing guides, grosses a minimum of four hundred dollars per square foot annually (in either U.S. or Canadian dollars, depending on location). In this stage of village planning, Intrawest's mania for control is most apparent.

"We don't call ourselves leasing agents; we're casting managers," says Bassel, who auditions prospective tenants. For each retail location, the company wants to hear a pitch. As with the chocolatier at Copper Mountain, Intrawest judges its would-be tenants based on their experience, their concept, and their financial strength. Before auditions begin, The Village People know exactly which business will go in each retail space, and how it will be operated. There will be only one chocolatier, only one baker, only one pizza shop.

All of this is detailed in the village plan. A breakfast nook will be situated on the way to the ski lifts. A high-end restaurant will be tucked in a corner where visitors have to discover it. The chocolate shop will be set where children can peer in the windows and watch the chocolate being made—windows of non-reflective glass that have been shielded from the sun, both to protect the chocolate and allow for better viewing from the walkway. For, Bassel says, the chocolate must be made in the window; that will be part of the lease agreement. The chocolate cannot be made in the back of the store. To do so would mean missing an opportunity to provide an experience, an experience in which the kids inevitably urge their parents to come inside and purchase a few chocolate-covered pretzels—just the sort of thing that Bassel and his colleagues know they can cause to happen, if they assemble all the village's pieces appropriately. Such a result is the key to Eldon Beck's "entertainment retail."

"The Dalai Lama says shopping is the museums of the twentieth century, or something like that," Bassel tells me. "What's happened in the leisure world is, many people now are not only going for whimsical shopping; vacation is actually their time to go do some shopping. That's when they stock up on clothes and stuff."[6] As a consequence, the villages are made for shopping. "We try to create places where people feel comfortable just to be, just to relax and slow down and admire all the things going on around them." Tourists can be sped up or slowed down simply by altering the patterns of the paving stones: straight lines accelerate people, arcs or other curving patterns slow them.

Slowing people down is important, because ultimately, Intrawest wants its visitors to wander into stores. Bassel designs a variety of "neighborhoods" in each village. At Blue Mountain, Ontario, a typical project, they include Arrival, Town Square, Main Street, Provisions, Events Plaza, Skier Plaza, Play Zone, the Docks, People Place, Lake Plaza, Georgian Way, and Waters Way, all within a few acres. At each of these "neighborhoods," there are opportunities for "experiences."

"You really don't go to a resort with the intention of stopping in all these stores to buy things," Bassel admits. "When I create a Main Street, the neighborhood I put on Main Street in my mind is called 'small indulgences and quick and easy decisions.' You don't need it, and probably in a year from now you're going to throw it out." Bassel's typical examples of the stores likely to fit this bill include a place selling "inexpensive artwork, beads, small totem poles, artifacts of the region," and a candle store. ("No one needs more candles," Bassel confides, "but it's a small treat.") For Main Street food offerings he will station a juice bar or a soup place that serves passersby through a window. "You don't go to Tremblant saying, 'I've got to go and get a juice,' but as you're walking down the street you can say, 'That's an interesting attraction.'"

What you won't find on Main Street is a high-end jewelry store, an expensive restaurant, a furrier. Those are hidden on byways where they can be "discovered" by committed shoppers. "If I feel a village is sympathetic to people's behavior in a twenty-four-hour clock, I think we've won," says Bassel. "But if I've created a commercial experience within those villages that matches with what people expect to find, it's logical: 'I expect that to be there, it's a no-brainer.' From their point of view, 'It should be there, everybody knows that, it's logic'—that takes careful planning. To give you another example, when I create a neighborhood for provisions, I will put a butcher, a baker, a wine store, [and] a bank machine all in the same area. I will think about people's needs and that wonderful sort of Ping-Pong effect: 'I'm going here to get my cheese; I'm going here to get some great meat; I'll go here to get some great wine; and I'm going to make sure that in that grocery store there's going to be take-out food that I may never even buy at home, because I'm treating myself.'

"If I can create a pocket of experience, as opposed to conventional malls—supermarket at one end, liquor store at the other, bank machine may be anywhere within the thing, that doesn't create that type of experience where people are having these fun sort of multi-experiences. And when I ask people at our resorts what they like most about them, they say there's so much to do. Part of the village experience is creating so much to do at different times."

✳ ✳ ✳

This extraordinary control over the village can be viewed two ways by the business operators who sign on as tenants. On the one hand, it is very comforting to know that Intrawest cares deeply about each tenant's commercial success and is willing to offer professional design and other services to make sure each business succeeds. Intrawest clearly perceives that the success of its villages depends on the success of each element within them and will devote enormous resources to ensuring that success.

On the other hand, if ever there was a company town, the Village at Copper Mountain is it. For all the lip service given by Eldon Beck and the rest of the Intrawest team to the idea of "diversity" and "individuality" in the businesses, the reality is written right in the lease: Intrawest's way or the highway. What's diverse in this game is what Intrawest says is diverse. Nothing is left to chance if it can be controlled.

The New Ski Villages themselves are not physically large; one could walk from one end of the Village at Copper Mountain to the other in three minutes. Susan Byers, Intrawest's commercial leasing manager there, takes me on a tour to show how the place keeps visitors amused for a week. The ski area lies to the south, the main passenger drop-off point to the north. A walkway through the village connects the two across a creek, clearly revealing the ski slopes from the drop-off. "The Beach" is a large plaza at the base of the ski area. Surrounding tenants include Indian Motorcycle Cafe and Lounge, a Toronto-born clone of the Hard Rock Cafe; on the eastern side a fast-food stand will be set up, a Canadian franchise called Beavertails that sells a trademark chocolate-covered sweet. On the western side of the village, a small plaza is dominated by an artificial rock climbing tower, which will be run by an adjacent outdoor store. Byers stops beside the tower.

"Let's say you're a guy from Texas or St. Louis, and you climb this forty-two-foot-high climbing wall, and you go back to the office on Monday morning," says Byers, a blond woman in her forties who wore a black pants suit and street shoes for our January tour. "You go, 'Goddamn, I climbed this forty-two-foot climbing wall, and I got myself an ice ax.' You know you're never going to use the ice ax, but you're going to bring the ice ax back as a memento of your trip. It's all about creating that feel, creating that experience and then creating the memories."[7]

Experience and memories translate into a commercial transaction; that's the equation underlying everything Intrawest does. I have to wonder if the company doesn't deeply overestimate the stupidity or gullibility of its visitors—I fail, for instance, to see the $150 ice-ax purchase ever happening—but then again, the firm's profitability suggests otherwise.

On the east side of the village, Intrawest is developing a boardwalk around a two-acre man-made pond. Vacationers will be able to visit nine "character buildings," such as an "antiqued" log cabin, a post-and-beam-built structure, and so on, each connected by a boardwalk and containing a small business: a gelato shop, a place to buy cheap jewelry. The criteria for such businesses, Byers says, is that they would offer "real authentic Colorado things, gifts and things, wonderful sculpture, do-it-yourself pottery." Visitors will be able to rent boats to row around on the pond—"not the cheesy blue boats, these are authentic rowboats that are really indicative of a high-alpine kind of town," Byers says with conviction.

Despite nearly two decades of residence in small mountain towns in Colorado, I have never seen any watercraft that are "indicative of a high-alpine kind of town," since high-alpine towns here don't normally come equipped with lakes. In my experience, Intrawest's impending boats are the product of a too-fertile imagination at the corporate offices. Besides, the vaunted "authenticity" seems somehow diminished by the unpleasant and very authentic reality of Interstate 70, situated four hundred yards beyond the boat docks. Here beside the pond, the roar of tractor-trailers hammering down from Vail Pass is constant.

At this point in my tour, despite Byers's obvious sincerity and genuine niceness, I've about had it. Bassel has talked about strategically positioning stores that sell stuff visitors will throw away in a year, and making sure a village has a minimum of Gap, Starbucks, and Nike stores to satisfy shoppers' expectations. Byers is describing tchotchke shops that sell "Indian" dream catchers, rubber tomahawks, and cheap silver jewelry, and chain stores like the Color Me Mine do-it-yourself pottery franchises. Both have told me they are "incubating" Indian Motorcycle and Beavertails in other resorts and hope to franchise them into still more Intrawest destinations, along with the Canadian clothing retailer Roots. Byers has said if she finds a store she likes in another resort or city, she'll try to recruit it to Copper Mountain, and perhaps then incubate it for other resorts as well.

Both have insisted to me that each Intrawest resort is different and special, yet when pressed, the only thing Bassel and Byers can say about *how* they are different and special is that they are built in geographically different places. "There will never be another Copper," Byers says, and she is absolutely right. But there certainly will be another Village at Copper Mountain, or something that feels and functions much like it. Sure, the buildings will be laid out a little differently, the store fronts will be painted other hues. But a visitor will find many of the same options and "experiences" at Keystone, Stratton, Mt. Tremblant, Whistler, Mammoth, and the rest of Intrawest's properties. Despite strenuous assertions to the contrary from Joe Houssian and everyone on down the ranks, the fact is that Intrawest is very guilty indeed of cookie-cutter development at its base areas—not because the buildings look identical, but because the theory, objectives, and manipulations underlying New Ski Village development are unvarying. Consequently, all efforts to the contrary notwithstanding, the finished products are going to seem—and to be—remarkably similar. Lorne Bassel admitted as much when he told me, "It's the Holiday Inn thing of having no surprises."

* * *

Most New Ski Villages cover a few dozen acres. But even with such relatively concentrated development (some buildings at the base of Vail ski area, for instance, reach up eight stories), sprawl still happens. In fact, it may be even more likely to happen. Vail Village was the mother of all North American ski villages, built in a tight cluster. Today, the Vail community is generally considered to run for at least eighteen miles along the valley floor, which is broadly covered by condominiums, single-family homes, and ten golf courses.[8] All of this happened, it is fair to say, because of the success of the original Vail Village.

Ski-resort development is an attraction that leads to sprawl as real estate prices go up. Absent the absolute prohibition of construction on surrounding lands—which is possible only if they are purchased as open space or the development rights are retired via conservation easements—those lands are almost sure to be developed, and that can be disastrous for a resort's neighbors. The American Farmland Trust concluded:

> Private valley lands near ski resorts are prized as noncommercial ranchettes. The market price is potentially well above the $2,500 per acre paid for large ranches. It is this virtually unconstrained market pressure, encouraging the sale of working ranches to absentee owners, that is seen as the principal threat to the ongoing viability of the traditional ranching communities.[9]

Despite all this, New Ski Villages are popular. The appeal is visceral. These places suggest the small towns where we grew up, or where we wish we had grown up, or they remind us vaguely of the pre-automobile hamlets of Europe. They are scaled for pedestrians, not cars. They feel safe. And they are full of the most benign and comfortable incarnations of the things that we like about our modern lives.

There's a walled quality to them, just as there is to a cruise ship, even though there are no walls. Like a cruise ship, they contain everything a well-off visitor needs; they import a wholly safe, rich, luxurious experience into an exotic environment wherein you don't have to *travel,* to open yourself up, to put yourself at risk at all. The staff members live somewhere in the bowels of the ship—or an hour's drive away—and always behave politely, even if they don't speak English very well. You never have to mingle with people who aren't like you. You pretend you live in the tourist zone of the village, just as you pretend you live in a stateroom. The tourist zone in a New Ski Village comprises places where visitors are expected to spend their time. It is a corporately envisioned, architecturally executed form of social engineering that gives visitors no obvious reason to venture out to where the real people live, where they might risk an actual, authentic encounter with someone who truly lives here—an organic, unscripted, noncommercial experience. (Isn't that what we crave?) Indeed, such wandering by tourists would be alarming to village developers if it occurred on any significant scale, since it raises the possibility that visitors would spend their money outside the defined tourist zone, thus depriving the developer of its cut. That would defeat the whole purpose of the New Ski Village.

These villages aren't about going somewhere else so much as they are the social, architectural, and economic sine qua non of taking the most pleasant, least threatening aspects of the upscale mall, the revitalized urban downtown, and the suburban McMansion, reducing them to their essences, and cobbling them together near some ski slopes.

Intrawest's incarnation of the New Ski Village is a breathtaking tour de force of consumer manipulation. Everything is just where it should be, where you'd like it to be without having ever thought about it. "When people are up at our resorts, they're on vacation," Bassel says. "It's kind of more exciting if they don't have to think about it." Or perhaps, it's better for Intrawest if they don't think too hard about it. For Intrawest has gone one better than Disneyland and the rest of the theme park world. When you visit Disneyland, you walk through the gates and know you are in a place where everything is connected to the Walt Disney Company. You know every dollar you spend goes to that company. But when you visit Copper Mountain, you don't know that. You are actively manipulated into spending more than you intended to, and you do so under the illusion that you are putting your money into the coffers of many different small businesses. Although that is technically true, what is unspoken is that you also are always—every time you reach for your wallet—putting your money into the hands of the corporation that is the man behind the curtain in the Emerald Cities of the modern ski industry.

CHAPTER 7

Smokey the Bear,
the Ski Industry's Best Friend

In the winter of 1999–2000, Breckenridge, Colorado, became the most popular ski resort in the United States. The previous March, Vail Resorts, which owns the Breckenridge ski area and operates it on Forest Service land, had unveiled expansion plans for three new villages at the northern edges of this sprawling, 2,043-acre resort. The existing base development at Peak 8, the northernmost summit of the ski area, would be razed and replaced with condominiums and a "mountain Victorian–style" lodge, plus retail and rental space along a mountainside plaza. New ski terrain would be developed on Peak 7, adding 165 acres of trails and pushing the ski area boundary farther north. At the base of Peak 7, a new village, including a five-screen movie theater, convention center, ice rink, retail shops, and restaurants, would be built. This would be connected by road and gondola to parking lots on the valley floor near the town of Breckenridge, a nineteenth-century gold mining town that has been overrun by resort kitsch.

All told, the proposal would add 853 new condos, town homes, and houses to the slopes above the town, plus sixty-three-thousand square feet of new commercial space.[1] What's unusual about this development is not the numbingly familiar proposal, but how it came about. For years, Vail Resorts denied it had any specific plans for base-village development at

Peak 7. It presented the terrain expansion and new lift on Peak 7 as a freestanding proposal, unconnected to any real estate development plans, and asked the Forest Service to see it that way as well. Vail Resorts insisted that this was the only possible way to consider the Peak 7 expansion.

This was an important strategy. The National Environmental Policy Act (NEPA) requires that new developments proposed for public lands undergo an evaluation that looks at the likely effects of the development according to a variety of alternatives, from "no action" to full development. This evaluation is undertaken via the compilation of exhaustive and expensive environmental impact statements or more cursory environmental assessments. Both are paid for by the developers.[2] Under NEPA, the Forest Service is obliged to consider not only the direct effects of development but also the indirect, off-site impacts. The agency can deny approval for a project if it finds there will be too many negative impacts. Without Forest Service approval of a "special use permit," Vail Resorts could not expand its ski terrain on Peak 7. If Vail could prevent the Forest Service from prying into the likely domino effects of base-area development, it would keep the lid on an expensive and inconvenient regulatory can of worms—and keep the public in the dark about what might be the company's true agenda and that agenda's true costs.

The salaries of Forest Service staff working on a NEPA project are paid for, in whole or in part, by the developer. This makes sense on one hand: since review of a proposed development can add to a ranger district's workload, the potential beneficiary (the developer) should pay the costs. But although the money to pay staff salaries is funneled through the Forest Service, the practice raises the question of whether Forest Service staff are able to be truly objective in their reviews. On the White River National Forest, this funding is effectively permanent. "In the four years I've been here," said Forest Supervisor Martha Ketelle, "there's always been some level of ski-area-funded work that's partially paying for one or more [staff] positions."[3]

When it first reviewed the Peak 7 expansion plans in 1998, the Forest Service accepted Vail's characterization of the project. In its environmental assessment of the Peak 7 expansion, the agency insisted it could not review the development potential of 283 acres of land owned by Vail Resorts Development Corporation (VRDC) that just happened to lie at the base of the proposed Peak 7 access lift. Environmentalists cried foul, claiming the Forest Service was blind to the obvious.

Vail stonewalled, insisting it had no development plans for the base of Peak 7, and White River National Forest rangers held firm. "It's speculative to say there will be a base area, there will be this, there will be that," said Tere O'Rourke, district ranger at the local office overseeing Summit County. "We don't have a single plan in front of us. We don't know when or what it will be."[4] Her language seemed to echo a letter from Robert Barrett, an attorney with Arnold and Porter, the most ubiquitous and powerful law firm representing Colorado ski resorts. Barrett's letter, addressed to the U.S. Army Corps of Engineers—an agency also reviewing the expansion proposal—insisted there was no possible link between any on-mountain expansion and base-area development on and just above the VRDC-owned lands at the base of Peak 7, known as Cucumber Gulch.[5] Environmentalists, including the Land and Water Fund of the Rockies, the local chapter of the Sierra Club, and Colorado Wild, didn't buy it. The Land and Water Fund sued the Forest Service, insisting the agency must consider the base's development potential when pondering the expansion.

The lawsuit went nowhere. But somebody else—the U.S. Environmental Protection Agency—smelled a skunk. In repeated correspondence to the Forest Service and the Corps of Engineers, officials with the EPA's Region VIII office in Denver hammered on those agencies' refusals to acknowledge the reality and consequences of the link between on-mountain and base development. The EPA was doubly concerned because Cucumber Gulch contains a wetlands area the agency deemed to be of "national importance": agency staff had tallied the loss of twenty-four hundred acres of wetlands since 1962 in Summit County—almost all of it directly or indirectly related to skiing or the construction of Dillon Reservoir—and found only thirteen hundred acres remained. Cucumber Gulch was exemplary as far as high alpine wetlands go. The seventy-seven-acre patchwork of forested wetlands, bogs, wet meadows, and streams was home to one of only twelve Colorado breeding colonies known to exist at the time for the boreal toad, a species facing extirpation in the southern Rockies. There was evidence that endangered Colorado river otters were using the wetlands, and the complex hydrology of the Cucumber Gulch area included fens—peatlike depositions of soil that accumulate at rates of only four to sixteen inches per thousand years. "We believe these wetland ecosystems are for all practical purposes nonrenewable and irreplaceable," the EPA concluded.[6] EPA staff worried that storm-water runoff from the new developments would damage the wetlands, and that foundation construction would alter the flow of groundwater that feeds them.

In 1997, Cynthia Cody, chief of the EPA's NEPA Unit in the Ecosystems Protection Program, had chided District Ranger O'Rourke for the Forest Service's apparent inability to defend the public trust when it came to ski areas in Summit County:

It is my understanding that despite efforts by your staff to reduce impacts, significant direct and indirect adverse impacts may still occur to waters of the U.S. from the ski area expansions as currently proposed. We are also concerned about environmental impacts of the Forest Service's special use permit decisions [for ski areas] on National Forest lands, which directly and indirectly affect land development activities at the base and surrounding areas. These seemingly minor permit decisions on Forest lands can initiate significant water and air quality issues resulting from residential/commercial/recreational development and associated increased emissions sources. . . . [W]e believe that change in land values associated with ski area expansions, including upgrades of the mountain and base facilities, can be significant and measurable. The property values and cost of development in these areas then drive the type and density of development, and invariably, adverse impacts to aquatic ecosystems. These economic factors, combined with the types and locations of wetlands in the basin, lay the ground for the train wrecks on 404 [water quality] permits we have been experiencing in the Blue River Basin.[7]

The pressure stayed on. In May of 1998, Cody again wrote to O'Rourke, asserting that the Forest Service had failed to demonstrate a need for the Peak 7 expansion, had looked at too few alternatives, and still was not fully disclosing the impacts of the project.[8]

O'Rourke was trying. She had formed a working group with several other federal agencies to orchestrate a coordinated analysis of the project. But Forest Service officials in both the White River Forest headquarters in Glenwood Springs and the regional Forest Service office near Denver were not as aggressive toward Vail Resorts as the EPA's staff were.

The EPA also went after the Corps of Engineers, which had fallen in line behind the Forest Service and was buying Vail's argument that there was no connection between lifts and base-area development. The Forest Service soon took the easy way out: White River forest supervisor Martha Ketelle approved the Peak 7 lift plans in August 1998 without acknowledging the base-area development that probably would result. But the EPA and the corps still were pondering what to do. As 1998 drew to a close, EPA staff in Denver continued to lean on the corps. The EPA's biggest fear was that building the Peak 7 lifts would have the effect of making a village at the base of them—right in the middle of Cucumber Gulch—a fait accompli. In other words, agency staff argued, there's no logical place to build a village *except* where skiers can reasonably get on and off the ski hill, which happens to be where the bottom of the lift is. Approve the lift, and for all intents and purposes you've approved the village, too.[9]

By late September, with the Forest Service a lost cause, the EPA advised the corps that the Peak 7 proposal stood a real chance of running afoul of the Clean Water Act and the President's Council on Environmental Quality and that EPA staff in Denver were pushing the review of the project higher up the administrative ladder. The implication was clear: the Corps of Engineers would be well advised to think carefully about its next move, or it could find any approval of the Peak 7 expansion reversed.[10]

The corps blinked and finally pressured VRDC in late 1998 to show its hand on how it planned to develop Cucumber Gulch before any approval would be given for Peak 7.[11] The company capitulated. Suddenly, in mid-February 1999, VRDC opened an "Information Center" in downtown Breckenridge, featuring careful drawings of the new villages planned for the bases of Peaks 7 and 8. These plans were precisely what environmentalists had insisted Vail had up its sleeve, and what Vail Resorts' attorneys had insisted they did not. Vail personnel manning the Information Center reportedly told visitors that the company planned to break ground on the new developments in a few months, during the spring of 1999—a highly ambitious schedule.[12] For a company that ostensibly did not have any such plans at all only a few months earlier, Vail Resorts had produced them suspiciously fast.

Unable to ignore the connection that the other agencies had ferreted out, White River forest supervisor Ketelle reversed herself in March. Her approval of the Peak 7 expansion would be held up until there was "resolution of the base area development by the Town of Breckenridge and Summit County."[13] In late 2000, Ketelle apparently reversed herself again, approving construction of an access road on Peak 7 before the town had approved the base development, an action that drew criticism from Breckenridge officials and the EPA.[14]

The whole process reeked. In a situation where the Forest Service was toeing the line of the company it was supposed to regulate, the Environmental Protection Agency found itself obliged to ride to the rescue, force Vail Resorts to come clean on its plans, and give the town of Breckenridge, as well as the federal government, an honest shot at evaluating them.

❋ ❋ ❋

The U.S. Forest Service is landlord to ski areas on sixty-two national forests in eighteen states. These ski areas account for about 50 to 55 percent of the more than fifty million skier days tallied each winter.[15] In 1996, Congress overhauled the Forest Service's lease arrangement with ski areas, so that bigger operators now tend to pay more, and smaller ones less. Previously, the agency had tried to capture as lease income some of the money resorts earned from development on adjacent private land—for instance, from base area restaurants. The agency's rationale was the "positive externality" argument: such developments made money as a result of the lifts and trails built on Forest Service land. This truth, however, angered ski-area operators, who turned to Congress for relief. The resulting legislative "reform" put an end to the Forest Service's attempts to claim a piece of the pie earned outside public land boundaries. The result is a deal for ski areas. Total lease fees paid by all ski areas nationwide to the Forest Service amount to between $17 million and $19 million annually, or between seventy-one and eighty cents per skier day. A draft analysis compiled by the agency in 2001 indicated that the federal government was collecting 6 percent less money than it would have under the old leasing system.[16]

Vail Mountain paid $2.6 million in Forest Service land rent in 1998—a sizable sum, but only 4 percent of the gross revenues Vail Resorts says it gathered from public lands on Vail Mountain the previous year. Four percent of the gross is the maximum the Forest Service can charge. (The low end of the rent scale is 1.5 percent of revenues.) All told, in 1998 the federal government collected $10.2 million from Colorado ski areas for leases covering approximately seventy thousand acres, equal to about $145 an acre.[17] In 1998, Vail Resorts could have paid the entire rental bill for every Colorado ski area on Forest Service land; the tab would have amounted to 2.5 percent of that corporation's gross revenues.

Consider what ski-area developers get for their money. Under the 1996 reforms, leases were lengthened and standardized at forty years, and language was introduced to allow leases to be renewed without environmental review under NEPA. The net effect of that loophole is a de facto permanent leasehold on public land. Ski resorts "couldn't get Congress to give them the land outright, so now they're trying for the next best thing: no oversight when the permit comes up for renewal," said Ted Zukoski, an attorney for the Land and Water Fund of the Rockies in Boulder, Colorado.[18]

This Forest Service leasehold creates an economic rationale for profitable base-village construction, ancillary businesses, and the inevitable associated sprawl. Without the ski area, there's no justification for a village. As developers themselves point out, the ski area is not only the reason to build real estate developments; it's also the amenity that drives real estate prices sharply higher. This connection should be self-evident, yet for some people it apparently isn't. The Forest Service has been reluctant, at times even truculent, about seeing what appears obvious to many industry observers and ski-town residents: ski-area expansion fosters base-area development and off-mountain impacts. As the agency primarily responsible for overseeing and regulating the ski industry, the Forest Service should take the lead in defending the public estate. Yet some Forest Service offices seem to turn a willfully blind eye to the connections between on-mountain development and off-mountain impacts, as well as to the negative side of ski-area development in general. As one Forest Service veteran of ski industry battles said: "My goal was to treat the industry like every other permitee, not give special treatment but to follow NEPA, the Endangered Species Act, the Clean Water Act. What I found out was the ski industry, they play by a different set of rules, and the Forest Service goes along with it. Congress and the administration supports the ski industry. They come out and have a great time, but they don't get it. It took me a year to catch on with what was going on, and then I thought, Oh my God, what can I do?" The answer, this individual said, was not much.[19]

Although the Forest Service presents itself as a steward of the public lands, the truth is that it is no longer capable of acting as one. The agency has become badly compromised in its ability to regulate the ski industry because it is formally in partnership with that industry—a textbook example of conflict of interest that leaves the public holding the bag.

Why wasn't Smokey the Bear standing up for the White River National Forest during the Peak 7 debates? At the end of the twentieth century, as its traditional mission—logging public lands—was dissolved, the Forest Service bureaucracy was busy looking out for itself rather than the public trust. It needed a new public mandate. Top managers, especially political appointees, believe they found one in recreation. In practical terms, that means the agency now is in the business of defending the interests of recreation as it once defended logging companies. A direct line cannot be drawn between recent shifts in Forest Service policy and what did—and didn't—happen in the Breckenridge fiasco. But an indistinct line does exist—after all, policy is supposed to drive what happens in the field offices. The reality in the U.S. Forest Service now, a reality driven down through the agency by Congress and the Clinton administration (and embraced by the Bush administration), is that the agency is out of the logging business and has jumped into the recreation business with both feet.

※ ※ ※

The Forest Service was formed a century ago to manage the public lands that were known at the time as "forest reserves" and eventually became the nation's 155 national forests. This land was to be used, not protected in the manner of national parks. The earliest mandates to the agency directed it to maintain a supply of wood and clean water for the nation. In 1960, the federal Multiple-Use and Sustained-Yield Act directed the service to manage its lands for range, timber, watershed, wildlife, fish, and recreational purposes. The agency accommodated these needs in part by zoning forests for different uses. In wilderness areas, for example, there is no motorized recreation or logging. To help satisfy the national need for timber, other lands are clear-cut. Still others are developed for recreation with campgrounds and boat launches.

The agency is part of the U.S. Department of Agriculture, and "getting the cut out," or logging, remained its primary focus through most of the twentieth century. In the late 1980s, logging on national forest lands peaked at about twelve billion board feet per year.[20] During the next decade it declined to about one-quarter of that amount. Environmentalists, judges, and the Clinton administration, particularly Forest Service chief Mike Dombeck, spent the 1990s weaning the agency off logging.

This was not an easy thing to do, since cutting trees generated revenue for the service. Although audits during the 1990s would show that the agency had lost money on many of its timber sales over the years, as far as officials in district ranger offices were concerned, selling timber to logging companies meant bringing revenue in the front door, which in turn kept that district's or that forest's budget healthy for the following year.

Like all bureaucracies, the Forest Service as an institution has a different embodied mentality from the individuals who comprise it. For a bureaucracy, self-preservation is the paramount goal. The writing was on the wall during the 1990s that high-volume logging was coming to an end. The agency needed to find a new mission—and a new cash cow. Salvation came in the guise of the recreation industry.

Today, the Forest Service portrays itself as a "recreation provider." Floyd Thompson of the Forest Service Office of Recreation, Heritage, and Wilderness Resources declared:

> The goal of the Forest Service is to provide the highest quality outdoor recreation settings. . . . Marketing plans and business plans are now becoming part of the Forest Service lingo. Travel and tourism is [sic] being recognized as one of the major benefits of National Forests. Outfitter and guide service operations and other private concessions are now being seen more as partners in serving our forest visitors. Collaboration with communities to set common visions for tourism potential and development in their areas is now part of the way business is done.[21]

Forest Service officials calculated that by 2000, national forests would contribute $131 billion to the gross domestic product—and three-quarters of that would be in the form of recreation.[22] Clearly, if the agency wanted to begin to defend its $3 billion annual budget in front of Congress, it was going to have to figure out how to get a piece of that recreation pie. The de facto bureaucratic unit of measure for the agency would no longer be the board foot of timber; it would be the visitor day of a recreationist.

The problem was, recreation on national forests traditionally has been free to individuals, with the exception of small fees charged concessionaires such as guides, outfitters, and ski areas that run their business on public land and pass those costs on to customers. The agency set about attempting to scrape money off recreationists in several ways. The most visible and controversial is the Recreation Fee, instituted by Congress as a three-year pilot program in 1996, then repeatedly extended. In essence, the program embodies the principle of pay-to-play. At test sites around the country, visitors to national forest lands were charged to use trails, climb peaks, park at trailheads, enter visitors' centers, and so on. In 1999, the agency pulled in $26.5 million—chicken feed relative to its budget, but the take at the door wasn't the point. The objective was to establish the principle of charging for recreation, and by 2000, Forest Service officials were pushing toward a regional or national pass system to charge for public access to national forest lands.

The Recreation Fee was not created solely because logging revenues were dropping. Congress had been cutting Forest Service appropriations in real terms for a decade by the time the fee was instituted, part of a Republican (and, under President Clinton, bipartisan) effort to reduce the size of the federal government—or at least of those parts not related to defense and entitlement spending. Between 1994 and 1999, the congressional appropriation for the Forest Service's recreation budget dropped one-fifth—more, if adjusted for inflation.[23] Unlike logging revenues, which must be remitted to the U.S. Treasury, recreation fees largely are retained by the forest that collects them—strong incentive for a cash-starved agency in which rangers on the ground may be unable to scrape together the money for basic tasks such as trail maintenance and patrols.[24]

More significant than user fees in terms of the agency's changing management strategy are the partnerships the Forest Service has entered into with the recreation industry. These, too, are a product of congressional budget cutting. As the appropriations funding tap has been tightened, Forest Service officials have had little choice but to turn to the recreation industry in search of money to help them do their jobs. This is an unholy alliance that forces the agency into the arms of the recreation industry, an industry that includes the Walt Disney Company, Kawasaki, and other heavy-hitters who want to profit from development on and use of public lands. "We find corporate-financed congressmen, cash-strapped land managers and recreation industry leaders working cooperatively to create an entirely new management paradigm," says Scott Silver, director of the Oregon-based nonprofit group Wild Wilderness, which opposes the recreation fee and corporate control of public lands.[25] "There is a concerted effort by Congress and the . . . administration to defund all federal agencies and programs so as to encourage them—force them—to function more like private businesses. There has been, likewise, a concerted effort to promote privatization of those parts of government that can, in the opinion of the promoters, better operate within the private sector."[26]

In its new recreation-friendly, business-buddy mode, the Forest Service is cozying up to the very industries it is supposed to be regulating. "Both our deteriorating infrastructure and our recreation customers are demanding more attention," declares the agency's Recreation Agenda, completed in September 2000.

Management of these cherished resources requires a long-term viewpoint and investment strategies. Years of declining budgets and a dwindling recreation workforce have made the challenges even more formidable. The agency has responded with innovative efforts such as the fee demonstration program, permit streamlining, *nongovernmental partnerships*, and help from volunteers.[27] [Emphasis added.]

Among the many problems the agency faced in 2000 was a deferred maintenance backlog of $812 million on public lands. By 2006, the Forest Service wants to cut that to $609 million, and it doesn't expect significant help from Congress, so it was considering private investment on public lands.[28] That sounds reasonable on its face—a campground concessionaire, for instance, might install new outhouses as part of its lease arrangement and get a break on the rent. But the quid pro quo can go both ways, and deals like these raise legitimate questions about the ability of the Forest Service to adequately regulate industries that profit from public lands development—from off-highway vehicle and Jet Ski manufacturers to the ski industry. If the Forest Service becomes dependent on its corporate partners to do some of what used to be the government's job, how clear-eyed will the agency be when it regulates those partners?

"The Forest Service's job is to properly manage and protect the resources entrusted to its care," says Silver. He continues:

> The ski industry's job is to make money for its shareholders. The Forest Service does not have the will, the courage or the financial motivation to tell the ski industry "no." There are many times when "no" is the only correct answer. By joining the fate of the Forest Service to the financial success of their partnership with the private sector, the objectivity of the Forest Service is, I suggest, compromised.
>
> Recreation is replacing the traditional extractive industries. The agencies are pretty much the same as they've always been. All that's changing is the use, the PR spin and the rhetoric. The Forest Service has mismanaged logging, mining and grazing for nearly a hundred years. Financially these commodities have, for the most part, all been played out. So the Forest Service is moving onto something new, and this time

they are expected to do something they never did in the past. They are expected to run their new businesses in partnership with the private sector and they expect that, in partnership, they will actually make some money. In that regard, the "wreckreation" agenda is potentially much worse than the resource extraction agenda. The Forest Service was never before so directly motivated by the need to make a profit as they are today. Likewise, the Forest Service was never so totally outclassed as they are when they play ball with the sorts of recreation, media, real-estate and entertainment companies they are dealing with today.[29]

The ski industry is a shining example of a willing mate for the "nongovernmental partnerships" the Forest Service is seeking. "We're building partnerships more than ever before, and we know that high-quality outdoor recreation experiences are the product of public/private partnership," Undersecretary of Agriculture James Lyons told the industry-heavy American Recreation Coalition in 1998. "Just look at the alpine skiing that occurs on the national forests. The Winter Sports Partnership was our first adventure in aggressively promoting the benefits of working together to promote our brand of outdoor recreation. We think it's paid off—for the ski areas, for the Forest Service, and for the customers we serve."[30]

There's a lot of talk like that from the Forest Service these days—talk about "customers," "branding," "marketing," "thinking like a business." The roots of this strategy trace back to a 1994 agreement between the Forest Service and two trade groups, National Ski Areas Association and U.S. Skiing, to create the National Winter Sports Partnership. The agreement lays out the agency's obligations to the ski industry, including promoting development of recreational facilities and using recreation on public lands to promote local economies. The partnership is a window into how the Forest Service perceives its relationship with the industry it oversees, and the view it provides is disconcerting. "Our success in achieving the goals of the Winter Sports Partnership is dependent on the strength of our relationship with our ski industry partners," declares a 1996 overview document. *"These relationships are, in large measure, based on how we as an agency help our partners achieve business success."*[31] As far as today's Forest Service is concerned, its job is not to protect the public estate from abuse of overdevelopment; it is to help the ski industry "achieve business success." Toward that goal, the federal government, through the Winter Sports Partnership, helped pay for a number of programs near and dear to the ski industry's heart. In 1996, the Forest Service agreed to commit $500,000 to furthering the partnership, and the National Ski Areas Association was quick to suggest how to spend it. NSAA president Michael Berry asked for money to help market skiing to people under the age of twenty-three, to study ski-lift technology, and to introduce beginners to skiing, among other requests.[32] The agency did agree to spend $45,000 getting kids interested in skiing and snowboarding.[33] In subsequent years, the Forest Service paid $30,000 to subsidize NSAA's creation of an "Environmental Charter" for the ski industry; $10,000 to the industry trade group Colorado Ski Country USA to encourage fifth-graders to ski; $8,000 to help SnowSports Industries of America develop a ski industry press kit; $10,000 to help the Sporting Goods Manufacturers Association develop a school workbook for kids that teaches them "about equipping themselves for winter-time outdoor fun"; and $55,000 to help a film production company called SIRDAR create a twenty-three-minute movie targeted at kids in grades K–6. According to Forest Service documents, "SIRDAR . . . is committed to creating youth programs about the benefits of being active in the outdoors. SIRDAR works closely with the ski and snowboard industry to create kid-friendly programs which do this."[34]

These are some of the ways in which the Forest Service spends taxpayer money to promote the industry it regulates.

It's obvious what the ski industry gets out of the deal; what does the Forest Service get? Good publicity. Among dozens of documents I examined that concern the Winter Sports Partnership, almost every one emphasized the idea that the Forest Service must obtain good visibility around ski areas. Of that first $500,000 committed in 1996, $50,000 was dedicated to "relationship building, communication strategy and national visibility."[35] Again and again, Forest Service officials insisted in documents that the agency get "recognition," that signs and logos and banners be placed in and around ski areas and events, even that Forest Service banners be positioned so they would be within camera range at ski races. A major problem the agency faces, according to the documents, is that few people know that the agency "provides" all this great skiing terrain they're enjoying. Consequently, they must be educated to that fact, apparently to drum up public support for the agency's new recreation mission.

Like the partners in a bad marriage who stay together to maintain their public image, the Forest Service and the ski industry are using each other. Through their partnership with the agency, ski areas are able to put a green veneer on their operations. They can install taxpayer-funded kiosks and dioramas about geology and animal tracks on ski mountains and then issue press releases about their sensitivity to the environment. The agency, for its part, can assert it is "providing" skiing opportunities by dint of happening to control the land where the skiing is taking place, erect lots of signs reminding visitors of that fact, and thereby claim a constituency.

In such an arrangement, neither partner is likely to rock the boat too hard. Are the fruits of this partnership apparent in—to take one example—the Forest Service's kid-glove treatment of Vail Resorts over the Breckenridge Peak 7 expansion? Is the fox guarding the henhouse? The answer is not clear, but there is the scent of a fox in many places, not just Breckenridge.

In Utah's Wasatch-Cache National Forest, ski resorts are aching to expand their operations, especially in Big Cottonwood and Little Cottonwood Canyons, home to Solitude, Brighton, Alta, and Snowbird resorts. Forest supervisor Bernie Weingardt seemed eager to accommodate ski-area interests. In June 1997, Weingardt overruled his staff and gave a thumbs-up to a summer alpine slide development at Solitude ski area, one of Intrawest's properties. "We have a national policy to help create four-season resorts at the ski areas and that is a policy we are trying to push here," Weingardt told critics.[36] Yet the Forest Service Manual, the agency's guiding policy document, does not seem to support him on the alpine slide, or on many of the other improvements ski-area developers want and often get. Recreation policy, according to the manual, should "[e]ncourage summertime use of ski area facilities where that use is compatible with or enhances natural resource-based recreation opportunities and does not require additional specialized facilities." Forest managers should "authorize concession developments only where there is a demonstrated public need. Do not permit concession development either solely for the purpose of establishing a profit-making enterprise or where satisfactory public service could be provided on nearby public or other private lands."[37]

Is an alpine slide a public need? It certainly is an "additional specialized facility." What about the expansion of Snowbird that Weingardt approved in 1999, an expansion that includes a land trade to enlarge the ski area, new ski runs, and new lodges, including one building covering fifty thousand square feet on the summit of Hidden Peak in Little Cottonwood Canyon? What about the proposed three new lifts, base-area "people-mover," bigger lodges, and mountain-bike trails proposed at Solitude, in Big Cottonwood? The Cottonwood Canyons provide drinking water to four hundred thousand people in Salt Lake City and already are suffering from water quality degradation.[38] Is more recreation there a public need?

Given the demonstrably flat and probably declining ski industry, a reasonable observer might wonder why the Forest Service has not taken a nationwide look at how much ski-area development is appropriate, where, and why. Indeed, since the battle for market share is presently a zero-sum game, the Forest Service probably is helping some parts of the industry while hurting others—which prompts the question, Why isn't the ski industry itself pushing for a nationwide review of expansion and development on Forest Service lands?

Some ski industry opponents, in the form of the Colorado-based Ski Area Citizens Coalition, a consortium of environmental groups, have agitated for just such an analysis as a way to short-circuit the resort arms race that now leaves Utah competing against Colorado, the Northwest against California, and the New England states against one another in a cutthroat fight for the same fifty million skier days. The demand was echoed by the *Denver Post* editorial board in early 2001.[39] As of summer 2001, however, the Forest Service had expressed no interest in undertaking such a nationwide analysis. To do so would undermine the agency's partnership with the industry. It would cut against the bureaucratic tendency to try to make each Forest Service fiefdom bigger and thus more successful, even if the net result is a "tragedy of the commons" on public lands.[40] So the Forest Service finds itself standing aside as ski areas undertake bizarre developments such as Vail Mountain's Adventure Ridge mountain-top amusement park, a place where kids can play video games and their parents can trade stocks online, hold a meeting, or send a fax.[41] By almost no stretch of the imagination can such a place qualify as fulfilling a public need—after all, one does not need a Colorado mountain in order to build an amusement park or conference center—although it does serve to add to the industry's bottom lines ("achieve business success") and to fatten the local Forest Service office's lease revenues and its count of the new bureaucratic currency, visitor days.

* * *

Wasatch-Cache forest supervisor Bernie Weingardt allegedly said he wanted to "fuzz the boundaries," and he evidently did so in 1997, when he went skiing on his free ski pass at Snowbird. Weingardt was spotted by another Forest Service employee, skiing out of uniform on a complimentary pass—an act that may not have been illegal at the time, but that did get Weingardt investigated and found in partial violation of the agency's ethical standards, since he appeared to be taking a freebie from a corporation he oversaw. Weingardt told investigators that he holds free season passes to six ski areas and uses them often.[42]

A season ski pass is a valuable thing, worth fifteen hundred dollars or more at some resorts. Forest Service policy holds that season passes are to be used for official business only, and that "season passes are limited to those employees normally required to spend at least one day a week at the facility during the operating season."[43] On national forests across the country, from New Hampshire's White Mountain to California's Eldorado, agency officials routinely ask for and get season passes and day passes. Typically, forest supervisors submit a list to local ski resorts specifying who should be given a season pass. At small ski areas, only two or three people typically request season passes each year, usually the local district ranger and a recreation or snow science specialist. Alternatively, an official may be named on a master list at the ticket office; he or she would obtain a free day ticket as needed to do the day's government business.

Agency staff must be able to visit a ski area to determine whether it is being operated according to permit conditions, to monitor boundaries, and so on. But the season pass can be problematic. Once a skier possesses such a pass, he or she has an open ticket to the slopes any time the lifts are running. Lists of Forest Service employees who were issued free ski passes during the 1990s range from two individuals per year at Winter Park to as many as nine at Vail, plus others who are entitled to day passes. Who really needs to be on a ski area every week to supervise operations? Likely candidates include the district ranger, winter sports administrator, and snow ranger. On some forests, including the Grand Mesa–Uncompahgre–Gunnison (GMUG) in Colorado and Tahoe in California, forest supervisors don't ask for season passes for themselves, only for the right to a day ticket if they have business on the slopes. On other forests, including Utah's Wasatch-Cache, where Weingardt runs the show, and Colorado's White River, supervised by Martha Ketelle, the forest supervisors obtain season passes for themselves from every ski area in their jurisdictions—about a half-dozen on each. If one is to believe these supervisors are living within the letter of Forest Service policy about season passes—policy holding that a pass is justified by skiing at a resort on business at least one day per week—then these busy supervisors ski every working day of every winter week.[44]

There is no evidence that these forest supervisors or their employees are breaking the law. But there is no significant safeguard, either, beyond an employee's integrity, that prevents Forest Service workers from using their ski passes as a perk. In all likelihood, few pass holders abuse their privileges. But the murkiness of who has ski passes and when they use them can raise doubts in the public mind about whether the Forest Service is being impartial when it reviews ski-area operations and expansions. Nobody, after all, is inclined to bite the hand that feeds him.

✳ ✳ ✳

Ski passes aside, there's plenty of other evidence to suggest that the agency is not impartial. In 1996, Jeff Burch, a Forest Service planner with the GMUG National Forest, sent a letter to each member of the board of directors of Telluride's Sheep Mountain Alliance (SMA). SMA was fighting the agency's recent approval of plans by the Telluride Company, parent of the Telluride ski resort, to enlarge the ski area from 1,050 acres to 1,783. Burch was the planner overseeing the expansion application and its review. SMA had won some of the changes it wanted through an administrative appeal and was contemplating court action to force additional changes when Burch's letter, excerpted here, arrived. His three-page missive is an apparent attempt to intimidate SMA's board into dropping its plans to appeal the expansion again:

> First of all, I would like to convince you that you do not have a legal case. . . . We have done a very careful job of ensuring that our decisions are supportable with legal process. Our consultant was one of the best. Our EIS is the best I know of. . . . You stand nothing to gain by litigation.
>
> Second, I would like to convince you that litigation will result in excessive, unnecessary and even, in some cases, unfair costs; costs to everyone. These costs will be real to you, to the Telluride Company, and to the people of the entire Telluride region. . . . From your perspective, you will bear both the financial and personal costs associated with such a lawsuit. . . . [M]ore than just money, it will cost you personally, each of you and as an organization in Telluride. . . . And speaking for the Forest Service and for myself personally, it will be impossible to work together in the same good spirit we have been, on the many issues in which we have common interest, if we are at war in court. And make no mistake, litigation is war.
>
> In addition to these costs to you, your actions will result in very real costs to the Telluride [C]ompany in terms of legal fees and the costs associated with delay. It is my belief that the Telluride Company is a friend to Telluride. They are the economic engine that supports the region. They contribute more than their minimum share to the community. . . . [Y]our chance of gaining more at the costs I just outlined is, I honestly

believe, low to none. You may be getting advice from others that indicate [sic] otherwise, but as I have outlined here, I honestly believe they are wrong.

I suspect your attorneys are advising you (apparently from the start) to go to court; that you can win. I believe they are wrong, also. Your legal counsel has not represented you well. . . .

I am appealing to you personally to accept (even grudgingly would be understandable) the [Forest Service] appeal decision and pursue no further redress. You can come out the winner by doing so. You will be embraced as reasonable and community minded while having acted on your principle [sic] throughout the process. I assure you that announcement of your intention not to go further will bring public praise, and real support, from the entire community. It certainly would result in public praise from the Forest Service.[45]

Burch's letter drew a quick disavowal from his boss, GMUG forest supervisor Robert Storch. The matter was investigated and Burch taken off the Telluride job, but as of 2001 he still worked for the agency under Storch's command. Sheep Mountain Alliance pressed ahead with its suit against the Forest Service in federal court in Denver. The day before the trial was to begin, Storch rescinded his entire approval of the ski-area expansion and took the project back to square one. The agency began the review process all over again. In the second round, SMA gained significant support for its position from the Telluride community. When Forest Service approval was issued again in 1999, the Telluride town council considered filing an appeal over the project's continuing deficiencies. Both the town and SMA felt the Forest Service had done a poor job of acknowledging the off-site, socioeconomic effects (higher housing costs, greater commuting times for workers), and the air quality reduction that would result from the expansion. In December 1999, as another round of litigation began, a frustrated Telluride Company CEO Ron Allred interceded and mediated a court-approved agreement between SMA, his firm and the Forest Service—the agency that is supposed to be protecting the public trust.[46]

❋ ❋ ❋

Jeff Burch's bias in favor of the ski area, and his evident belief that it is the Forest Service's job to promote the local economy through ski-area development, is not unique to him. The most extraordinary example of agency bias may well be the draft environmental impact statement on the new White River Forest Plan, released in 1999. A forest plan is perhaps the most important document produced by the agency, for it determines what actually happens on the ground. The White River plan would set the course for that forest's management for the next fifteen years and was widely viewed as a test case for new forest plans nationwide. Yet the 1999 draft asserted that management alternatives that proposed the *most* ski-area development and the most aerial travel corridors for gondolas and chairlifts would result in the *least* negative environmental impact. It's an assertion that seems laughable on its face, yet it passed agency review all the way to the point of the plan's being issued for public comment. The Environmental Protection Agency took it upon itself to point this ludicrous assertion out to the Forest Service, which took the comment under advisement.

In Klamath Falls, Oregon, District Ranger Rob Schull saw no conflict of interest in his appointment as president of the local chamber of commerce in 1998. Schull was deeply involved in the Forest Service's review of plans by Jeld-Wen, Inc., to build a new, thirty-six-million-dollar ski resort on nearby Pelican Butte. Yet he reportedly said more than once that he took the chamber of commerce job to help promote the ski-area project, which is closely tied to a large Jeld-Wen real estate project, the

Running Y Ranch Resort. In October 1998, Schull joined a contingent of local businessmen who flew, at no cost to themselves, on a Jeld-Wen corporate jet to St. George, Utah, to lobby Sky West Airlines for air service between Klamath Falls and Sacramento or San Francisco—a key to making the resort financially viable. Schull insisted that his trip on the Jeld-Wen jet had nothing to do with the ski resort, but others on the junket said that the Running Y Ranch was discussed; they "could not recall" whether the ski-area plans came up.[47] Schull was suspended by Forest Service officials after the junket was publicized but still worked for the agency as of 2000.[48]

In Utah, billionaire Earl Holding wanted to trade the Forest Service some of his land for property at the base of his Snowbasin ski resort northeast of Salt Lake City. A private man, Holding is by all accounts dogged and usually gets what he wants. Snowbasin would be no exception, and the result was not the Forest Service's finest hour. In addition to Snowbasin, Holding owns Sun Valley resort—W. Averell Harriman's creation that started the destination-resort boom—and numerous other businesses, most notably Sinclair Oil, which counted an estimated $1.9 billion in sales in 2000; the Little America and Grand America hotel chains, which he started in Rock Springs, Wyoming; and approximately five hundred thousand acres of western property.[49] He reportedly wanted to create a jet-setter's enclave by developing a high-end base village at Snowbasin. In 1990, Dale Bosworth, then the supervisor of the Wasatch-Cache forest, decided Holding needed two hundred acres at the base to do the job and agreed to a land trade of that size. Holding desired a lot more; seven months later, higher-ups in the agency, under intense political pressure from Utah officials, reluctantly agreed to trade seven hundred acres. Holding still wasn't satisfied; he eventually went to Utah's congressional delegation to make an end run around Forest Service regulations. They jumped at his bidding, which was to be expected: between

1993 and 1998, Holding and his wife, Carol, gave almost $100,000 to Utah's Republican representatives in Congress and to Governor Mike Leavitt.

Representative Jim Hansen (R-Utah) introduced legislation in Congress ordering a 1,320-acre land exchange—more than two square miles of property at the base of Snowbasin's ski runs. Grey Reynolds, then deputy chief of the Forest Service, drew up the legislation, which slipped through Congress on the last night of business in 1996, attached to a seven-hundred-page omnibus bill. Like many such late-night deals, it was the kind of legislative rider that would wither under public scrutiny. The bill exempted the first phase of development on Holding's new land from environmental review and obliged the Forest Service to build a fifteen-million-dollar access road across two active mud-slide sites. (In the spring of 2001, the new road started sliding down the hill, as expected).[50] Representative Tom Petri, a Wisconsin Republican, gave the road bill a Porker Award as an example of wasteful federal spending. Grey Reynolds soon quit the Forest Service; six months later he was Holding's general manager at Snowbasin resort. Reynolds's move left many Forest Service veterans shaking their heads at an apparently tawdry quid pro quo, and it deeply damaged the agency's credibility.[51]

※ ※ ※

No ski area land trade has been the result of such obvious political arm-twisting at the expense of the environment as the one at Snowbasin. Grey Reynolds's departure from Washington in favor of the corner office at Snowbasin aside, many Forest Service employees opposed the trade on environmental grounds. But many land trades do go through, and they are becoming increasingly popular among ski-resort developers who covet land at the base of ski runs. Typically, the developer acquires or holds property the Forest Service wants and will trade that land to the government in exchange for Forest Service property the developer desires. Since 1988, the Forest Service has traded an annual average of 70,755 acres of federal property in exchange for 124,470 acres of nonfederal lands, with each side officially valued around $90 million.[52] (This includes all trades for all purposes—ski-area-related trades were a small fraction of the total.) Yet a U.S. General Accounting Office review of land trades made by the Bureau of Land Management and the Forest Service concluded that the trades don't serve the public interest and should be abandoned altogether. "The agencies have given more than fair market value for nonfederal land they acquired and accepted less than fair market value for lands they conveyed," the GAO stated in 2000. "We believe Congress may wish to consider directing the Service and the Bureau to discontinue their land exchange programs."[53]

For the moment, land trades are continuing. In regard to ski areas, land trades raise many questions about the Forest Service's determination or ability to defend the public interest—again, questions that are shadowed by doubts over whether the agency can adequately regulate an industry that is its financial partner. One dubious trade is proposed at Grand Targhee, the resort near Driggs, Idaho, that is owned by George Gillett, founder of Booth Creek Ski Holdings. Gillett proposed trading 385 acres of habitat used by grizzly bears (a threatened species), which he owns in the Targhee National Forest, for 195 acres of public land at the ski-area base. The resulting development could accommodate 970 lodging units, a 36-acre village of shops and restaurants, and 55 acres of single and multifamily homes.[54] Opposition to the trade ran four-to-one among the four thousand people who registered comments on it.[55]

The trade was shelved in the mid-1990s, then revived under intense scrutiny. As at Breckenridge, the Environmental Protection Agency found itself squaring off against the Forest Service. Although the EPA supported the idea of obtaining

Booth Creek's inholding (known as Squirrel Meadows, it was surrounded by public lands and faced the threat of development), it had significant problems with the Forest Service's analysis of the impacts of the trade. Again, as at Breckenridge, the EPA criticized the service for failing to acknowledge that base-area development and its associated impacts are related to the Forest Service's action—in this case, the trade.[56] Peter Morton, an economist employed by the Wilderness Society, hammered the socioeconomic analysis in the land swap's draft environmental impact statement for failing to consider off-site impacts, underestimating the expected resulting home construction and its effects on local schools and transportation, and promoting the trade at the expense of the local community and environment. (The socioeconomic analysis was written by Ford Frick, a Colorado consultant who often works for the ski industry.) "What is best for the ski corporation is not the same as what is best for local communities and the American people who own the land," Morton wrote. "While developing a four-season resort on public land might be in the best interest of shareholders of [then-owner] Booth Creek Holding Company, the development will be associated with off-site negative impacts on local residents and businesses. Why is the agency concerned about the economic vitality of the resort?"[57]

The Forest Service ultimately approved the trade in late 2000, swapping 120 acres at Grand Targhee's base for 400 acres in Squirrel Meadows. Agency officials concluded in their assessment that the trade wouldn't make much difference either way in terms of what happened in the Teton Valley and Driggs area. The region is going to grow anyway, the agency said, so development at the ski-area base—or lack of it—doesn't matter.[58] In August of 2001 a federal judge halted the Grand Targhee trade, ruling that the Forest Service had failed to disclose the trade's full environmental effects, thus violating the National Environmental Policy Act.[59]

At Grand Targhee the Forest Service offered another *Through the Looking Glass* type of argument: everything will happen and yet nothing can be done because everything will happen. This approach completely repudiates the concept of analyzing development for its cumulative impacts, ignores the history of ski-resort sprawl across the country, and incorrectly asserts that the Forest Service has neither the mandate nor the ability to control ski-area growth or off-site impacts. The agency wishes to throw control of the base area—at the edge of a federal wilderness—into the hands of George Gillett. To top things off, it valued the land at the base at $28,000 per acre, although land at nearby Jackson Hole is selling for $50,000 to $100,000 per acre.[60]

Despite the complaints of the General Accounting Office, land trades are proliferating in the ski industry:

- In Vermont, American Skiing Company's Sugarbush resort traded 213 acres of private land and $415,000 to the Forest Service for 58 acres at the bottom of the ski hill.[61]
- A three-way land trade between Crested Butte Mountain Resort, the Colorado State Land Board, and the U.S. Forest Service netted the resort 558 prime base acres.[62]
- Vail Resorts is seeking to swap 463 private acres for 568 acres of Forest Service land near the town of Avon.[63]
- Intrawest wants to trade unspecified land for 100 acres of Forest Service property at the entrance to Copper Mountain Resort.[64]
- At Ski Cooper—a tiny ski area south of Vail that was developed as the original training area for the Tenth Mountain Division during World War II and that has no residential base development—the government of Lake County, which operates it, proposed a swap to gain 850 acres of base area land. The resulting village would radically alter the ecosystems, not to mention the peace and quiet, of Tennessee Pass, where Ski Cooper sits.

The Ski Cooper trade is yet another instance in which the EPA found it necessary to remind the Forest Service that it must address cumulative and indirect impacts in its environmental analysis—something the agency failed to do in this case, as it has in so many others.[65] In 2000, when the Forest Service belatedly indicated that a full environmental impact statement would be required, Lake County withdrew the exchange proposal.[66]

The EPA is no knight in shining armor. But time and again during recent years it has found itself in the role that should be played by the U.S. Forest Service: providing a counterweight against corporations' profit motive in debates over ski-area development on national forest lands. Whether EPA officials will be encouraged or even able to continue doing this during the Bush administration remains, at the time of this writing, unknown. If they are not, if the EPA adopts more of a hands-off attitude toward ski-resort development, the evidence suggests that the federal government will do very little to rein in the industry. There are plenty of individuals in the Forest Service who recognize their agency is falling down on the job and who wish things were different. But so long as the agency is obliged by Congress to find its funding in places beyond Capitol Hill, it is going to be compromised in its stewardship of America's public lands. Those who pay the highest price for this co-opting reside in the communities, both natural and human, situated near ski resorts.

CHAPTER 8

Resort Roadkill
The Environmental Price Tag

The lynx had survived the terrifying experience of being trapped in Canada and transported to Colorado. Now the cat was well-fed and healthy. Released during the early summer of 1999 into the South San Juan Mountains near the New Mexico border, it had migrated north and west during the past five months, seeking food and territory in this strange new terrain. It had traversed the ten thousand square miles of the San Juan Mountains, crossing the great, ancient volcanic caldera that formed these youngest of Colorado peaks. It had passed the dilapidated former mining town of Silverton and slipped over two-lane U.S. Highway 550. It had skirted the bustling ski resort complex of Telluride and Mountain Village, drifting west down into the drainage of the Dolores River.

By the end of October, the cat was in good country, finding its way in the world. It lived amid long rolling hills covered with conifers, land full of rabbits and coyotes and marmots—good game for the shy, rare, bobcatlike carnivore. This was the southernmost part of the Canada lynx's range, and many hopes were riding on this particular animal and several others. If the reintroduction of the lynx to Colorado went well, these cats might establish themselves again as a viable predator in these mountains.

Some environmentalists insisted that the species was still

present, that despite decades of hunting and trapping and re-lentless encroachment into its habitat, the cat never had vanished from Colorado. There was no need to reintroduce it, they said; these Canadian imports were the product of politics. There was some truth to that. When the reintroduction program began that February with the release of the first five cats, the federal government had just announced it would list the lynx as a threatened species under the Endangered Species Act. If the Colorado Division of Wildlife showed that it could successfully reintroduce the animal, the feds would be more likely to let the state agency manage the mandated recovery program in Colorado's mountains. That's what state officials and business groups wanted. If the lynx was going to get federal protection—something that rankled a lot of folks at the state capitol in Denver—at least the local boys could run the show.

The lynx near the Dolores didn't know any of this. Nor did it know that of the first five cats introduced, four had starved to death and the fifth had to be recaptured to prevent it from suffering the same fate. In fact, of the forty-one lynx introduced in Colorado that spring, seventeen already had died, including five starved, five killed by cars, and two shot. The cat padding through the forests of the Dolores River basin was present in large part because Vail Resorts wanted it to be there—to be *there*, that is, and not somewhere close to Vail, where its presence might be, well, inconvenient. The corporation had paid two hundred thousand dollars toward the state effort to reintroduce the animals—good public relations, perhaps, but also an investment that bought Vail Resorts a seat at the table when decisions were made about just how the reintroduction program was going to work. For the executives at Vail, lynx were fine and dandy—just not in their backyard, thank you.

The state of Colorado could finesse the problem that lynx reintroduction posed to developers; that's why it was dumping animals in the woods near New Mexico. That April, Ed

Quillen, a *Denver Post* columnist, had described the emperor's clothing:

> Various endangered-species laws might interfere with Vail's plans, but if Colorado had lynx populations elsewhere in the state, then that obstacle to Vail's expansion would be removed. As we all know, our state government delights in assisting needy corporations like Vail Resorts, and when Vail needs something like a bigger highway or some lynx to run around in a distant part of the state, the wheels start to turn. Thus the lynx trapped in Canada and Alaska have become pawns in a statewide chess game. They get to starve and Vail gets to enhance its bottom line.[1]

The lynx near the Dolores had survived a lot, and it was in good shape to make it through the winter. But on Halloween, it crossed paths with Lloyd Mulkey. Visiting from Louisiana, Mulkey was in the woods on an all-terrain vehicle, toting his .270-caliber rifle and hunting elk. His permit was for elk and elk only. But that apparently didn't matter to Mulkey. Nor did the fact that the lynx in his sights was wearing a radio tracking collar. He rammed a cartridge into the breech of his rifle and promptly shot and killed the cat.[2]

"The next time anyone feels compelled to capture some predators," Quillen wrote, "[to] tag them with computer chips and then turn them loose in a deep-snow wilderness until they die of starvation, [go] catch some Vail executives."[3]

✳ ✳ ✳

I meet Bill Heicher in a bar in Eagle, Colorado, on a quiet summer afternoon. Sandwiched between his thinning brown hair and uneven mustache, Heicher's eyes are tired. He looks worn out. Since 1972, he has worked in the Eagle River Valley as a field officer for the Colorado Division of Wildlife. During that time he has watched the landscape, and his job, change in ways he has been almost powerless to influence. The wildlife of the Eagle River Valley—the mule deer and elk, the sage grouse and jackrabbits, Canada lynx and boreal toads—are disappearing, falling back before the relentless development that is rooted in the ski industry.

The Eagle River begins at the Continental Divide near Ski Cooper, the small ski area at Tennessee Pass. The river flows north through the flats where Camp Hale, the Tenth Mountain Division's barracks, once stood and slices a deep canyon between the ridges that are home to Vail Mountain ski area to the east and Beaver Creek resort to the west. After thirty-one miles, at Dowd Junction, the Eagle merges with Gore Creek, a tumbling brook that begins twenty-five miles to the east at Vail Pass and flows through the town of Vail. Here the Eagle turns west and runs through almost forty miles of fertile river bottom, finally pouring itself into the Colorado River near the mouth of Glenwood Canyon. This flat, open part of the Eagle River Valley was ranch country when Heicher arrived in 1972. Vail was a fledging resort along a two-lane road at the eastern end of Eagle County. The town of Eagle was a one-horse sort of place, and Avon, the condo metropolis sprawled at the feet of what is now Beaver Creek ski resort, didn't exist.

Back then, hunters came to Eagle County to chase one of the largest mule deer herds in the state, and to bag some of the biggest bucks found anywhere. Today, the deer herd is in steep decline. The valley and its tributaries are filled with an increasingly dense sprawl of homes and businesses. Along the ridges and against the ski slopes, luxurious second homes have sprouted. Farther down the valley there are town homes and condominiums and trailer parks for the growing number of people who work to support the resort and construction industries, people who commute along Interstate 70, which was built through here in the 1970s. Planners estimate that Eagle County, which in 1980 contained 13,320 residents and in 1999 was home to 34,950, may have a population of more than 80,000 by 2020.[4]

From the ski slopes to the riverbeds, this population explosion has been devastating to wildlife. The story of what happens to wild creatures near ski resorts is almost always the same, almost always negative, and almost always hidden, obfuscated, lied about or ignored by ski industry representatives. Although ski resorts work hard to present an environmentally friendly face, the reality on the ground does not match up to the rhetoric.

✳ ✳ ✳

For most wildlife in ski country, winter habitat and spring calving or nesting grounds are the two most critical elements to a population's survival. Ungulates such as elk spend their summers and autumns at altitudes of ten thousand feet or higher in the boreal forests; in Colorado, most such land is national forest and often is protected as designated wilderness. When heavy snows accumulate in late autumn, they migrate to traditional wintering areas lower down, seeking a combination of good cover, available food, and less snow. Here they winter over, trying to find enough to eat to hang on until spring. Wintering areas, however, are also the places humans like to develop: valley floors, low hills with south-facing slopes, river bottoms.

Prior to the development of Beaver Creek resort in the late 1970s, several hundred elk wintered on what would become the ski slopes. Once the ski lifts began running, those elk crowded into Bachelor Gulch, a pocket of undeveloped land lying west of Beaver Creek near the small, independent ski area of Arrowhead. In the 1990s Arrowhead was purchased by Vail Resorts and connected with lifts and trails to Beaver Creek. The undeveloped pocket of Bachelor Gulch was filled with lifts and luxury homes, to the detriment of the resident elk. "It was the last spot that remained," Heicher says. "There's no place for those suckers to go. There's nothing left for them."[5]

Public officials are not entirely unmindful of the fate of wildlife. Development approvals often include requirements to "mitigate" impacts; Heicher spends about 40 percent of his time making recommendations (his suggestions are not legally binding) to land managers and county commissioners regarding building projects in the Eagle River Valley. The Beaver Creek elk herd has been the subject of "mitigation" three times since the 1970s. In each case, developers set aside land for the elk, then came back later with a reason why they needed to develop that land, and explained how the elk could go somewhere else. It is a pattern of treatment that might sound familiar to American Indians.

During the winters of the late 1990s, the Beaver Creek elk herd, now desperate for food, did something unprecedented. Finding the low slopes and valley floors developed with homes, condos, and golf courses, and unable to tolerate the people, dogs, and traffic in what had been their winter range, they literally charged Interstate 70, Colorado's principal east-west artery. Several hundred elk surged across the four-lane highway in a panicked hunt for forage on the north side of the road. Four times in three winters the Colorado State Patrol was forced to close the highway for several hours in order to allow the elk to cross.

The risks to the animals—and to drivers, who can easily be killed in a collision with a thousand-pound elk—are obvious. But they are not limited to the obvious. The low hills the elk reached on the north side of the interstate are not empty; this is an area grazed by mule deer, which cannot compete effectively with elk. There is, in most of nature and certainly in ski country, no "empty" land that wildlife can be pushed into. When Heicher makes presentations at elementary schools, he sometimes leads children through an exercise. If all the elk have enough food to get through the winter, and then the food is taken away from half the elk, what would you do? Most kids suggest that the hungry half should join the half that has food, and everyone should share. The idea has a feel-good logic about it—except in the real world outside the classroom, none of the elk will have enough food to survive, and so all of them will die.

"People are astounded—[the elk] all died!" Heicher says ruefully of the inevitable results of the school exercise. "This is a pretty good example of what happens if deer or elk are pushed from one area to another, if the other area is at a high carrying capacity. The end result is you're going to have a loss of animals, and probably sooner or later you're going to have a loss of habitat. But we go and tell county commissioners this, and they just go, 'Eighty percent of Eagle County is public land, why don't they just go eat on that?' It's like knocking your head into a brick wall." The great majority of public land in Eagle County and much of ski country is unsuitable as winter habitat; it consists of steep, forested slopes, high rock, and ice. Proposing that elk winter there is like insisting that a homeowner should be able to survive easily in the rest of his house after the kitchen burns down.

Compounding the situation, the federal land the animals reached in their cross-highway forays was being considered in 2000 for a land trade to the Town of Avon and Vail Resorts, which both want to build employee housing there to provide workers for the ski area. Where will the elk go then? Some people have proposed building high wire fences along either side of the Interstate to keep the elk from crossing and endangering themselves and drivers. "If that happens," Heicher says, "you're going to have a couple hundred elk on the south side who are going to die." They will starve, and that will be that. The Beaver Creek elk will have been mitigated out of existence.

Heicher has been deeply demoralized by the venality he witnesses in his territory, by everyone cashing in on the boom. If he argues that a development is going to affect wildlife, "those folks will just fight you tooth and nail." But as soon as a development clears regulatory hurdles, advertisements pop up saying, "'Build Your House Right Next to a Deer and Elk Migration Corridor,'" Heicher says, and shakes his head. "Everybody wants their share. They want that big chunk of money."

Ski-area executives protest that these impacts on wildlife are not their fault. It is a disingenuous argument. Although ski-resort development may not directly kill much wildlife, it is the identifiable and undeniable beginning of a chain of development events, and so it is indirectly responsible for much of what follows. Away from major cities, many western river valleys remain bucolic and agrarian. In Colorado's river valleys where the most significant development-induced wildlife and habitat problems are to be found, so are ski areas: the Snake River near Arapaho Basin and Keystone; the Blue River beside Breckenridge; the Roaring Fork threading past Aspen and Snowmass; the Fraser Valley, which includes Winter Park; and Vail and Beaver Creek's Eagle River. Yet examples also abound of Colorado valleys that do not face such problems: the North Platte in North Park; the North Fork, Lake Fork, and Tomichi Creek of the Gunnison; the Dolores, the Conejos, the Rio Grande. Apart from Colorado's booming Front Range cities and the retirement meccas of Grand Junction and Montrose, it is difficult to find a Colorado valley being filled with sprawl and new development that is not also close to a ski resort; it is impossible to find a major ski area that is not associated with sprawl and its attendant environmental messes. If ski areas have nothing to do with the environmental problems plaguing these valleys, there certainly are a lot of coincidences being built in ski country.

❋　❋　❋

The effects of modern ski-resort development are perhaps most visible in Colorado because that state is host to more skiing, and more skiers, than any other. But these effects can be found at ski areas nationwide. At Earl Holding's Snowbasin resort in northeastern Utah, for example, elk and moose are getting the short end of the stick. "Snowbasin is a real estate development masquerading as a ski resort," says Ron Younger, a former U.S. Bureau of Land Management field biologist. "The development there is a real estate development, including an eighteen-hole golf course. There's no place else for them to go. The elk can go east to mostly private land, but there's already some elk over there. They're invading other territories. That other habitat is not a vacuum; the same species are there. It makes wildlife fight for their own territory."[6]

In Whitefish, Montana, development of an 840-acre private golf community on the flanks of the Big Mountain ski resort has had the effect of funneling migrating grizzly bears down into the town center. The golf community links up to the ski slopes to create an enormous swath of open space the bears don't want to cross; they move downhill looking for cover, which leads them into town, where they are likely to come into conflict with humans—a conflict bears inevitably lose. "What was a huckleberry landscape is becoming a household landscape," says Tim Manley, a bear management specialist.[7]

In the Greater Yellowstone region of Wyoming, Montana, and Idaho, eight ski areas plan to build two million square feet of new commercial space, fourteen thousand hotel beds, and five hundred dwelling units at their base areas. Ninety percent of all subdivisions built in Greater Yellowstone—built in part because of the attractions those ski areas provide—were constructed without consideration of their impact on wildlife or water quality.[8]

At Squaw Valley USA ski resort in California, a dozen federal agents raided the resort's corporate offices on behalf of the Environmental Protection Agency, seeking information on a series of alleged environmental violations that are said to have gone on for years. A year later, as that investigation was continuing, the local water control board called on the California attorney general to open his own investigation into what water quality officials called Squaw's "systematic" and ongoing habit of polluting local waterways.[9]

Setting aside the philosophical question of what level of human development is appropriate in mountain valleys, ski-resort development greatly accelerates the urbanization of these places, to the detriment of wildlife, water, clean air, and other communal resources. The development and expansion of large ski resorts on public lands degrades the natural environment in ways that are as pervasive, far reaching, and difficult to remediate as those caused by excessive logging, grazing, and mining. Around ski resorts, these consequences are effectively permanent. The deleterious effects of road kills, loss of habitat, and air and water pollution are obvious to all but the most willfully blind observers. (In Colorado alone, an estimated five thousand deer are killed annually by drivers on the state's roads, along with hundreds of elk and dozens of bighorn sheep, moose, bears, mountain lions, and even eagles.)[10]

The road kills are an obvious red flag. More subtle is the nearly invisible erosion of biodiversity and ecological richness that accompanies ski-area growth. Both on the ski mountain and off, wildlife habitat is fragmented by roads, trails, and ski slopes; water quality and quantity diminish as water is drawn from rivers for snowmaking, golf-course irrigation, car washes, and household use, and as runoff from roads and golf courses carries silt, oil, gasoline, snow-melting chemicals, pesticides, and herbicides into wetlands and waterways.[11] Sensitive species such as Canada lynx, marten, and many migrating neotropical songbirds, unable to tolerate increased human presence, flee not only the disturbed areas, but also much larger regions around them.[12] The indirect effects of ski resorts, particularly as they morph into four-season destinations, degrade bio-diversity. As more people undertake more activities in or near ski areas, they generate more impacts—regardless of their good intentions. Researchers found that in areas where there was moderate use of all-terrain vehicles on trails, 50 percent fewer songbirds and 24 percent fewer breeding songbird pairs resided than in areas without ATVs. If ATV use was heavy, there were no breeding pairs at all. Simply hiking along trails had dele-terious effects on species such as western wood peewees, Townsend's solitaires, and solitary vireos.[13] The end result is that what looks from a distance like undisturbed forest around a ski area is probably a much less biologically diverse place than it was before resort development.

There is perhaps no illustration of this phenomenon that is so egregious, or so offensive, as the impact of Vail's Cate-gory III expansion on the Canada lynx. Political machinations cost the lynx its last, best chance in central Colorado, and very likely cost it a foothold in the entire Southern Rockies, from central Colorado to northern New Mexico. In this political game, the lynx was the loser. The winner? Vail Resorts.

* * *

The ski-terrain expansion plan known as Category III at Vail was conditionally approved by the U.S. Forest Service in 1986 and fully approved a decade later. Category I was the original ski area; Category II, an expansion to the southeast, added Mongolia Bowl, Siberia Bowl, and China Bowl. Category III en-compassed 4,100 acres of additional terrain to the south, sufficient land to double the permit area. This included Com-mando, Pete's, East Pete's, Super, and West Super Bowls. As part of Category III, the Forest Service also approved develop-ment of about 855 acres of cleared, lift-served terrain in Pete's, East Pete's, and the eastern part of Super Bowl—about 25 percent more terrain than the entire Aspen Mountain ski area. The development includes three lifts, a restaurant, warming huts, and ski patrol shacks, plus access roads.[14] The approval acknowledges that although not all of the terrain will be actively developed, all of it will see substantial increases in human traffic as a result of the ski-area expansion.

This expansion was planned for what biologists agree was some of the last, best habitat in Colorado for the Canada lynx, a thirty- to thirty-five-pound feline with wide, furry paws that specializes in hunting snowshoe hares in deep snow. The lynx is very habitat specific, preferring dense, high-altitude boreal forests, especially old-growth timber. Historically, lynx existed in forested lands from Alaska south to the Cascades; in the Rocky Mountains of Colorado and Utah; and from the extreme northeastern United States east to Newfoundland. Today, viable populations are found only in Washington and Montana in the lower forty-eight states; remnant populations are believed to exist in Maine, Wyoming, Idaho, Michigan, Wisconsin, Oregon, Utah, and Colorado.[15] Hunting and trapping reduced lynx populations in Colorado and elsewhere, but the animals—protected by Colorado in 1970—persisted in diminished numbers. "There is no question that lynx exist in the Vail Ski Area and surrounding mountains," biologists concluded in 1989; a decade later, although studies were few, many biologists continued to hold that opinion.[16]

This presence was problematic, because in February 1998, the U.S. Fish and Wildlife Service announced that it intended to list the lynx as a threatened species under the U.S. Endangered Species Act in June of that year. Such a listing meant that lynx would have special protection under the law, and that the federal government would begin working to increase lynx populations to a stable and self-sustaining level. The designation of the lynx as a threatened species, in fact, held the potential to cause serious problems for the Category III ski-area expansion.

If federal biologists concluded that the development could adversely affect lynx, political pressure to scrap it would be intense.

To head that off, Vail Resorts and the U.S. Forest Service requested a formal conference with U.S. Fish and Wildlife Service biologists. Those biologists would be studying and formally commenting on the Category III development; if they issued a "jeopardy" finding, that would mean they had concluded that the ski-area expansion would jeopardize lynx survival or recovery efforts. Category III—neatly shortened to Cat III in the popular lexicon—then would have to be changed or abandoned and might not be able to earn approval from the Forest Service. Neither that agency nor Vail Resorts wanted Cat III stymied, so in the spring of 1998 they proposed a proactive strategy to keep Cat III on track. They hoped to work with the FWS to create a development and mitigation plan that treated the lynx as a threatened species yet would still allow the development to proceed. The key to the strategy was that the FWS biologists must reach a "no jeopardy" decision about Cat III.[17] That would inoculate the development against the planned listing of the lynx under the Endangered Species Act.

The conference, a several-month review and debate of scientific data and projections by all three parties and the Colorado Division of Wildlife, began in mid-1998. The FWS entered the conference with the following premises:

> The Canada lynx population in the Southern Rockies currently [is] critically and imminently imperiled based on existing conditions in the ecosystem, including historic, ongoing and planned human actions. . . . This population [in the Southern Rockies] is ecologically disjunct from all other Canada lynx populations. . . . The Canada lynx population in the Southern Rockies is in imminent danger of extinction.[18]

The second point is a critical one. It is an assertion that the lynx living south of Interstate 70 might constitute a distinct species group, possibly different from lynx elsewhere and deserving of full and separate protection and restoration.

The final conference report, released in March 1999, paints a grim picture for the lynx, not only on the Cat III lands but on hundreds of thousands of surrounding acres. "Most lynx habitat in Category III will be directly and adversely impacted [by the development]," the report states.[19] Of greater concern, and more significant, is the way Cat III likely would sever the remaining, tenuous connections between the lynx population south of Interstate 70 and those lynx living north of the highway. State wildlife officials liken the highway to the Berlin Wall.[20] Human development along the interstate spans the width of Colorado's Rockies; it runs almost continuously for 112 miles from Georgetown, in the foothills to the east, to Glenwood Springs in the west. It effectively creates a barrier to lynx migration, migration necessary to prevent the development of a potentially unsustainable "island" population of the animals south of the interstate.[21] The remaining north-south connection is no more than a handful of drainages bridged by the interstate on the west side of Vail Pass. The Fish and Wildlife Service concluded that if Cat III were built, those connections would effectively be cut.[22]

Throughout the ninety-one-page report, the biologists who prepared it (principally Gary Patton, the service's most experienced lynx specialist in Colorado), make clear their belief that the lynx population south of Interstate 70—the Southern Rockies "distinct population segment"—would be badly damaged and quite possibly eliminated by Cat III. The likely final nail in the coffin, they write, would be massive real estate development associated with Cat III. The potential for such development seemed very high when the report was being assembled. A six-thousand-acre parcel of private land situated a mile southwest of the Cat III boundary and encompassing the abandoned mining town of Gilman along U.S. Highway 24 presented an opportunity to create an entire new village and "portal" into the back side of the Vail ski area (with the addition of Cat III, Vail Mountain sprawls over more than twelve square miles). A connecting ski lift to provide access over the mile of intervening Forest Service terrain could make that private holding very valuable indeed.

Vail Resorts just happened to hold an option to buy half of the company that in 1998 owned the Gilman land. Yet throughout the entire Cat III review process, Vail officials denied they had any plans to develop that property. As at Breckenridge, Vail insisted the conferees should blind themselves to the possibility of development at Gilman. "Vail [does not] currently have any development plans for the Property," Vail attorney James S. Mandel stated in a letter to the FWS.[23] But nowhere in the carefully worded, fifteen-page document is there an outright assertion that Vail Resorts and its partners don't desire to develop Gilman at some point in the future.

Such a qualified denial seemed suspicious to those who fought the expansion, and with good reason. At Breckenridge, Vail Resorts had repeatedly denied that it had base-area development plans for Peak 7—until the company suddenly produced them under sharp prodding by the U.S. Army Corps of Engineers. Would the same thing happen at Gilman? The FWS accepted Vail's assertions that it didn't plan development or connection to Gilman, but admitted it was worried about the possibility.[24]

Even without development there, the biologists believed Cat III would be disastrous for the lynx. Near the end of the report they wrote:

> The proposed action [developing Cat III] risks both the survival of any extant lynx population and our ability to recover lynx in this area. This, in turn, risks the residual Southern Rockies population and our ability to recover that population to a healthy status capable of sustaining itself

into the distant future [as required by law under the Endangered Species Act]. . . . The massive development and burgeoning human presence associated with ski area development in Eagle and Summit Counties, and the presence of I-70, have resulted in large-scale losses of lynx habitat, creation of a substantial barrier to movement at the landscape level, and introduction of widespread and locally intense disturbance. Lynx are, apparently, now rare in the assessment area, no doubt in part [due] to these very factors. Thus, development and activity associated with the Vail resorts likely have already contributed to the lynx decline in the area and are a risk to future viability of lynx . . . perhaps in the entire Southern Rockies ecosystem. Because of the now precarious position of lynx in this ecosystem, any future action taken in the area that further preempts what may have been historically important habitat, or which further compounds serious constraints on landscape level movement, is likely to have adverse effects disproportionately great to their apparent scale. This may well be the case with Cat III.[25]

Despite this clear indictment of Cat III as the straw that would break the lynx's back, a curious thing happened when it came time to write the formal conclusion to the conference report. This conclusion states: "It is the Service's biological opinion that the proposed project is not likely to jeopardize the continued existence of the contiguous United States population of the lynx. . . . The Service also finds that the project, as proposed, is likely to adversely affect the lynx, and may contribute to the ultimate extirpation and diminish the potential for recovery of the lynx, in the Southern Rockies ecosystem." In the very next sentence, the report's authors state that if certain "mitigation" efforts are completed "the project will be unlikely to contribute to the extirpation of the lynx or substantially diminish the recovery potential of lynx in the Southern Rockies ecosystem."[26]

If it sounds confusing, it was meant to. The opinion that was rendered was the coveted "no jeopardy" decision. For Vail

Resorts, it was a grand slam, a determination by the federal government that Cat III won't harm lynx populations in a meaningful way. Yet how did such a conclusion get drawn when the body of the report clearly states that the development would irreparably damage the Southern Rockies population—a population that U.S. Fish and Wildlife Service biologists consider distinct and important to preserve? In a single word: politics.

At the eleventh hour, Washington political appointees countermanded the entire conference strategy, effectively mandating from on high that the report would reach a no-jeopardy decision regardless of the facts on the ground. On November 4, 1998, Richard Hannan, an official in the endangered species office at FWS headquarters in Washington, D.C., e-mailed Joe Webster, the associate regional director in Lakewood, Colorado (and Gary Patton's boss), and torpedoed the six-month lynx conference effort. The service, Hannan declared on behalf of Director Jamie Clark, would not recognize a "distinct population segment" of lynx in the Southern Rockies, despite the strong opinions of federal field biologists in Colorado—and the conference's entire premise—that just such a distinction was necessary and justified. The net effect of Director Clark's decision was to defy the premise of the conference and to allow a conclusion that the lynx population south of Interstate 70 may be sacrificed to development without endangering the species as a whole.[27] That is the wholly political conclusion the report reaches.

Washington politicians had nullified the biologists' strategy of trying to protect the Southern Rockies lynx as part of a larger effort to protect the lynx nationwide. The service's regional director had subsequently determined that—because the Southern Rockies lynx had been deemed expendable for political purposes—the project did not jeopardize the lynx as a species, and so a no-jeopardy decision was appropriate. The Endangered Species Act does not say a developer can't *harm* a species; it is only illegal to jeopardize the survival and recovery of the species. What these two decisions on Cat III did was dismiss the Southern Rockies population (and, not incidentally, those in the Northeast and Great Lakes states) as unimportant. They effectively took away the service's ability to make a jeopardy call on any development and made lynx recovery actions in those geographic areas improbable. Thanks to Clark's decision about Cat III, unless a Canada lynx happens to be living in Washington State or Montana, it is unlikely now to find any shelter under the Endangered Species Act.

Like the lynx itself, those who pulled the strings on this decision left few tracks. There is no smoking gun, but money buys access, and access buys influence, and Vail Resorts certainly knows that. Vail officers give generously to Colorado's congressional delegation, and ski industry officials are no strangers to Washington's corridors of power.

* * *

Service biologists who had worked for more than five hundred hours on the report were stunned and furious at the interference. They pointed out that, Hannan's protests to the contrary notwithstanding, the conference report had been discussed with Washington officials—indeed, the whole purpose of the report was to analyze the Southern Rockies lynx as a potential distinct population. "We know we got our legs cut out from under us by Wash.," wrote Colorado Field Office Supervisor LeRoy Carlson in an e-mail message to Webster. "We wind up [sic] looking like chumps."[28]

Biologist Gary Patton was disappointed. He wrote in an e-mail:

> The sudden change by the Service is bound to look suspicious. Because this entire process is documented in the administrative record, we will

have to demonstrate the request and rationale for, and agreement with the dual analysis [distinct population] approach taken; then have to explain a last-minute decision by the Service to do a complete about-face. The administrative record is clear, precluding any option of simply leaving the original approach out of the consultation history. Again, this is unlikely to look good to anyone.[29]

Patton was right—the whole thing looks bad. In the end, Vail Resorts got what it wanted; the first of the Cat III bowls, 520 acres now called Blue Sky Basin, opened to skiers on January 6, 2000.

Patton had argued strongly in internal Fish and Wildlife Service debates for listing the lynx as a threatened or endangered species. There was a strong sentiment against listing, but the final debate just prior to the decision swung the service toward a threatened species listing, and Patton believes his efforts contributed to that decision. He now feels the service has become so sensitive to political agendas to defang the Endangered Species Act that there is excessive accommodation in Washington to defuse controversy and political pressure. This results in an erosion of crucial natural resources such as the Canada lynx. Rather than giving species the benefit of the doubt, the service is now shifting toward demanding absolute proof that something is harmful to the species before beginning to take a stand.

In early 2001, Patton was taken off all lynx work for the service. He was given a desk job filing papers for water withdrawals on the South Platte River. He believes he's been busted down as retribution for his lynx advocacy. "I've been put in a hole," he says. "They've put me in a place where I'm doing something nobody cares about. They've put me in a hole and shoveled in the dirt. I work on average one or two hours every day. Essentially, I've been told to sit here and do nothing and waste taxpayer money. They told the public I was urgently needed to work on the Platte River program, but I haven't done anything on the Platte River program for over a year." The whole process has left him somewhat saddened and bitter, and he thinks the emasculation of the lynx conference report will neuter the entire Endangered Species Act. "At the end, they pulled the rug out from under us," Patton says. "The reason we really fought for the jeopardy call was the precedent it set for future consultations. If we couldn't call jeopardy in this situation, we couldn't call jeopardy in any situation."[30]

In the spring of 1998, federal biologists wanted to err on the side of caution when they assessed the impact of Cat III on the lynx; in autumn of that year, politicians told them they could not do so. It is true that Vail Resorts, the Forest Service, the Colorado Division of Wildlife, and the U.S. Fish and Wildlife Service agreed to a number of mitigation measures, but it is also true that the combination of continuing development and diminished lynx populations have created a situation in which no mitigation may be sufficient. As the Beaver Creek elk herd demonstrated, "mitigation" is a reassuring word for what very likely may be futile attempts to spare wildlife the messy and fatal effects of human activity. Unlike that of the elk who dash across highways, however, the plight of the lynx won't be obvious to the public. They will simply vanish quietly, one more dropped thread in central Colorado's tattered web of biodiversity.

✳ ✳ ✳

The story of the lynx is unusual in that it involves a high-profile, well-documented example of how a single development will affect a single species. Yet it is the combined direct and indirect effects of ski-resort development and its associated sprawl that, cumulatively, are most damaging. As part of its unending demand for growth, the ski business today regularly hammers the environment.

At Copper Mountain, Intrawest proposes to fill 8.5 acres of wetlands—more than at either Cat III or Cucumber Gulch. Ninety percent of Colorado's animal species make use of such riparian areas, which constitute less than 2 percent of the state's land area.

At Loveland, a ski area on the Continental Divide along Interstate 70 where Forest Service officials had approved a seventeen-hundred-foot-long surface lift, the ski area instead "inadvertently" built a forty-eight-hundred-foot-long chairlift over the land bridge above the Eisenhower Tunnel, effectively cutting off the last major wildlife migration corridor across the interstate east of Vail Pass.[31]

Telluride Ski and Golf company (Telski) illegally obliterated approximately seventy acres of wetlands to build a golf course. The violation was discovered by sheer luck by the Environmental Protection Agency, which subsequently obtained a court settlement that leveled the largest wetlands-related penalty ever—on anyone—against Telski. The company was obliged to pay $1.1 million in fines and create nineteen acres of new wetlands.*

Such environmental insults pale in the face of the devastation that would be wrought by the planned Pelican Butte resort in southern Oregon. This new ski area proposed near Klamath Falls would be built beside the Upper Klamath National Wildlife Refuge. It would draw an estimated 390,000 new visitors to

---

* Author telephone interview with confidential source at EPA, Aug. 20, 2001. Lingering community anger resurfaced when Telski was on the verge of gaining approval for a 733-acre ski-area expansion in 2000. Anonymous, handwritten posters appeared around Telluride, reading: "Is your rent too low? Wetlands got you down? Is the air too easy to breathe? Are the trees in the way of your views? Do you want Telluride to look and feel like Aspen? Try new Ski Area Expansion, sponsored by Telluride Chamber of Commerce. Coming soon! Guaranteed to drive all the working class out."

the region. Fifty percent of the ski development would be within old-growth forest critical to the survival of endangered northern spotted owls. Much of this territory would be clear-cut for ski runs and lift lines. Fuel spills and pollution would be expected to occur in Klamath Lake's Pelican Bay, the one part of the lake that has relatively good water quality because springs from Pelican Butte enter there. These springs likely would be disrupted, with significant consequences for Klamath Lake as a whole. A two-thousand-car parking lot would be built on Forest Service land in a designated bald eagle nesting area. Thirty-four threatened, endangered, or sensitive indicator species—species whose overall health and population distribution indicate the health of the ecosystem they inhabit—would be affected.[32] Because the resort is to be built a mere twenty-five miles south of Crater Lake National Park, Park Service officials expect it to create a smoggy haze there.[33] The ski area's developers are also building a new community, the Running Y Ranch, of 1,425 housing units.[34] Added to the ski resort, it is likely to degrade regional air and water quality and harm old-growth forests and their inhabitants, according to the U.S. Fish and Wildlife Service.[35]

Concerns about the environmental consequences of new ski resorts are the norm and, combined with the miserable economics and demographics of the ski business, explain why no major ski areas have opened in the United States since 1980. Similar or worse litanies almost certainly could have been recited for the consequences of ski areas that opened in the 1950s, 1960s, and 1970s before the passage of the Clean Air Act, Clean Water Act, Endangered Species Act, and National Environmental Protection Act. A generation or two ago, Americans and their government simply did not pay attention to environmental issues the way they do now. The great postwar ski-area building boom took advantage not only of the demographic bubble of Baby Boomers, but also of a regulatory window of opportunity.

Today, as more scrutiny is applied to ski areas, more problems are being identified.

Few skiers probably know or think deeply about the environment implications of their sport (although many consider themselves to be environmentalists). Yet paying to ski on man-made snow—to take a single illustration—supports an extraordinarily destructive set of environmental practices.

In the market-share war, snowmaking has become a critical weapon. Les Otten proved its value when he built up Sunday River's share of the Northeastern market via unprecedented investment in snowmaking and grooming. That growth eventually allowed him to leverage a buying spree that made American Skiing Company the largest ski operator in the United States. The lesson was well-learned by others. "Make snow and they will come," says Jim Felton, a spokesman for Breckenridge ski area. "Snowmaking allows us to open in October and gives us a reputation for having a long season with good snow. So, when people turn on the Weather Channel in October or November and see Breckenridge is open for skiing, it gives us a competitive advantage when they're deciding where to book a ski vacation."[36]

Snowmaking happens in great volume during October, November, and December as ski areas scramble to produce enough fake snow to cover several runs and begin operating lifts. Colorado's Front Range resorts—Keystone, Loveland, Arapahoe Basin, Breckenridge, Vail, Winter Park, and Copper Mountain—hold a much publicized race to be the first to open for the season. Usually, a few runs are ready by early or mid-October. That achievement is sure to get the winning resort on the Denver nightly news, and from there onto the national news shows. A brief spot on the *Today Show* or its equivalent can cause a spike in the most profitable vacation bookings; destination visitors are much more profitable than day visitors to ski resorts. But creating snow takes a lot of water and an enormous quantity of electricity to drive pumps and high-volume air compressors. If the water is drawn from local streams, as it usually is (in some cases, however, water gathered during high runoff earlier in the year is stored in man-made ponds), it has the effect of exacerbating low-flow conditions. Lower water flows expose more of a streambed to the air, killing invertebrate life and fish eggs through drying or freezing. Anchor ice, which adheres to the bottom of rivers and renders them uninhabitable, forms in shallow water and effectively sterilizes even more stream bottom. Fewer deep pools exist, which means less wintering-over terrain for fish.

Snowmaking, in other words, creates or exacerbates drought conditions in streams, sometimes prolonging normal late-summer low flows for months. Some states have minimum stream-flow requirements to prevent total dewatering by snowmakers or other water users, but even where these rules exist, they may be arbitrary and insufficient to sustain a trout fishery, the rule-of-thumb standard for a healthy river. Concerted snowmaking makes a mockery of the carefully crafted image ski resorts project of the benign, refreshing, back-to-nature experience visitors can enjoy, but resort developers nevertheless spin their ostensibly green imagery aggressively and hope customers believe them. In a now characteristic piece of ski industry disinformation, on Earth Day 2001, Keystone Resort officials unveiled an "environmentally friendly" Information Center at River Run. Recycled materials are used in the building's construction, and solar-powered lights help cut the electric bill. The goal, according to Keystone's environmental coordinator, is to "educate and motivate guests to make Earth Day every day."[37]

If Keystone were serious about environmental stewardship, the first thing the resort would do is stop making snow. The Snake is one of the most degraded rivers in the West, in part because of snowmaking, yet its adjacent ski areas—Arapahoe

Basin and Keystone—want to take still more water from it. Keystone withdraws water from the Snake River to feed its snow guns, and—the feel-good Information Center along its banks notwithstanding—this practice wreaks havoc on the Snake. The Army Corps of Engineers has found that the state's minimum stream-flow requirements leave insufficient water in the river to support trout, yet snowmakers regularly push flows down toward that minimum.[38]

An additional problem the Snake faces is heavy-metal contamination leaching from old gold and silver mines. That contamination includes copper, lead, cadmium, and manganese, and Keystone snowmakers allegedly are spreading these pollutants into previously clean tributaries. During 2000, federal officials determined Keystone was pumping water out of a polluted drainage and using it to make snow along two formerly unpolluted creeks. Keystone Resort, while not admitting it had created a problem, did agree that it ought to be studied. Meanwhile, the resort with the solar panels on its Information Center pushed ahead with an application to more than double its snowmaking water withdrawals from the Snake to 1,350 acre-feet per year.[39] The application was granted in late 2000.

To compound problems for the Snake, the owners of Arapahoe Basin applied in 1999 for permission to build a snowmaking system that conceivably could allow that high-altitude ski hill to run year-round. The associated water withdrawal, however, would destroy at least a quarter of the trout-spawning habitat in the North Fork of the Snake. "It defies logic," declared Melinda Kassen, Colorado director of Trout Unlimited, "to believe that the federal government needs to allow its lands to be used for year-round skiing at a small Colorado resort that, even with this project, can provide only a few runs of artificial snow (over 40 acres) for an additional 17 days on average during the summer and late fall."[40] Arapahoe Basin's withdrawals would take clean water out of the North Fork—water that now diluted the polluted main stem of the river—thus increasing pollution levels in the main stem by 8 percent, according to one study.[41]

In New England, nobody knows how much water snow-makers use. Vermont and New Hampshire count thirty-four ski resorts between them, yet state regulators there have little idea how much water is being turned into snow. This is especially troubling, because snow is made more aggressively, and in larger quantities, in New England than anywhere else in the country. "Snowmaking is creating deserts out of our rivers," says David Carle, executive director of the New Hampshire environmental group Conservation Action Project. "[Water withdrawals have] been found to be harmful in every industry except skiing, and that's [only] because nobody's looking."[42]

There are also more distant effects of making snow. When skiers go up on the slopes to carve turns on several new inches of man-made powder, they are benefiting from a system that carefully and actively externalizes the true environmental costs to some other place. Snowmaking isn't a zero-pollution activity; it's an elsewhere-pollution activity. In Vermont, four of the state's six largest nitrous-oxide air pollution sources are ski resort diesel generators that make electricity to run snowmaking air compressors and water pumps.[43] (Nitrous oxide is a contributor to smog.) In the West, where most electricity is produced by coal-burning power plants that release significant quantities of sulfur dioxide, the precursor to acid rain, the air pollution impacts of snowmaking are exponentially greater. Here, snowmaking is a form of alchemy, of turning coal into snow.

In Colorado, 94 percent of electricity is generated by coal-burning power plants. If a ski area pays a million dollars over the course of a winter for electricity to run its snowmaking compressors—not an unreasonable amount by today's standards—it has paid its utility company to burn fourteen million pounds of coal, which produces thirty million pounds of airborne carbon dioxide, the leading greenhouse gas that causes global warming and, by extension, may be altering weather patterns in ways that will make commercial skiing in the United States a thing of the past during the twenty-first century.[44] In Colorado, much of a ski resort's electricity is likely to be generated at the Craig and Hayden power plants, located in the northwestern part of the state. In the mid-1990s, a federal court found that the Hayden plant, the largest producer of sulfur dioxide in the region, had violated clean air standards nineteen thousand times in five years. (The Environmental Protection Agency believes there were an additional ten thousand violations.) Acid snow and rain from the Craig and Hayden plants falls in the nearby Mt. Zirkel wilderness, a 160,000-acre wilderness area north of Steamboat Springs. The U.S. Geological Survey determined that such pollution kills and cripples 40 to 100 percent of the amphibians in the ponds of that wilderness, breaking one of the critical links in that ecosystem's food chains.[45] In the simplest terms, a high-altitude wilderness is being poisoned so that ski resorts can compete for early-season reservations—and the U.S. Forest Service is complicit in this practice.

The Forest Service, in its final environmental assessment of expansion plans at Breckenridge, agreed with the industry's "need" for snowmaking, noting "reliable early season coverage is critical in obtaining advanced reservations from out-of-state destination visitors."[46] So the Forest Service's position is essentially identical to that of the resort industry: snowmaking is a good marketing tool to increase ski operators' profits. That is not surprising, in light of the agency's stated definition of success, which under the Winter Sports Partnership is "based on how we as an agency help our [recreation] partners achieve business success." But early-season snowmaking doesn't serve a demonstrable public need; only a tiny percentage of skier days are counted before the traditional opening day of Thanksgiving.

In terms of real numbers, the ski season doesn't get rolling until Christmas and never has. Early-season snowmaking is a marketing tool, period. Once again, the Forest Service appears to be in the pocket of industry.

* * *

"The environment is a ski area's number one asset," declares Michael Berry, president of the National Ski Areas Association, in his introduction to *Sustainable Slopes: The Environmental Charter for Ski Areas.*[47] Released in June 2000, the NSAA's charter was paid for in part by the U.S. Forest Service, which pitched in thirty thousand dollars under the auspices of the Winter Sports Partnership. The document was hailed by ski resorts as proof that the sport really is environmentally friendly, yet it was roundly condemned by environmental groups as greenwash. The charter contains some nice ideas: resource efficiency, pedestrian-friendly development, waste recycling, minimizing impacts on wildlife and air quality, fostering environmental education. But nothing in the charter obliges any ski area to do anything, and in very fine type the document (printed on recycled paper) includes the following notation: "These principles are voluntary and are not intended to create new legal liabilities, expand existing rights or obligations, waive legal defenses, or otherwise affect the legal position of any endorsing company, and are not intended to be used against an endorser in any legal proceeding for any purpose."[48]

The text is peppered with such phrases as "where appropriate," "in a responsible manner," "where possible," "explore opportunities," and "minimize." A typical principle is to "[m]inimize impacts to fish and wildlife and their habitat and maintain or improve habitat where possible."[49] What does that really mean? Federal regulations almost universally oblige ski resorts under threat of law to "minimize impacts to fish and wildlife."

The charter has some good ideas for ski-area managers who are looking to do a better job. But it also has listed many actions that would be obligatory anyway and included them as "Options for Getting There." Ski areas apparently hope to claim environmental good-guy credit simply for following the law.[50]

Daniel Glick, the author of *Powder Burn: Arson, Money, and Mystery on Vail Mountain*, nicely summed up the criticism of *Sustainable Slopes* when he said, "Recycling the Perrier bottles at [Vail Mountain's] Two Elk Restaurant somehow doesn't cut it."[51] This view may be a cynical one, but the ski industry has become a very environmentally unfriendly business that invites such cynicism by actively attempting to deceive skiers about its record and practices.

The industry has a perception problem with environmentally conscious consumers—its own customers.[52] The urban experience, and urban levels of pollution, are not what people want when they go skiing. So the ski industry released its environmental charter to much fanfare at the National Press Club in Washington, D.C., insisting it is green at heart. Saying does not make something so, but the industry appears committed to an aggressive spin campaign to portray itself as environmentally friendly in the face of countervailing facts. This kind of strategy was captured neatly by Groucho Marx when he demanded, "Who you gonna believe? Me or your lying eyes?"

CHAPTER 9

Commuters or Communities?

Two miles high in the Colorado Rockies, in the alpine head-waters of the Arkansas River along the eastern side of the Continental Divide, a little piece of Mexico straddles Colorado Highway 24. Almost every adult living along the dusty lanes running between the uneven rows of trailer homes in the Mountain View Trailer Park was born south of the border, most of them in northern Mexico. The kids who live here attend school in nearby Leadville, but Spanish is the language that greets a visitor to this enclave.

The trailer park flanking the highway possesses a stupendous view of the fourteen-thousand-foot peaks of Mt. Evans and Mt. Massive. They loom above the Sawatch Range, the great spine of central Colorado. The people of Mountain View aren't here for the scenery, however. Many of them may go weeks during the winter without even seeing it. They leave for work "over the hill" in the ski resorts along Interstate 70 before the sun comes up and return long after it has set. They live here because they can afford to.

Winters are long at ten thousand feet. The aspen leaves have not yet appeared when I drive to Mountain View on a mid-May evening. A late-model sedan and pickup truck are parked outside the beige trailer that is my destination. Two dogs bark within a small cyclone-fence pen. Inside, the television is tuned to a Spanish-language station. Kids run in and out the door or flop on the plush matching living room set. Elena and Jesús García are eating their dinners in the kitchen, which is clean and bright, finished in white linoleum and set with varnished oak furniture. These are not their real names; the Garcías and other Latino workers agreed to talk openly with me about their lives in the ski resorts only if I blurred their descriptions. They worry about retribution from their employers.

This could be any middle-American trailer home any-where in the country. The Garcías, who left northern Mexico to pick vegetables in eastern Colorado, came to ski country in the late 1980s. By the standards of immigrant Latino work-ers, they have done very well for themselves and are proud of what they have achieved. They make a decent living and are saving to put their three children through college. They have become American citizens. They have a 401-k retirement plan and health insurance through Vail Resorts, where they both work.

But they have not achieved their success because of their ski-resort jobs; they have achieved it in spite of them. After eleven years with Vail Resorts, Jesús earns only $14 an hour; Elena, $10.50. Consequently, both of them hold down second jobs. Jesús starts the one-hour drive over Tennessee Pass to Vail at 7 in the morning, works a full day as a laborer for Vail Re-sorts, then goes immediately to his second job. Most nights he is not home until 11 P.M. Elena works seven days a week, and on many mornings she has to be up as early as 2 A.M. to work a half-shift at her second job in the Eagle River Valley before starting her regular office job for Vail Resorts. She gets home at 6 or 7 at night. To achieve what they have on the wages they earn, the Garcías each work sixty-five hours or more per week and commute another ten to fourteen hours.

This is the modern and largely invisible face of the corpo-rate ski industry: hardworking, foreign-born, often semiliterate laborers, many of them illegal, who commute long distances to work the menial jobs that keep four-season ski resorts functioning. The starkest examples in the nation of what happens when real estate prices rise and workers get pushed out of ski towns can be found in five counties in central Colorado known to bureaucrats as the Rural Resort Region: Pitkin, Summit, Eagle, Lake, and Garfield. Pitkin, Summit, and Eagle Counties are home to Aspen, Aspen Highlands, Buttermilk, Snowmass, Keystone, Arapahoe Basin, Breckenridge, Copper Mountain, Vail, and Beaver Creek ski areas. Garfield County and Lake County—the Mountain View Trailer Park is in the latter—have become bedroom communities for many workers in these ski resorts.

The Garcías' life is hard, but for many foreign resort workers life is much harder. In Lake County and throughout ski country, as many as twenty newly arrived Latino workers may live in a single trailer or condominium, sleeping in shifts on the floor, saving their money to send home. The Garcías, and many others who have not succeeded nearly so well as they, embody a complex set of problems that has been spawned by resort development and can be summed up this way: mountain communities are disintegrating, both metaphorically and literally (that is, dis-integrating) in the face of corporate skiing. A ski-town worker's life increasingly is a commuter's life, defined by the constant struggle to get by in a world of below-average pay and above-average costs. The most successful ski towns today, in terms of size and market share, lie at the uphill end of a daily chain of traffic jams, deadly accidents, road rage, domestic violence, substance abuse, troubled children, suburban sprawl, and overburdened schools, police departments, and social agencies.

Such social costs as these are pointedly not counted in the calculus of publicly traded ski companies when they measure their success. Just as they try to distance themselves from many of the effects of their business on the natural environment, ski industry executives insist they did not create the social problems surrounding their resorts. However, the deteriorating human condition in the hinterlands around major ski areas is indirectly but inextricably linked to the presence and expansion of those resorts. Although it may be true that ski executives have little ability to solve social problems fifty or a hundred miles away, it is disingenuous of them to disavow all responsibility when their workers live there.

✳   ✳   ✳

"We used to kid about these places being for the haves and the have-mores," says Myles Rademan. For thirty years, Rademan worked in ski-town governments, first as a planner in Crested Butte, more recently as director of communications in Park City, Utah. He may be the most traveled pundit in the mountain-resort business. During the 1990s, he crisscrossed the country with a speech and a carousel of slides, talking about the costs of growth and earning the sobriquet "The Prophet of Boom." He has a graying, close-cropped brown beard and reveals long upper teeth when he smiles. Two years before the 2002 Winter Olympics came to Utah—an event that generated its own boom—Rademan lounged behind his desk in Park City, ate a breakfast of yogurt, and reflected on the changes he has seen. "That social divide has become much more significant with the number of people that are moving to these places and paying cash for five-million-dollar homes," he says. "A resentment seeps in, and that resentment can be destructive to the community fabric."[1]

The root of the word *community* is the Latin *communis*, or common. A community is a group of people who have something in common. In today's ski country, there may be more people living, working, and visiting, but they have less in common than ever. A half-page newspaper advertisement that could have—and perhaps should have—been a parody, but was not, summed up the problem nicely with this headline: "This May Be Your Last Chance to Build an 18,729 sq ft Home in Aspen."[2]

Much has been written about the growing wealth and income disparity in the United States. In few places, however, will you see so much wealth and so much poverty revolving around the same center point—the ski resort. The displacement caused by this disparity is so neatly and fully realized in ski country that an op-ed columnist in the *New York Times* termed it "the Aspen effect." In ski areas such as Aspen, the columnist explained, almost nobody who works there lives there, which precipitates massive daily traffic problems. The Aspen effect is seen to lesser degrees all over the country. The top 1 percent of American families have more than doubled their incomes since 1980, while the bottom 20 percent saw their incomes fall in real terms (the median family's income rose a modest 10 percent). That disparity has pushed many workers farther and farther from their urban workplaces and has much to do with why traffic jams in the United States are getting worse.[3] The income gap is almost the sole reason why affordable housing and transportation have become the biggest, most complex, and most contentious issues in ski resorts around the country.

✳ ✳ ✳

The lack of housing is a consequence, sometimes intended, sometimes not, of industry strategies. Real estate prices in and near ski resorts skyrocketed during the 1980s and 1990s. The amenity value of a ski area of four-season resort drives up the price of property, as Vail Resorts so adeptly demonstrated when its real estate sales division put a ski lift into Bachelor Gulch and then sold the surrounding home sites for an average price of $750,000. During the late 1990s, the average price of a single-family home sold in Aspen topped a million dollars, then quickly topped two million. The rising real estate values around resorts ultimately is what many ski-area executives desire, since they underpin the business strategies of the Big Three and other operators who have linked their bottom lines to real estate sales and management.

Resort workers—even those in places where the starting wage is ten dollar an hour or higher—are in no position to buy property that sells for several hundred dollars per square foot, as is now the norm in established ski towns, even for a twenty-year-old condominium. Nor is renting a real option. The Garcías spent fourteen thousand dollars on rent during a single year in a Vail condo before buying their trailer in Mountain View. They couldn't begin to sustain those rent payments, Jesús says. Yet they were getting a deal. A two-bedroom condominium in Jackson Hole, Vail, Telluride, or Aspen will rent easily for fifteen hundred dollars a month, maybe twice that. One reason rents are so high is that most homes simply are vacant. In Breckenridge, 80 percent of the homes stand empty; in Vail, 70 percent.[4] People who can afford to buy top-end vacation properties can't be bothered with renting them out to locals, and don't need to.

The price of real estate in ski towns in now comparable to that of residential property in San Francisco, New York, or Dallas.[5] In the face of these prices, a common urban pattern develops: workers commute. In 1991, Eagle County was home to about 6,500 more resident workers than jobs. By 1999, the situation had reversed; it had 7,000 more jobs than workers. Similar trends hold for Summit and Pitkin Counties. A government study of Eagle, Summit, Pitkin, and two adjacent counties to the north, Grand and Jackson, showed that about 24,000 people commuted during 1997 from outside those five counties to fill jobs within them. The study projected that by 2020, almost 59,000 people will make that daily commute, and nearly 8,000 jobs simply will go unfilled.[6]

✲ ✲ ✲

Cordillera is a forty-one-hundred acre, gated "mountain-top community" built around the idea of exclusivity. The baronial mansions dotting the landscape look as if they belong in Europe. If you don't have a good reason to go to this private enclave a few miles west of Beaver Creek, you don't get in. Cordillera's glossy promotional materials feature happy, smiling white people dining in elegance, playing golf, riding horses. There are evocative, dusky pictures of long, virginal golf fairways that seem to ache for the touch of a CEO's four-iron, fairways manicured in precise patterns by people like Jesús García—that is, by people in the bottom 20 percent of the income scale. Cordillera's employees don't live there and certainly would not be welcome if they weren't working. Home sites—not homes—sell for half a million dollars or more. At the foot of the hill upon which Cordillera is perched, rows of trailers are lined up beside the Interstate. Beneath this exclusive resort whose name is the Spanish word for "mountain range," the trailer homes are filled with Spanish-speaking laborers.

Places like Cordillera are becoming the norm in ski country, rather than the exception. North of Winter Park, the tiny (287-acre) ski area of Silver Creek was purchased at the end of the 1990s by a Brazilian airline heir who then traded other property to the Bureau of Land Management to acquire a thousand acres at the base of the ski hill. Her plans: to build five thousand single-family homes and condominiums. Condos on the drawing board in 2000 were priced between $198,000 and $550,000.[7] As with Cordillera and so many other gated retreats, thousands of workers will be needed to keep the silver polished, the greens buffed, and the sidewalks shoveled at what the heir renamed Sol Vista. They will come from somewhere— hopefully, somewhere out of sight—and they will be expected to leave at the end of the day. This is classic colonial behavior: outside capital exploiting the undeveloped region for maximum financial gain, with little regard to how it affects the place and its people.

✳ ✳ ✳

To a greater or lesser degree, all major ski resorts face housing problems. The New Ski Village and its Cordillera-style brethren promise high levels of service, which imply lots of workers. Many, many people are required to do the laundry, run the snow guns, mix drinks, empty trash cans, load lifts. People in the Rural Resort Region of central Colorado live farther from their work than ever before because they must. A typical Pitkin County family pays eight times the national average for housing, which means a lot of truly typical families don't live there at all. The average Eagle County family spends 41 percent of its income on housing, compared to 16 percent nationwide. Even in Glenwood Springs, a service town of big-box stores and car dealerships situated more than forty miles from a major resort, housing costs are twice the national average. Yet wages in Glenwood Springs are only 81 percent of that average.[8] The social costs of this calculus can be brutal: 17 percent of Glenwood Springs's public-school teachers resigned in 2000, in part, they said, because they could not afford a place to live.[9]

Across the Continental Divide, in Leadville and surrounding Lake County, homes cost far, far less. In 1997, the median home price there was $86,000.[10] The price of affordability is an hour's drive or more across Fremont Pass on Colorado Highway 91 or Tennessee Pass on U.S. Highway 24, winding roads that can be deadly in winter and are now dotted with memorial crosses. Housing is more affordable too as you travel west along I-70 down the Colorado River from Glenwood Springs to Rifle, Silt, New Castle, Parachute, and even Grand Junction, 90 miles from Glenwood Springs and 135 miles from Aspen. Despite the distances, people commute daily from these and other remote locales. At 6:30 on a weekday morning, the I-70 on-ramp at Rifle is backed up with workers headed to Aspen, 71 miles away.

Within the Roaring Fork Valley, anchored at one end by Aspen (habitat for the Last 18,729 sq ft Home) and at the other by Glenwood Springs, an estimated fifteen hundred people qualify for a very low cost house built by the charity Habitat for Humanity.[11] Such inequities led Francis Stafford, then the archbishop of the Roman Catholic Archdiocese of Denver, to scold the resort industry. "The tent and trailer camps, sometimes without electricity or running water, that today house so many service workers on the Western Slope [of Colorado], raise troubling questions about the kind of society emerging there," Stafford wrote in a 1995 pastoral letter (the church's equivalent of a white paper). "What we risk creating is a theme-park 'alternative reality' for those who have the money to purchase entrance. Around this Rocky Mountain theme park will sprawl a growing buffer of the working poor."[12]

The former archbishop's fears (he was made a cardinal by the Vatican in 1998) largely have been realized. Despite efforts to create affordable subsidized housing for workers, the problem is growing faster than the solution. Vail Resorts can house three thousand workers in company-owned beds—but employs about ten thousand people. Aspen and Pitkin County have built approximately fifteen hundred units of government-subsidized employee housing but have not markedly increased the percentage of resort workers living in town. Scores of Telluride and Crested Butte employees live, semipermanently and in some cases year-round, in makeshift illegal structures on Forest Service lands surrounding those towns.[13]

* * *

"At least 50 percent of our time is spent dealing with the un-documented alien," says Lake County Sheriff George Sheers. "It puts a real burden on a small sheriff's office."[14] The Lake County sheriff's office is in back of the Lake County Court-house, an ugly postwar accretion of concrete and brick plopped in the middle of the faded Victoriana of Leadville's national his-toric district. Officers can be summoned via an intercom to speak to visitors through a cage. There is no entrance for the public. To meet with Sheers I have to wend my way through the building and enter through a locked internal door.

Sheers, born and raised in Leadville, is a friendly, slightly harried man of Hispanic ancestry in his mid-forties. Thick, dark hair lies close against his head above square glasses and a close-cropped salt-and-pepper mustache. His office is small, little more than a cubicle containing a government-issue steel desk and chairs. The place is covered with messy stacks of paper. Sheers, short two deputies on the day of our interview, never takes off his nylon patrol jacket during our talk. He seems ready to bolt out the door if necessary.

Between 1990 and 2000, the official Latino population of Lake County more than doubled, to 36 percent.[15] Unofficially, it's almost certainly higher. But the Latinos largely live in a separate world. With the exception of a few contact points— the school system, the local hospital, the law—Latinos rarely mix with Anglos. "Your could live here a long time and not in-teract with that community at all," says one social worker.[16] Yet this is the place where the challenges, problems, and oppor-tunities of the modern ski resort's workforce are drawn in sharpest relief, and where those workers have put the great-est strain on the system. Probably no other place has been changed so much, or so quickly, by the immigrant workers on whom the contemporary ski industry now depends as Lake County.

The vibrancy and striving of the Latino community does not mesh with the depressed public face of Leadville, a town that once competed with Denver to be Colorado's state capital. Founded as one of the state's earliest gold mining towns in 1860, Leadville seemed to be on the decline when silver was discovered in the gulches of the Mosquito Range, which rises gentle and treeless east of town, in 1875. The city exploded to a population of almost thirty thousand and was one of the wildest, most dangerous places in the West.

The silver crash of 1893 put a damper on things, but mining continued, and Leadville, with the usual ups and downs of a single-industry town, waxed and waned. The only city in Lake County, Leadville was fat and prosperous as recently as 1982, thanks to the Climax molybdenum mine northeast of town on the Continental Divide at Fremont Pass. The Climax was a modern mine; the work there entailed tearing down the better part of a mountain, processing out the molybdenum (a metal used in the manufacture of steel alloys), and filling a pair of adjoining valleys with the waste rock. Almost four thousand employees labored there; a man with a high school degree could earn the equivalent of forty dollars an hour in today's wages. Lake County raked in millions of dollars in property taxes.

It all changed in 1982, when the Climax mine closed. Lake County and Leadville's economies crashed. Lake County quickly went from being one of the richest counties in the region to being the poorest. Many people left; others, with few options, found work in the growing ski resorts an hour's drive to the north along the I-70 corridor: Copper Mountain, Vail, and Beaver Creek. Today, Leadville's assessed property values are one-fifth of what they were, and per capita income is down.[17] Leadville limps along on some summer tourism, capitalizing on its mining glory days. But 35 percent of Lake County's workers head north every morning, mostly to service and construction jobs.[18] Leadville has been transformed from one of Colorado's wealthier towns into a poor bedroom community, barracks for the ski industry's foot soldiers. Many of these people spend so much time in Summit and Eagle Counties that they shop there, bank there, even keep a post office box there. But if they need something from the government, they turn to Lake County's tattered safety net. The situation is a litany of struggle. Within the five-county Rural Resort Region, Lake County:

- Has the lowest high school graduation rates and the second-lowest revenues per pupil, after Garfield County.
- Has the highest unemployment rate and the highest percentage of workers without health insurance. Enrollment in Medicaid increased 234 percent between 1996 and 1999.
- And has the highest percentage of children living in poverty.
- Average wages in Lake County are the lowest among the five counties and equal to only 61 percent of the statewide average.[19]
- Assessed value and retail sales per capita in Lake County are one-sixth of what they are in Eagle and Summit Counties, while property and sales tax rates in Lake County are twice that of Eagle and Summit.[20]
- Foster care expenses, travel time to work, percentage of income spent on housing, domestic violence, and substance abuse are all on the rise in Lake County. Divorce rates are among the highest in the state. Drugs are easily available in local schools, and violence is common. Almost two in five students have dropped out, been suspended, or been expelled.[21]

The rise of a commuting workforce in ski country has created a geographical separation between where tax money is and

where it's needed. Aspen, Vail, and Breckenridge each generate hundreds of millions of dollars in annual retail sales and
may top a billion dollars in annual real estate sales, all of which
pads the checkbooks of local governments. Yet unlike workers,
that money does not readily cross county borders.

"They don't want to share at all," says Alice Pugh, who has
worked in Lake County social services since 1990. A forceful
and articulate woman with hazel eyes, a tan face, and dark, graying hair pulled back into a bun, Pugh started Full Circle, a men-
toring and support program for kids, in 1991. The program
enrolled 260 children in 2000.

"There's a real attitude," Pugh continues, sitting at a folding table in a small, cinder-block building on Leadville's western edge. "There's a real lack of understanding, particularly in
Eagle County. They want to keep their money in Eagle County.
They have no concept of how different it is up here with people
who don't have any resources. Our rec center pool just shut
down because we can't afford to fix it, while they build new rec
centers over there."

During the 1990s, Colorado state representatives repeatedly introduced legislation to allow the Rural Resort Region
counties to retain and share some of the state sales tax funds
they raised, rather than remitting all revenues to Denver. That
would be a way to spread resort wealth to poor bedroom counties. But the legislation failed. Pugh and other social workers
would like desperately to see that sort of government-revenue
sharing, but they believe the resort industry itself also has a responsibility to help its workers—and the industry is not doing
enough.

"Ethically, there needs to be a more equal distribution of
resources," Pugh says when I ask her about what role the private sector should play. "I think a lot of it is a misunderstand-
ing about the lack of services here. I think [resort companies]
are trying to maintain their own costs. They don't care about

some poor trailer park that none of their guests are ever going to see. They don't really care about the transient nature of their employees. It's like, 'Okay, we'll get some more.' I don't think they [workers] become people for them. They're expendable."

I ask Pugh, who knows many of Leadville's retired miners, if she thinks that the ski corporations are emulating the company-town behavior of the mining firms that preceded them. She demurs, noting that at least the mining companies "took care of their workers, whereas [with] the ski resorts, I don't see them being taken care of."

Lake County has become a dumping ground for the resort industry. County officials were openly frustrated when Copper Mountain executives proposed situating laundry, employee housing, vehicle maintenance, and reservations facilities in their jurisdiction. "Lake County is shouldering a disproportionate share of the burden of new development, principally due to housing of employees," county commissioners wrote in response. "We cannot even come close to providing for our own constituents a level of service that is blatantly obvious just miles away where a majority of our labor force works."[22]

Pugh summed up more pungently the prevailing sentiment about how the ski industry views Lake County: "'You can have our trash, our garbage; you can have our poor workers, and in that sense you're part of us. But we wouldn't want you to have anything positive.' I guess we feel like the poor, distant cousins. 'If you come for a visit, that's okay as long as you clean up good. But I don't want you living next door to me.'"

❋ ❋ ❋

Elena García doesn't like to go into Leadville from her home in Mountain View Trailer Park. "Let me tell you something," she says, passion rising in her voice, her body leaning forward over her kitchen table. "I never go to town. I don't like to go when they're doing parties in the schools, Cinco de Mayo, or whatever. I don't like to go, because I feel I'm not welcome there. They're kind of snotty, they're not friendly, because they're thinking we're in their country or we bother their towns."[23]

Latinos and Anglos agree that racism is a new and pervasive problem in Leadville. Old-timers, Anglo and Hispanic alike, commonly refer to Spanish-speaking newcomers as "wetbacks." "In third grade some kid was calling me a *mojado,* a wetback," says Elena's youngest son, who was born in the United States and is wearing an oversize Denver Broncos football jersey. "I go to the teachers, but the teachers don't do something."

Elena and Jésus are frustrated by the public schools. When Elena confronted the principal about other kids calling her children illegal, he denied it could happen in his school, she says. Jésus nods in agreement. He has a habit of pressing his lips together, tilting his head to the side, and raising his eyebrows as he makes a point. The effect is to convey the sentiment that "it's obvious, isn't it, that this is a stupid or ridiculous thing?" He does that now, and again as he relates how, for no apparent reason other than harassment, local cops keep stopping Latinos cruising in their cars. He does it yet again when he describes the ineffectual and cursory police investigation of a string of burglaries at the trailer park. Through the lens by which the Garcías and many other Latinos view America, this is racism; these slights are directed at them because of how they look and speak.

Every Latino I speak with has a story of frustration about dealing with the system. Some of this can be chalked up to clashing cultures and simple bureaucracy. But the consistency of the tales suggests the Latino community has real problems with some aspects of life in Lake County. The racism here is subtle, a smiling unwillingness to be helpful. The message many Latinos get is that they and their business are not especially welcome. The usual Latino reaction to rejection or frustration here is to pull back and disengage, rather than fight for something. This disengagement from and resentment about American society, say social workers, leads some Latinos to drug and alcohol abuse, a persistent problem here. Many Lake County officials, businesses, and individuals clearly do care a great deal about the new arrivals and worry about such problems. Others, apparently, do not.

Martina, a woman with seven children who lives in Mountain View, takes a break from washing her car and pours out a story in frustrated Spanish. The Leadville school administrators ignored her requests that her oldest son, whose first language is English, be placed in the English-speaking class, she says. He was put in a Spanish-language class, led by a teacher who didn't even speak Spanish well, and that teacher gave him excellent grades although Martina saw he was doing terrible work.

Lucinda, a sad-faced, resigned, twenty-six-year-old with bleached hair, is sitting in a small living room in a block of apartments on Leadville's outskirts when I visit. A rotted hulk of a Chevy pickup truck, its windows broken and tires gone, noses down into a corner of the parking lot. The complex of apartments is dirty and worn, the paint peeling, the grounds untended. Spanish TV is playing in Lucinda's living room. A few framed family pictures grace the wall above the flickering box. Lucinda's life is devoted to her two children. Her five-year-old son was born with a major birth defect. He is unresponsive in his small reclining chair, an oxygen tube up his nose, his eyes rolled back. Another son, a year old, his dark hair tousled, rocks contentedly in a wind-up swing. This is her life, day after day, with no prospect for change. She stays here because her first son, born in America, needs constant medical attention. Help is not readily forthcoming, however. She asked for food stamps for him, but did not receive any. "I needed a little help because I only worked two days a week," she says. She had a job in a Vail hotel laundry, earning $7.25 an hour, pushed by her supervisor to complete eight hours' worth of work in a six-hour shift. Now Lucinda doesn't work at all. She is supported by her husband, who works construction when he can but receives no benefits. "I never got any [food stamps], because I'm Hispanic," Lucinda says. "I don't have any papers, but my son is a citizen. I never asked for help for me, I asked for help for him. But I didn't get it."

✳ ✳ ✳

Life for today's ski-town worker usually entails a lot of time on mountain highways—time that can be dangerous and frustrating. "We're seeing lots of road rage," says Captain Scott Friend. A twenty-two-year veteran of the Colorado State Patrol, Friend supervises officers whose beat extends from Vail Pass to Aspen. Friend's first reaction, upon being posted from eastern Colorado to Glenwood Springs, was, "Holy mackerel, what's going on here?" The level of crowding, anger, and accidents alarmed him, and he does not expect it to improve.[24]

"You've got more and more people driving farther and farther as upvalley keeps expanding, and that's just more and more traffic on Highway 82 [the road to Aspen]," he says. "It's just tough. We had quite a few fatals before I got here, and those fatal accidents are continuing. It's unfortunate. You can design the best highway in the world and take a lot of things into consideration, but you still have a lot of human beings driving the cars. They're still trying to beat that red light after work or going to work. People are hitting the accelerator and not the brakes. Then you get following too close, weaving in and out of traffic and all these other aggressive things. People are just in a hurry, they've worked a long hard day, they need to get back home. They may have an hour's commute or more every day. People are just stressed out."

As traffic volumes, vehicle sizes, and speeds increase (although there is more total traffic, many ski-country highways are being improved, which allows for faster driving), traffic accidents grow deadlier. Those who pay the ultimate price often are the low-rung workers. Used automobiles trickle down through the workforce, so that the poorest workers usually end up driving the least expensive, and least road worthy, vehicles. More and more visitors and wealthy residents drive big, heavy sport utility vehicles, which often are deadly to smaller cars, while many poor workers find themselves behind the wheel of a smaller, older, less reliable sedan, pickup truck, or hatchback. These workers regularly travel early in the morning or late at night, when roads may not have been sufficiently cleared of snow and ice. They may not spend money on good snow tires and regular maintenance, say ski-country law officers, since many send their earnings home to their families in Mexico or Central America and keep only the barest amount to get by. But on the highways, just getting by is risky.

Colorado law enforcement agencies do not track the race of individuals involved in road accidents, but anecdotal information suggests that Latino workers in particular are involved in more, and more dangerous, accidents per capita than Anglos. Although Latinos now make up 20 to 40 percent of the population in central Colorado counties, one veteran ski-country lawman estimated that about 50 percent of reported accidents in his jurisdiction involved Latino drivers. He went on to note that the reporting party was "always an Anglo." Latinos may drive vehicles without proper insurance or registration and may be in the country illegally, he explained; typically, they won't report an accident if they can avoid doing so. Alcohol and drugs frequently are involved, he said, and even if they are not, many Latinos, extrapolating from corruption in their home countries, fear American police officers. He believes many accidents involving Latinos simply go unreported and undiscovered.

"Very often we will find a car in the ditch or out in some field with many Latinos building a road to get back on their way," the officer said, adding, "every now and again the emergency room will call if there is someone requiring medical attention that they suspect was caused in an accident." In one instance, a passing officer checked on a car that had been upside down by the road for several days and found a Latino family trying to surreptitiously extricate a dead relative who had been pinned beneath it. "Cars can sit for weeks before they are towed or looked under," the officer said, explaining that law enforcement agencies are stretched thin. Underpatrolled highways, he said, can be "a veritable graveyard," with no true accounting of the accidents happening on them.[25]

✳ ✳ ✳

Social service agencies in central Colorado's bedroom counties find themselves dealing with a slow-motion disaster. Many service workers are drawn to ski country by what one observer calls "the Tiffany wages." Ten dollars or more per hour looks like decent money from a distance, but the official poverty line in Garfield and Eagle Counties is set 85 percent above the federal standard. A family of four that earned less than $2,629 per month in 2000 fell below that adjusted poverty line.[26] Margaret Long, Garfield County's social services director since the mid-1980s, thinks a more realistic poverty line would be 125 percent higher than the federal standard. That implies an annual income of more than thirty-eight thousand dollars. What sounds like a decent middle-class living in many parts of America—nineteen dollars an hour for a single wage earner supporting that family of four—amounts to just getting by in Glenwood Springs and other Garfield County towns.

"People come here from all different parts of the county.

They hear about the construction jobs and the other jobs that are available, but they have no clue what it costs to live here," says Steve Carcaterra.[27] A former county agricultural extension agent, Carcaterra left that career in the mid-1990s when agriculture largely vanished from the valleys around ski resorts—and with it, his job at Colorado State University. Now he runs Life Inter-Faith Team on Unemployment and Poverty (LIFT-UP), a nonprofit safety net supported by a variety of Garfield County churches and businesses. Founded in 1982 in the wake of the collapse of western Colorado's oil shale business, LIFT-UP has seen steady increases in the number of people appearing at its doors for a soup kitchen meal, a voucher to stay at a motel, a tank of gas, help filling a prescription, some canned goods. With three hundreds volunteers working at five county offices and an annual cash and in-kind budget totaling seven hundred thousand dollars, LIFT-UP is a paradox, helping many people in a region whose economy—now based almost entirely on recreation and construction—boomed through the 1990s. In 2000, LIFT-UP provided emergency services to more than seventeen thousand individuals and served more than five thousand meals at its soup kitchen in a church basement on a quiet residential street in Glenwood Springs. Its total caseload was up 21 percent that year over 1998.

Many of Carcaterra's clients are the working poor who live one paycheck from catastrophe: "If they get sick, if they get injured, they can't work. They typically don't have much if any buffer in terms of any savings they can rely on, so they come to us for food, they come to us for help with rent, they come to us because they're running out of funds and they haven't been able to secure jobs that are going to afford them the kinds of protection they need through benefits [so] that they can weather some of those storms."

The church basement where Carcaterra and I meet is worn and bare except for a few benches and folding tables. Several shelves are full of donated canned goods: tomatoes, pumpkin puree, green beans. The soup kitchen opens here each evening. "People don't like to come here," Carcaterra says. "It's difficult for them to even look you in the eye, and you can tell. They're men and women just devastated by life's circumstances. These aren't lazy people. These aren't people who deserve what they're getting by any stretch."

Down the street, Garfield County social services director Margaret Long saw her agency's caseload of children placed in foster homes nearly triple from 1987 to 1999. "The increase clearly was [due to] stressed families," Long says. "It was families at risk because of long commutes, because of not being able to make ends meet, because of some ill-advised coping mechanisms with substance abuse. I think all of this combines to make stressed-out families and kids who get into trouble."

The burgeoning Latino community in Garfield County worries Long. By most estimates, somewhere between 35 and 50 percent of the thousands of Latinos in the central Colorado region are in the country illegally and therefore subject to deportation if they are caught by the Immigration and Naturalization Service. "If I'm an undocumented woman," Long says, explaining that in many families only the men who work can afford working papers, either real or forged, "I'm in a potentially vulnerable position. My husband may have papers, but if I don't have papers, let's say he decides to beat me. What am I going to do?"

✳ ✳ ✳

Foreign workers have become the backbone of the modern ski resort. Some are recruited from places like Sweden and Australia to be the public face of the company in front desk posts, teaching skiing, loading lifts. In the harder, less glamorous jobs, the workers mostly come from Latin America, often illegally; some are brought over by job brokers from Africa and Eastern

Europe. Employers like them because they work for relatively low wages and don't ski much, if at all.[28] African workers who were shipped to Summit County by a New York employment agency complained to a reporter of high job-placement fees, hard work at menial tasks such as cleaning hotel rooms, crowded living arrangements, and low wages.[29] Their situation is typical for many workers in the industry.

In 1999, the mayor of Douglas, Arizona, Ray Borane, wrote an extraordinary letter to the editor of the *Aspen Daily News*, laying the human tragedy of the Mexican-American border war at the feet of the ski industry. By the late 1990s, Douglas had become the most bitterly contested place in the daily Sisyphean battle between U.S. Border Patrol agents and those who wish to come to the United States to work illegally. More illegal immigrants were apprehended in and around Douglas in 1999 than in any other sector of the border: an astonishing 470,000 arrests in this sector alone, almost ten times the number caught in 1995.[30] Borane's letter is a catalog of anger and disgust directed at the ski industry and its offshoots, some of the many magnets drawing illegal workers through his town:

> When you hire illegal aliens because you have forgotten, or never knew how, to make your own beds, mow your own lawns and cook your own meals, it causes our open fields to be littered with thousands of plastic water jugs and pieces of clothing. It means ranchers' water lines are cut and their cattle die from ingesting discarded plastic.
>
> When you hire illegal aliens, our elderly are forced to live in constant fear because of the marauding hordes who trespass their homes and properties every night.
>
> When you hire illegal aliens to work in your homes, hotels, restaurants, landscaping businesses, fields, orchards, factories and construction crews, our property values plunge because of the huge numbers of people who trample over our land.

Can you even begin to fathom the arduous, debasing journey these people travel for the opportunity to manicure your gardens, wash your dishes, build your homes and make up your hotel rooms? Would you place your loved ones at risk for this?

Polleros and *coyotes* [traffickers in human cargo] will stuff 20 people in a room with no restroom facilities as a staging area in our sister city of Agua Prieta, Mexico. Vans will transport them in conditions intolerable even for animals. Some will suffocate or die in rollovers as drivers attempt to outrun the U.S. Border Patrol. Just last week, 12 were injured in such an accident and had to be transported to the hospital in critical condition.[31]

Once, slaves and people who aided them risked their lives for freedom. Today, the undocumented alien risks his life and the lives of his family for poor living conditions and a job that often pays less than the minimum wage. This Underground Network ends right at your community's doorstep.[32]

The racism Latinos feel in Leadville is common in many ski towns and their outlying communities. But there is a broader, more nuanced frustration about the rapid change the Latino community represents, and it is felt not only by people such as Ray Borane, who live along the border. After a series of brawls involving Latinos in Carbondale, Colorado, a former coal-mining town that has become a bedroom community for Snowmass Village and Aspen, locals half-jokingly referred to it as "the knife-fight capital of the Roaring Fork Valley." There is truth and unease in the phrase, a shorthand that summarizes the view of many longtime residents in mountain communities who blame Latinos for a list of problems that includes drug dealing, vandalism, low wages, auto accidents, school violence, and more. According to this view, immigrants, legal and illegal, are destroying much of what makes Colorado attractive. Many critics of immigration, including former Colorado governor Richard Lamm, argue that the question isn't whether Americans should be compassionate toward Latino workers trying to get a leg up; the question is how to protect and defend the things Americans value, including open space and sense of community. A town such as Carbondale is different now than it was fifteen years ago. For some people, especially new arrivals, it is better than the place they left. But for those who were there before, who resent the rising crime and the impending big-box developments on the edge of town, it is worse. It is the story of immigration as it has played out in the United States for centuries, playing out now in ways and places where few people expected it less than a generation ago.

There are no obvious villains in this situation, and one can view it as a continuation of a long American tradition in which immigrants take low-end service jobs, work hard, send their kids to college, and so experience the best of the American Dream. Certainly, Latin American workers do many jobs that most Anglo Americans shun, from cleaning toilets to washing dishes. Some analysts believe illegal immigration contributed to the economic boom of the 1990s, a time when the stock market soared yet inflation was almost nonexistent—partly because of all that cheap labor flooding across the border. "Undocumented foreigners are keeping our strong economy afloat," declared the *Denver Post*.[33] While that may be true, it should not obscure the extraordinary human cost associated with the workings and appetites of the modern, high-volume ski resort. I asked many people in law enforcement and social services whether they believed my characterization of the ski-resort economy as a feudal arrangement was an overstatement. Nobody disagreed. Many seconded my suggestion that these places have been colonized, and none of them were willing to say that they felt the ski industry had made their part of the world better during the past fifteen years.

* * *

There is a great gnashing of teeth in mountain towns about the loss of social diversity, about how successful ski resorts are becoming empty "towns" made up of mostly empty houses. What is less apparent but is an important part of the problem is that some people in positions of power do not care. "For many people who choose to live in gated communities across the country, that's not an issue," says Myles Rademan, the industry observer in Park City. For these people, the "Rocky Mountain theme park" lamented by Archbishop Stafford is not a bad thing; it's a good thing. It's their playground. They are the reason that Cordillera exists, that Sol Vista is being built, that there are private hiking trails at Grey Head outside Telluride, and that the ranches outside Jackson Hole have been filled with trophy homes. Collectively, these people, attracted and coddled by a ski industry that has aimed at a market higher and higher up the economic ladder, lie at the core of the social problems facing ski towns.

Aspen's West End is a quiet, shaded residential area, thirty blocks of lush lawns overhung by big cottonwood trees. It is a still place, unnaturally so. Once the residential center of town, the West End has been almost completely taken over by second-home owners. There are few dogs and fewer children, because almost no one lives there. This is the flip side of the coin that is "the Aspen effect." On one side, there is traffic and sprawl. On the other, there is this too-quiet, depopulated neighborhood. The people who care for this place live somewhere else, just as the people who own it do. The West End illustrates what happens when a town is bought by outsiders: in many ways it resembles the Potemkin villages built by Intrawest, a hollowed-out simulacrum of a town. Those who own the homes in the West End, and those who care for their lawns and shovel their driveways, could hardly have less in common.

"People who work with and live in a community, prima facie, care more about the community than people who don't work and live in it," says Rademan. "Those places that have the largest workforce with a stake in the town, those people are like shareholders."

But employees and townspeople aren't the controlling shareholders of the Big Three ski corporations, who live and work elsewhere, and whose interests often sharply diverge from those of people who want a vibrant, sustainable, diverse community and economy at the base of a ski hill. "What we're talking about is a fundamental flaw in the structure of corporations," says Michael Kinsley, the community development consultant at Rocky Mountain Institute. "Corporations always have a short-term outlook. If a CEO does something that matters for the long term, he's out on his ass. If I was in the resort investment business in the short term, I wouldn't give a shit about any of this stuff. If I was in it for the long term, If I wanted my children to inherit my company, I would care deeply about the quality of the community in which I'm operating. If this is only another page in somebody's portfolio, then all they have to do is tear out the page."[34]

What the Big Three ski corporations care about first and foremost is growth and income, not elk, songbirds, or the quality of life of resort workers. They do not care sufficiently about the long-term viability of skiing, ski towns, or the natural environment in which the sport is rooted. In the past forty years, the sport of skiing has morphed from a more or less environmentally benign outdoor experience into a destructive extractive industry with a potential to cause permanent environmental damage on par with logging, ranching, and mining. That potential is now being realized thanks to publicly traded corporations that are making a short-term play on the great population slug of Baby Boomers. This strategy may warm the hearts of company shareholders, but it brings with it real costs that communities and regulatory agencies seem unable to manage very well.

These corporations are spearheading the urbanization of mountain retreats that traditionally have been places where Americans sought an alternative to mainstream culture. And these corporations are, particularly in the West, perpetuating an American economic development model that was created in the nineteenth century by industrialists who treated the nation's hinterlands as resource colonies. Today, things are little different. "Tourism," wrote author Hal K. Rothman, "is the most colonial of colonial economies."[35]

Critics of this view may contend that the ski industry has revived dying towns, that we are better off because of it. But who are "we"? Are "we" the lynx, the mitigated elk, the Townsend's solitaire seeking a quiet place to nest? Are "we" the struggling artist looking for an affordable and inspiring community? Are "we" the workers who commute long hours on dangerous roads for low wages? Such work may be a better option than poverty in a rural Mexican village, but it should not be a Hobson's choice. Those sorts of comparisons are a meaningless attempt to dodge responsibility, and they do not excuse the poor treatment given so many ski-resort workers who receive low wages, no health insurance, no benefits of any kind. Certainly, some individuals are better off, but their betterment clearly has come at a cost to other people, other places, to wildness and to nature. The rising economic tide in ski country has not lifted all boats by any stretch of the imagination. It has lifted some, but it has swamped many others.

The problems that have spread through ski country thanks to the rise of the modern ski corporation, both environmental and social, spring from this common source: the interests of ski corporations and the interests of people trying to build or sustain a community in ski country run at cross-purposes. The long-term solution to the problems the ski industry has created involves changing the industry's players. Publicly traded corporations, including the Big Three, should get out of the business—and they probably will as Baby Boomers age and return on investment dwindles. Ski towns and the people who live in them can and should take advantage of this coming shift to regain control of the ski business.

CHAPTER 10
Back to the Future

The entryway to the home of Aron Brill and Jen Ader is a small, glassed-in porch clogged with outdoor sports equipment. A narrow path winds through a collection of kayak paddles, old skis, bicycles, loose gloves, and clotted dog hair. The porch opens onto the living room, where I am assaulted by a huge, friendly Akita and a frantic, honey-eyed Border collie. Brill, a thirty-one-year-old snowboarder, slouches in an old armchair perched like a throne in the middle of the room. A visiting friend has been sleeping on the adjacent futon couch, which is jumbled with blankets. A poster of a New Zealand ski area hangs on the wall. It is spring, but snow is piled halfway up the west-facing window, and more is falling the day I visit. Snow may fall here well into May.

This century-old building on the main drag of Silverton, Colorado, is a classic ski bum's house. Yet the only ski area here is Kendall Mountain, a community-run rope tow that rises a few hundred feet from the southern edge of this moribund gold-mining town. It operates on Fridays and Saturdays; tickets cost six dollars, three dollars for kids.

Brill and Ader are not here to ski Kendall Mountain. They intend to put Silverton on the skiing world's map. After a year of searching the mountain ranges of the West, they have settled on a site six miles north of Silverton. On the huge, north-facing bowl of Velocity Peak and its flanking ridges, they will build the first large public ski area to open in the United States since 1980. Silverton Mountain ski area will, Brill says, offer one-thousand-six-hundred acres of skiing, putting it in the light-heavyweight category for sheer size.

Yet something different is happening here. There will be no real estate development at the ski area, beyond a few guest cabins and a dormitory at the base of the single, fixed-grip chairlift. Nor will there be any snowmaking, grooming, or man-made trails. The lift, a relic recycled from Intrawest's Mammoth Mountain, will carry skiers and snowboarders to the top of Silverton Mountain's west ridge. From there they can dive east or west down half a dozen avalanche chutes or climb on foot another thousand feet toward the summit of Velocity Peak. The skiing here is not for beginners.

Tickets will cost twenty-five dollars, and most customers are expected to come from western Colorado. Brill and Ader, helped by a few investors, a Small Business Administration loan, and an economic development grant from the State of Colorado, will build and open their ski area with an investment equal to "the cost of a moderate house in Telluride or Aspen," Brill says. They will break even if they count nine thousand skier days during a winter—less than half of Vail Mountain's maximum single-day capacity. By the spring of 2001, the chairlift line had been cut through the trees and the chairlift was on hand, ready to be installed when the snows melted. The ski area has drawn a flurry of media attention and generated phone calls to the little house on Greene Street from people as far away as New York, wanting to know how they can get tickets, and when.

"The hard-core skiers who can no longer afford to live in their favorite ski town really get no respect," says Brill. He is rangy and muscular, standing a little over six feet tall. He's good looking, with hazel eyes, light freckles, and tousled red hair, the sort of man who would have been a model for the 1930s Art Nouveau wall posters that promoted the glamour of skiing in Sun

Valley or Gstaad. "I lived in Park City, Steamboat, Tahoe, and Big Sky and got priced out of each and every one of those places."[1]

He shifts in his chair, grabbing one of the dogs to scratch its head. "Today's ski resorts are no longer about skiing," he says. "It's about golfing and just overall entertainment and leisure activity. If you read the industry reports, they compare it with having to compete with Disneyland and other vacations. I think that's where things have gone wrong."

Brill and Ader are taking a different path, charting their ski area's future by looking to the sport's origins. They may be the vanguard of a renaissance in the skiing world, part of a movement to bring skiing and ski areas back to their roots. Brill and Ader may succeed or they may fail, but they are not alone. From the board of the National Ski Areas Association on down, ski enthusiasts are questioning whether the Big Three have led the ski industry astray. Some are beginning to look for skiing's future in its past.

❋ ❋ ❋

The capital-intensive, high-cost, New Ski Village model of ski-resort development and operation, made so popular during the 1990s and pursued so slavishly by North America's largest resorts, is not inevitable. It is not even wise.

It has spread through the ski business because the Big Three have promoted it. Responsible for one in four of the lift tickets sold in the United States, Vail Resorts, Intrawest, and American Skiing Company set the pace for the rest of the ski business. Given the iconoclasm and independent thinking that characterized the development of America's downhill-skiing industry from the 1930s through the 1960s, there is a certain irony in the manner in which today's resort operators largely have mimicked the Big Three's strategies in the hope that somehow they will revive both the ski industry and their own profits.

But the truth is in the numbers, and the numbers show that the Big Three's strategies are reviving neither. The snow-induced bump in skier days during the winter of 2000 notwithstanding, skiing's participation remains essentially flat. "One of the promises of consolidation . . . was that all the new energy and promotional clout, brought to bear with the help of strategic partnerships and lucrative sponsorships, would give a lift to the whole sport that had not previously been possible," declared *Ski Area Management* magazine in the spring of 2001. "But, the simple fact is, this has not happened."[2] Despite all the fanfare surrounding the publicly traded companies and the changes they brought to skiing, they have been anything but resounding business successes. American Skiing Company's stock tumbled steadily from its opening price of $18.125 when the firm went public in 1997. By 2001, it was trading around $1 a share. Vail Resorts and Intrawest have not fared quite so badly, yet neither could they be called rousing successes. More than four years after it went public, Vail stock was trading around $20, roughly 10 percent below its initial public offering (IPO) price (from a high of $32, it eventually dropped to about $14 before recovering). Over the same time period, Intrawest's common stock rose from its 1997 IPO price of $17 to $21, then plunged to $11 before climbing back to trade around $19 a share by mid-2001. This is a less-than-stellar performance for the companies that are leading America's most popular winter sport, a mediocrity achieved during a record, decade-long run-up in the stock market.

More cracks were evident in the Big Three's business models in the wake of the busiest ski season on record. After logging a 7.6 percent increase in skier visits, Vail Resorts cut its staff during the spring of 2001. The company fired thirty-seven full-timers, noting that increasing competition and a drop in destination visitors had forced the cuts. American Skiing already was slashing costs and personnel for its own reasons.

Crested Butte Mountain Resort and the Aspen Skiing Company also laid off personnel that season.[3]

The cost of the ski industry's fling during the 1990s with the publicly traded corporate resort model has been high. Although some individuals have benefited, Vail, Intrawest, American Skiing Company, and their imitators have brought enormous disruption to ski towns across North America. They have contributed significantly to the urbanization and gentrification of some of America's most magnificent places. They have displaced human communities and damaged natural ones. They have accelerated the on-mountain arms race and jacked up the cost of skiing, helping to force other ski areas out of business. They have made the sport increasingly unaffordable, drying up the pool of new skiers. They have done all this in the search for greater wealth and profits—yet their shareholders have fared poorly at best, and at worst have lost their shirts.

Skiing is not simply dying; skiing is being killed. The very fact that skier days jump when the snow is good, as they did during the winter of 2000, shows that millions of Americans love to ski and want to do it. So why don't they do it more often?

Part of the answer is time poverty. But it's also fair to say that the ski industry is moving away from skiers. The New Ski Villages, high-speed lifts, ubiquitous snowmaking, and the rest of the modern corporate skiing experience are a product of desperation, of too many ski areas chasing a diminishing pool of wealthy Baby Boomers. It is true that the biggest corporate resorts are popular and outwardly successful, but that popularity has come at a cost that is not sustainable. The pursuit of the Baby Boomer demographic has perverted skiing and ski towns—a perversion knowingly undertaken by corporations that are using the sport of skiing, the vanishing charm of ski towns, and nature's scenic beauty as a front for profiteering at the expense of those places they depend on.

For those who are willing to look, the signs that the ski industry is going in the wrong direction are easy to see. "I remember Aspen to be a place that people visited annually for their ski trips," wrote Dominic Buscemi, a Marin County, California, resident who in 1999 penned a letter to the *Aspen Times* after visiting that town regularly during the 1980s and 1990s. "Now it has become a place that, if they are very lucky, [they] will be able to take a trip to once in their entire lifetime. That's a huge difference." Buscemi went on to relate the story of a shell-shocked family of five he encountered in the Aspen airport. In the course of two weeks they had spent fourteen thousand dollars. They would never be able to afford to return. Neither, added Buscemi, would he.[4]

Such a price tag is not exceptional at today's top-drawer resorts. Jonathan Stauffer, a Vail native and outspoken critic of Vail Resorts, calculated that a typical family of four from Chicago would spend $10,000 during a week's visit there in high season.[5] A survey during 2001 at twenty-seven ski areas revealed that the average ski trip of three or more nights cost an individual $1,608.[6] This sort of information is well known to ski industry executives; indeed, much of the modern resort's business strategy is dedicated to capturing more of that spending, rather than reducing visitors' costs.* But vacation expenses like these bode ill for those who want skiing to thrive for another century.

---

* In fact, many ski areas seem committed to increasing costs. A single-day private ski lesson at a major ski resort ranged from about $269 to $470 during the winter of 2000. After paying the instructor, the ski resorts are left with a gross profit as high as 60 percent, according to a former (and outraged) director of the Aspen Mountain Ski School ("Ski Instruction in America," *Mountain Gazette* 79, p. 36). Equipment costs are also prohibitive. In 1990, skiers replaced their equipment every 3.5 years; by 1998, they were replacing it every five years—perhaps because new, shaped skis cost an average of 37 percent more than traditional, straight skis that year ("The Booming Economy and Ski Industry Trends," sno.e news 11, no. 2, Summer 1998).

By many accounts, the land-boom economy that has de-rived from the sport is the biggest business of all in many ski regions. But ultimately the strategy is bad for skiing. By 2008, the last Baby Boomer will have turned forty-four, the age at which participation in skiing drops off a cliff. Increasingly, Boomers will turn to warm-weather destinations. Intrawest, looking to ride the Baby Boomer wave again, has begun in-vesting in warm-weather golf resorts. After all, it was Intrawest CEO Joe Houssian who said, "We don't consider ourselves in the ski business."

When the Baby Boomers have gone, what will be left? The New Ski Villages and the business strategies surrounding them evolved during one of the greatest expansions in Amer-ican economic history. The near-miraculous growth of the 1990s created wealth that midwifed the high-end vacation and real estate economy in ski resorts. By late 2001, the rolling good times of the 1990s seemed a distant memory. Even if the eco-nomic vitality of that decade is rekindled, this industry, so deeply dependent upon discretionary income, will find itself facing overbuilt ski villages; too much vacation property on the resale market and too few buyers; too many ski areas and too few skiers; and urban sprawl filling mountain valleys. In large part because of the strategies of the ski industry during the last decade, a smaller percentage of Gen-Xers who follow the Boomers will have learned to ski. There won't be nearly as many of them interested in buying mountain real estate, simply be-cause there aren't nearly as many of them, period.

Ski resorts that follow the Big Three's get-big-or-get-out model are effectively building their church for Easter Sunday. That church will be too big and too expensive to run once the Baby Boomers have wandered away to warmer climes. The Na-tional Ski Areas Association's somewhat panicked call to attract more first-time skiers and turn them into aficionados under-scores the bleak demographic reality facing the ski industry:

the Echo Boomers who were expected to fill their parents' places at these resorts seem increasingly unlikely to show up—and if they do, they very well may not be skiing.

The New Ski Villages attract mountain visitors but not necessarily skiers. No ski resort, no matter how slick, is going to out-Disney Disney, be more cruiselike than Carnival, more amusing than Universal Studios. So why are ski areas even trying? It's an old business maxim that in times of trouble, the companies that do well are those that focus on their core competency. Those ski areas that thrive will be those that respond to what skiers want.

✳ ✳ ✳

Only when control of skiing is wrested from publicly traded corporations, which value profit to the near exclusion of all other values, and vested with people committed to the long-term success of the sport and of mountain towns will skiing—and ski towns—have a fighting chance. This is not an exercise in nostalgia; skiing and ski towns will change no matter what happens. At issue is who will determine the direction and the beneficiaries of that change. For much of modern American history, rural towns have suffered from boom-bust economies precipitated by their colonial existence on the tip of the national economic whip. Ski towns today still live that colonial life. A relatively small change to the nation's economy was, and is, magnified in places that depend on a single commodity, be it silver ore, timber, or high-end vacations. Traditionally somebody else, somewhere else, called the shots. Residents of these places live at the mercy of remote owners and a fickle investment market.

Many residents in many ski towns remain economic captives of larger forces, particularly in those towns that host one of the Big Three's resorts. "The way you change that is exactly the way you kill it," says Park City's Myles Rademan. In his view, only urbanization can free small towns from colonial economics. Small towns that diversify their economies sufficiently to insulate themselves from the vagaries of the ski business and the local ski operator are not small towns anymore. They have become bigger, more diverse, more urban. "That's the dichotomy. You change it by enough people living there that they develop their own capital. I hear people rail that we're a resource colony. The alternative is—what? That we're Chicago?"[7]

Yet the world is changing, and a third way is emerging, an alternative to the two poles of Rademan's dichotomy. More and more people seek out mountain communities for the quality of life they offer. Unlike their predecessors during the 1950s and 1960s, these urban refugees are not coming to drop out of the mainstream, nor to give up their careers. With the help of technology, they are trying to blend the best of both urban and rural life.

This phenomenon has many aspects to it. The Center for the New West, a Denver think tank, uses the term *Lone Eagles* to refer to individuals leading this change. "Lone Eagles are the first wave of those who are changing the way we live, work, play, learn, and move around because of the telecommunications revolution," wrote center president Phil Burgess. "They may represent America's most important lifestyle change since the rise of the two-wage-earner family in the 1970s." Lone Eagles earn an average of eighty-one thousand dollars a year and garner 85 percent of their income from somewhere outside their home community.[8] Just as ranchers, loggers, and miners are in the export business, so are Lone Eagles; they export intellect. The are executives, stock traders, writers, photographers, software designers, and artists; or people who run advertising agencies, publishing houses, consulting firms, and the like. (Some observers say that the future of ski towns lies not in more industrial tourism, but in attracting technology companies.)[9]

The resort industry is in the export business, too. It exports experiences people carry away with them, and it exports real estate when people who live elsewhere own it. Vacation real estate development is the last in a long line of exploitative, colonial, export-driven, and unsustainable economies that typified the development of rural American mountain communities. Now, for the first time, a sustainable economy based on services, rather than products—based on the export of intellect—is rising in rural locales.

It is rising first in resort towns, where rural and urban interests collide. The process of moving to this more sustainable economy is a messy one that engenders its own set of problems, but the result is something new in America, neither rural nor urban nor suburban, but instead a physical juxtaposition of urban and rural worlds. Aspen, Colorado; Jackson Hole, Wyoming; Bozeman, Montana; Mammoth Lakes, California; and Stowe, Vermont, along with many other towns, have become places that offer urban-level amenities—and often suffer urban-style social problems—in a natural setting that is largely rural or even wild.

This economic and social transformation has significant implications for the ski industry. As more people move to mountain towns, as those who live in those towns earn more money, and as more of them earn their money from somewhere else, the potential customer base for a ski area changes. (This is a form of gentrification, but it is a far superior form to the version in which the gentry doesn't even live in these changing communities, which is the result when real estate is sold to second-home owners.) Ski-area customers do not have to come from distant places; they can come from closer to home. This flies in the face of the Big Three's New Ski Village strategy, which depends on high-spending destination visitors. But it also offers real opportunity for the future of the ski business.

* * *

"Having the ski areas here gave it original cachet," says Juli Beth Hoover, executive director of the Mad River [Vermont] Planning District. Hoover, a young mother who grew up skiing in Vermont, has watched the Lone Eagle phenomenon take place and seen how an increasing portion of the Mad River Valley's population is no longer connected to the economic fate of the local ski resorts. "It gave a reason for people to come here, and a reason for the grocery stores and the general stores to start selling thirty-five-dollar bottles of Bordeaux and the *New York Times*. [Now], a lot of people are in that professional class where they don't have to worry about when the next downturn comes."[10]

The Mad River Valley is the only place where the American Skiing Company was stopped in its tracks. A bitter battle ensued in the mid-1990s when American Skiing proposed a 155-room quarter-share hotel for the base of its Sugarbush ski area. With the help of a community plan, a powerful state environmental law known as Act 250, and endless town meetings, Mad River Valley residents forced American Skiing to modify its design so significantly that although the company eventually won approval for a hotel, executives chose not to build it. This happened, Hoover says, because the residents of the Mad River Valley generally shared a common vision. They had put some effort into collectively deciding what they wanted to be, and they were willing to hew to that agreement when a development that served the needs of an outside corporation—but not their own—was proposed. In the end, Mad River Valley residents determined that the ski resort would have to conform to the community, rather than the other way around. That victory may be a watershed event in the evolution of the business of skiing. With luck, it will be. In September 2001, American Skiing accepted an unsolicited offer from a group of Mad River Valley investors and sold Sugarbush to them for an undisclosed amount.

There are many differences between New England and the American West, but perhaps the most significant is symbolic. New England has been inhabited by Anglo Americans for the better part of 400 years. In the West, most Anglo American history reaches back no further than 150 years. The West can feel unfinished to people from other places. It still stands in Americans' collective psyche as the place where we go to reinvent ourselves, as a landscape of freedom and self-determination. That attitude hampers Western communities trying to stand up to an outside corporation, because belief in the primacy of individual rights and freedoms is much more keenly felt west of the Mississippi than in New England, where community often comes first and where the town meeting, rather than the Marlboro Man, is the defining cultural expression.

The Mad River Valley's residents are in many ways closer in their thinking to Europeans than they are to Coloradans or Montanans. "Switzerland is hardly a socialistic place, yet they realize this is all there is. They don't have any manifest destiny," says Terry Minger, the former town manager of both Vail and Whistler. Today he runs a consulting business in Denver, and he admits a certain remorse for the overdevelopment that happened at ski resorts on his watch. "In Europe, there are places that have held the line for a couple hundred years. We could learn from that. I think we could learn that in our country in general. We can't afford to screw up any more land. In that sense I think it's sort of a sacred trust. We've got to quit looking at these things as another development. This is defining who we are as Americans in the next go-round. I know that doesn't mean a lot to a banker or a big corporation from Vancouver, but I think it ought to be put on the table."[11]

As ski towns grow into the rural-urban, more economically independent hybrid, the biggest political battles will be about the shifting of power—about what matters and who gets to call the shots. "That is going to be the major battle of the next fifteen or twenty years," says Myles Rademan. "How you keep local control, how you keep culture when you come up against these big corporations."

In modern ski towns, what role does skiing hold? The old company-town, resource-colony models are falling away. Economies are diversifying as telecommuters and retirees bring in new sources of income. No longer does everyone depend on tourism and its reverberations as they once depended on the mine or the railroad. Vermont, for instance, follows only Florida and Nevada in terms of per capita nonwage income, as Juli Beth Hoover points out. That means more and more rural residents' livelihoods are disconnected from the local ski resort's marketing schemes. They have little interest in whether the beds are full during high season. As Baby Boomers fade away, what will happen to places like Sugarbush, Stratton, Wolf Creek, Crested Butte, Mammoth, Targhee, Steamboat, Taos, and the rest? There will always be a tourist market seeking out Vail and Aspen. But not everyone can afford to, or wants to, ski in top-drawer resorts. What will skiing in these other places be like, and who will it serve, in 2015 or 2020?

If skiing is going to thrive as a commercial concern for more than an elite few—if it is going to be something besides the members-only Yellowstone Club, besides "snow polo"—ski-area managers must return to skiing itself, to the simple beauty of being in nature in winter, of exercising and socializing with like-minded souls. The salvation of the ski industry lies not in more Potemkin villages, dewatered rivers, shopping arcades, on-mountain stock trading, and high-volume, high-speed lifts. In this age of virtual reality, skiing's salvation lies in affordability, authenticity, nature, and simplicity. For skiing to thrive, the industry must abandon the path being forged by the Big Three. Some ski areas already are doing that.

* * *

The origins of skiing are infused with *Idraet*. It was an idealistic philosophy, but at its core, *Idraet* describes why we ski. That philosophy is the touchstone of skiing; those ski-area executives who understand that, who are returning the sport to its roots, are taking skiing back to the future with noteworthy success.

In 1998, Mike Shirley, the CEO of Bogus Basin, Idaho, did something that—at least for the ski industry—was radical. He cut prices. The former vice president of finance and administration at the construction giant Morrison Knudsen, Inc., Shirley took the reins of the nonprofit twenty-six-hundred-acre ski area outside Boise in 1992. Bogus Basin is a member-owned cooperative ski area that has operated since 1938. There is no base village, no shopping district, no high-end fractional real estate. Just skiing and boarding. Shirley, a self-described "redneck conservative and total capitalist," didn't care about the nonprofit structure; he was irked by empty chairlifts. Bogus Basin already offered a good deal by industry standards, selling its season pass for only $500. Shirley dropped the price to $199, explaining, "A $200 expenditure for a season pass is almost pocket money. It's an easy decision." For those people who had never skied, Shirley threw in a season's worth of equipment rentals and four lessons free with the same $199 pass. Kids twelve and younger got a season pass for a mere $29.[12]

The lines to buy season passes went out the door. In 1997, Bogus Basin had sold 2,854 season passes at $500 apiece. For the winter of 1998, the co-op sold 25,000 at $199 each. In the spring of 2001, Shirley expected to sell 30,000 for the following winter. During a single year—in an industry that hasn't seen any sustained growth in two decades—skier days at Bogus

Basin jumped from 192,000 to 303,000. These weren't skiers stolen from a nearby competitor; these were Boise locals who wanted to ski. Between the winter of 1997 and the winter of 1999, skier-related revenue at Bogus Basin rose from $4.7 million to $7.7 million. Even though many new season-pass buyers previously had bought more-expensive day tickets, dollar yield per skier-day climbed 3 percent.

Shirley, who sits on the board of directors of the National Ski Areas Association, has taken to proselytizing. "We've got to start thinking about the day after tomorrow, rather than just this afternoon," he says. "We're not giving anything away by doing these cheap deals [at Bogus Basin]. We're making more money than we ever have."

After I spoke with Shirley, he sent me a fax:

> The ski industry in general is in the terrible bind of having all this brutal capital intensity in our mountains. There is ultimately little difference in how we act as a community-owned non-profit corporation versus a private, for-profit enterprise, except that maybe we have the luxury of sometimes being able to take the longer view—not totally consumed with immediate returns to investors. . . . The larger difference would be between the high-dollar (elitist?) destination resort, and places like Bogus Basin, the quintessential local, day ski area. Our places are skier/boarder factories and certainly [among] the less elite resorts, where one can go for weeks at a time without spotting a thousand-dollar Bogner outfit. We don't, however, have to take second place to anyone in terms of the actual skiing experience.

Several hundred miles east, in Montana's Bridger Mountains, Doug Wales is thinking the same thing. Wales is the director of marketing at Bridger Bowl, a cooperatively owned nonprofit ski area founded in 1954. Bridger offers a thousand acres of skiing and some of the best terrain in the state. One person in ten in the greater Bozeman area buys a season pass, which costs $475. Skier days have climbed from 125,000 annually in 1990 to 168,000 in 2000. Bridger Bowl throws off a very high 40 percent profit, money that is reinvested in the ski area's operations and that keeps Bridger debt free.

"People are looking for an opportunity to be outside, enjoy the outdoors and enjoy doing some fun, physical recreation," Wales says. "There's a very strong component to [skiing] of enjoying the outdoor world that people are looking to experience. I think that's being lost."[13] The Big Three's business strategies are pricing people out of skiing, Wales says, and he believes the shopping, real estate, and urban experiences that typify big resorts turn off a lot of potential skiers.

Perhaps the most famous nonprofit, cooperatively owned ski area in the nation is Mad River Glen, just a few miles up the Mad River Valley from Sugarbush ski area. It was founded in 1948 with a charter that reads, "[A] ski area is not just a place of business, a mountain amusement park, as it were. Instead it is a winter community whose members, both skiers and area personnel, are dedicated to the enjoyment of the sport." Today Mad River Glen, which has about two thousand co-op members, is a real village, not a Potemkin one. There are no buildings in this village, but there is a great deal of community among the people who ski here, along with all the messiness and contentiousness that comes in an authentic community where people care about what is at stake.

Mad River is open about 110 days a year, depending on snow (it makes almost none), and counts sixty thousand to eighty thousand skier visits annually. It's not big, but it's not going away. General manager Bob Ackland, the former American Skiing Company vice president, shakes his head and stares out at the gray March day when I ask him about the sport's future. "There are too many big ski areas," he begins. "I think these big ski areas are going to become more exclusive. They've become more expensive, and that can't bring new people into the sport. That's where there needs to be some shrinkage. You could rejuvenate the community ski area. Then you have a chance at generating new skiing revenue and generating new skiers."[14] Ackland will get his chance to find out. He is part of the group of Mad River Valley residents who purchased Sugarbush from American Skiing in late 2001. Ackland returned to his old stomping grounds as Sugarbush's mountain manager.

Mad River Glen, Bogus Basin, and Bridger Bowl have three elements in common: they are nonprofits owned in some form by their communities; they are low-cost operations offering affordable skiing; and they were started around World War II. It would be difficult to replicate today what the founders of those ski areas did a half-century ago. People typically don't get together and build a ski area these days.[15] What can be replicated, and what is critical to the future of skiing, is local control and low costs. Without external pressures to turn an ever increasing profit, these ski areas grow only to accommodate skier demand, not to satisfy Wall Street. Local control is a critical and necessary difference that changes everything, for it essentially aligns the ski area's interests with those of the Mad River Valley, Boise, and Bozeman, rather than against them.

Just such thinking lies behind a proposal floated in 2000 in Grand County, Colorado, to sell stock in the debt-ridden Winter Park ski area to county residents. The sixty-year-old ski area, owned by the City of Denver, had struggled during the ski wars of the 1990s. City officials concluded they needed to find a private firm with whom to partner to bail the resort out of twenty million dollars in accumulated debt. But Grand County resident Jay Erlandson had a different idea. He proposed to sell stock in 49 percent of Winter Park to county residents, with a goal of raising thirty-five million dollars. After paying off the debt, the resort would have about fifteen million dollars to invest; Denver would retain a controlling interest; locals would have a real say in how the place is run; and, as a for-profit operation, Winter Park would pay taxes to Grand County for the first time.[16]

Local control is not an untested strategy. Mad River Glen, Bogus Basin, and Bridger Bowl have been in business since the middle of the twentieth century, and they have shown how to turn a profit and use it to keep the skiing good and costs down. These three ski areas are the face of sustainable skiing. They are showing the way to the future, and they are being followed. When Mike Shirley cut season-pass prices to $199, lots of people in the industry paid attention; sixty ski areas restructured their pass prices during the next two winters.[17] Indirectly, Shirley started a price war among Colorado's Front Range resorts. During the winter of 2000, Vail Resorts sold more than a hundred thousand season passes for $299, valid at Breckenridge, Keystone, and Arapahoe Basin, plus several days at Vail or Beaver Creek. Copper Mountain and Winter Park followed suit. Seeing no other option, several smaller ski areas in central Colorado—Ski Copper, Loveland, Eldora, and Ski Sunlight—cut prices as well. Between the winter of 1998 and the winter of 2000, the number of season passes sold at Rocky Mountain resorts rose 145 percent, to almost one in five skiers. Skier days were up, helped by good snow and more affordable passes. Yet, according to the *Denver Post*, "the amount of money culled from snowriders has dropped steadily over the past four years, when the discounted season-pass programs first emerged on the resort scene."[18]

This declining yield is a problem for big and little operators alike. The bigger resorts can afford to sell lift tickets and passes at a loss for a while, subsidizing them with revenues from hotels, retail, and real estate operations. Little ski areas don't have that cushion. They are forced to compete on price with the bigger operators, who, while battling each other, may inadvertently be forcing smaller areas toward financial collapse.

That ultimately will shrink rather than expand the new-skier market.[19]

Yet loss-leader tickets and passes can't be sustained forever, even by the biggest operators, as the declining-yield problem illustrates. In the end, low prices only work in conjunction with low costs, and so the cheap passes pose an enormous challenge for high-cost operators as well, particularly the Big Three and their imitators. According to Doug Wales, a high-speed lift costs twice as much as a fixed-grip chair to buy and three times as much to maintain. Snowmaking can cost millions of dollars for the annual electricity bill alone. Free shuttle buses, ski concierges, on-mountain hosts, grooming machines—there is a reason a single-day lift ticket costs sixty dollars or more at a New Ski Village resort. If the trend is toward lower lift-ticket prices, as it may be, then New Ski Village operators will earn even less money from skiing and will turn their attention more aggressively to finding other forms of profit. That is all the more reason for ski-town residents to reject them and their business model.

American Skiing Company founder Les Otten dismissed the idea of a cheap lift ticket. But his company's stock has collapsed under the burden of debt, and in early 2001 Otten himself was out of a job, resigning after the Meristar merger fell apart.[20] Just down the road from Otten's first ski resort, Sunday River, Josh Burns is running a low-cost ski area at a profit. In the fall of 2000, Burns bought Mt. Abram during a foreclosure sale for $325,000 and began running it in the black. He got a good deal: eight hundred acres, five lifts, grooming and snowmaking equipment. Single-day tickets are cheap: $33 for an adult (compared to $51 at Sunday River), $20 for skiers six to seventeen, free for kids five and younger. It's a stripped-down operation, but it's providing cheap family skiing and seems to be finding a niche.[21]

The future of skiing may not be built around the New Ski

Villages, fast lifts, and snowmaking championed by the Big Three. Indeed, such high-cost operations that seemed so unstoppable during the 1990s may turn out to be dinosaurs, while the low-cost, locally owned ski areas are the furry mammals scurrying around their feet. Locally owned ski areas will not, of course, turn their backs on tourism. It seems highly unlikely that a ski area of any size could survive without visitors from afar, who generate a significant portion of skier days at Bogus Basin, Bridger Bowl, and Mad River Glen. These three areas do market themselves to tourists, and tourism will remain a significant part of the sport. But skiing tourists are welcomed at the co-op resorts as part of a larger strategy targeted toward long-term sustainability. They are not pursued at the expense of the greater community.

"I think many [business] models will emerge in the next decade or two," says Myles Rademan. "This corporate model you see now has been tried before. I've seen it tried several times over the last thirty years, not successfully for the most part." Perhaps, he says, locals will step up to the plate and buy failing ski resorts to run for themselves—as was proposed at Winter Park.

It's a bold idea, and in many places it couldn't work. A modern ski area easily could sell for millions, even tens of millions, of dollars; few communities would be interested in ponying up the money to buy one. But that does not mean the concept of community ownership should be dismissed out of hand. Community ownership—in the form of a for-profit business, municipal or freestanding nonprofit, or co-op—has the inestimable advantage of taking outside owners out of the equation. The root of the problem between ski towns and publicly traded corporations that own ski resorts is that they ultimately have irreconcilably different goals. Community sustainability and quality of life do not mesh with relentless quarter-over-quarter growth.

In the modern, rural-urban community being invented in America today, a ski area can be a community amenity, one more aspect to quality of life no different in type from the municipal pool or golf course. In Bozeman and Boise, it already is. "I think there is definitely a place for ski areas to operate that are simpler by design, that focus on the sport and the environment and the mountain," says Bridger's Doug Wales, who gets excited at the suggestion of a community-owned Crested Butte or Wolf Creek. "They can be very possible."

❋ ❋ ❋

The idea of a community taking control of a ski resort is not anticapitalist; it is the best realization of capitalism. That's what employees do when they buy companies through an employee stock-ownership plan, and America's employee pension funds are the largest owners of many corporations and mutual funds. What local ownership really accomplishes is to put a community more directly in charge of its fate (during the early 1990s, the Vail town government briefly considered purchasing Vail Associates out of bankruptcy). There's nothing un-American about doing this. Rather, it may be the only way to solve the conundrum facing small mountain towns, what Rademan calls "the tradegy of success."

"Everywhere I go I hear people say what they don't want to be," he says. "They used to say, 'We don't want to be Aspen.' Now they say they don't want to be Park City. Everywhere I go they don't want to be something, but they don't know what they do want to be. We're becoming what we don't want to be a lot faster than we're becoming what we do want to be, because we don't know what we do want to be."*

---

* One veteran Aspen skier, upon hearing this comment, said, "A lesson from skiing: when you ski the trees, focus on the spaces, not the trees. Stare at the trees and you'll hit one."

Small mountain towns will keep ending up as what they don't want to be until the people who live in them control the levers of power. There are other levers than ski areas, but for the communities built beside major ski resorts, these businesses almost certainly represent the biggest lever.

"I worry about these places," says Terry Minger. "I love skiing and I love the idea of mountain communities. Mountain people are different; they're good people living in the last of the best places. I just worry about what we're doing and what we've learned and where it all goes. We haven't evolved to the degree the Europeans have to recognizing that these are treasures. These aren't just subdivisions. These aren't just lifts."

Minger believes it is possible for American mountain communities to re-create themselves as something newer, rounder, and more complete than they ever have been. What I call the urban-rural hybrid he more mellifluously terms "the Chautauqua model," after the nineteenth-century colony in upstate New York dedicated to culture and enlightenment in natural surroundings. He describes it as "strictly an American idea."*

"I've been responsible for mucking around some of these places," Minger says of ski towns. "For a long time I think Eldon [Beck] and I both thought that you could solve a lot of these problems through good urban design and architecture and all that, and you can, but ultimately, it's still the people. It's the soul. Good architecture and good siting and planning are essential, but that's just the beginning. That's not the end of the thing. That's what's been missing.

"I'm a firm believer that the best resorts, the most enduring places, are because people actually live there," he says. "The ski world is a little bit behind this curve, I think. Words like

---

* This is almost exactly what Walter Paepcke had in mind when he selected Aspen in the 1940s for what became known as "the Aspen Idea."

sustainability are, to them, fighting words. How much is enough? That's a question we never ask ourselves in America."

Adds Rademan: "Our greatest challenge in the West is we have not been settlers. The only settlers were the Mormons. The rest of us have just been passing through. Our great challenge now is how to not be looking for the next place, which has been the traditional model, but to dig in for long enough—and generations of long enough—to settle. We camp out in the West, and that's different than settling."

❋ ❋ ❋

As the spring storm builds, Aron Brill fishtails his Chevy Blazer up the slushy dirt road north of Silverton. The windshield is cracked, and bits of rust show on the truck's fenders. Once, these steep mountainsides rang with industrial activity. The Silverton Caldera was one of the richest mineral deposits in America, veined with gold, silver, copper, and lead. Now Cement Creek runs orange beside the road, polluted by a century of gold mining to an acidity level akin to tomato juice. Much of the valuable ore has been removed from these mountains, leaving behind poisoned creeks, leaching piles of mine waste, and picturesque crumbling buildings. Silverton was a one-industry mining town, subject to the whims of distant markets and remote ownership. Since the last mine, the Sunnyside, closed in 1991, the town's population has dropped from eight-hundred to four-hundred. A popular summer steam train that runs here from Durango keeps the place bustling during the warm months, but in early spring, Silverton feels close to dead.

Silverton Mountain ski area lies in the middle of this abused yet still beautiful jumble of thirteen-thousand-foot peaks. We drive through snow that is blowing sideways. I have to crane my neck to see the steep ski runs, no more than narrow avalanche chutes between tight spruce trees, disappearing up into the clouds. Brill points out where Silverton Mountain ski area's lone chairlift will be set near a small, rough parking area. A few hundred yards downstream from the Sunnyside Mine we park, cross the ocher creek on foot, and begin slogging up a trail that zigzags steeply up the spruce-covered mountainside. Brill is on snowshoes and carrying his snowboard on his back; I have attached climbing skins to my skis so they will grip the snow.

The valley is quiet, and the snow and fog blot out my sense of place and time. As I follow Brill I feel a strange sense of both déjà vu and discovery. This must be what it felt like for Pete Siebert and Earl Eaton as they climbed the flanks of Vail Mountain for the first time in 1957, or for Count Felix Schaffgotsch as he sought just the right peak to become Sun Valley in 1935. This is what skiing is about; finding the right mountain, the right slope, and then riding it, experiencing it, loving it and the snow and the weather and the sense of being alive. It's about sharing that experience with kindred spirits and taking what nature has to offer on its own terms.

The spirit of skiing has been submerged beneath all the hype and marketing, the slick advertising campaigns and the distressed pine paneling in the condominiums, the heated sidewalks in the "villages" and traffic jams along the highways, the plight of illegal laborers scrubbing plates in the back of the designer-decorated restaurants, the on slope video arcades and private mountaintop clubs, the ski valets and snow guns and grooming machines. Perhaps, a generation or two from now, people who ski and snowboard will look to Silverton the way they look today to Sun Valley and Vail and Aspen. Perhaps they will trace the roots of skiing's renaissance back to the chairlift beside Cement Creek and the little ski bums' house on Greene Street, where a couple of folks who didn't like the status quo decided to change things, decided to reject what seemed inevitable and return to the roots that always have made this sport great.

The lesson from Europe and from our own destruction of communities in the name of progress is that the time has come for Americans to set aside the concept of manifest destiny. We have to decide, as Rademan says, to settle, to really be someplace for the long haul and to make it work. That's not the business model for a Wall Street corporation riding a demographic bubble. But it is the right approach for people who love and live in the mountains, who love skiing and who want to find a way to sustain both the sport of skiing and the places they live. At a June 2000 conference about the future of Telluride, one speaker summed up what sustainability means for mountain towns: "Don't just find a way to live here. Find a way to die here."

The urban-rural hybrid being created in the mountains of America is a step toward settling, because it is a step away from the colonial power arrangement that has characterized the history of rural towns for so long. Publicly traded ski corporations are the latest—and hopefully the last—incarnation of colonial power exerted over the towns that now host them. It will be neither simple nor easy for communities to gain control over ski resorts. In many ways, it will be much harder than letting someone from outside run the show. But opportunities to do so will arise. Local control is a solution to a problem that will produce its own problems, yet it also is an exercise in democracy and self-determination that will go a long way toward redressing many of the problems that have been created by corporate overdevelopment of the ski business and ski towns.

The future of skiing and ski towns can be bright if mountain communities find ways to take their fate into their hands. How to do that is for each community to determine on its own, but the motivation is clear: If we don't change the direction we are headed, we are likely to end up where we are going.

NOTES

CHAPTER 1

1. The before-tax profits are referred to by the companies involved as EBITDA: Earnings before Interest, Taxes, Depreciation, and Amortization. This is a commonly used but misleading figure. American Skiing Company, although showing a positive EBITDA, actually lost money in 2000 once those costs were factored in. See Intrawest Corporation Annual Report to Security Holders, Oct. 20, 2000, p. 28; Vail Resorts Inc. Annual Report, Oct. 27, 2000, p. 11; American Skiing Company Annual Report, Oct. 26, 2000, p. 19.

2. Intrawest Corporation Annual Information Form, fiscal year 1998, pp. 8–9; Vail Resorts Inc. Annual Report, fiscal year 1998, p. 6; American Skiing Company Annual Report, fiscal year 1998, p. 7 and 17; "Who Owns Which Mountain Resorts," National Ski Areas Association, Oct. 5, 2000.

3. Vail Resorts Inc. Annual Report, fiscal year 1998, p. 1.

4. Remarks of the Hon. James R. Lyons, Undersecretary for Natural Resources and Environment, U.S. Department of Agriculture, at the NSAA National Convention and OITAF International Congress, San Francisco, May 24, 1999, transcript p. 7.

5. E. John B. Allen, *From Skisport to Skiing: One Hundred Years of an American Sport, 1840–1940* (Amherst. University of Massachusetts Press, 1993), p. 4.

6. Ibid., p. 98. It was in Arlberg that Hannes Schneider developed the Arlberg turn, a stem turn that replaced the telemark turn Scandinavians had used and taught for turning while skiing downhill. See Abbott Fay, *Ski Tracks in the Rockies: A Century of Colorado Skiing* (n.p.: Cordillera Press, 1984), p. 1.

7. Fay, *Ski Tracks in the Rockies*, pp. 10–11.

8. Otto Schniebs, *Skiing for All* (New York: Leisure League of America, 1936), p. 12.

9. Fay, *Ski Tracks in the Rockies*, p. 1.

10. Allen, *From Skisport to Skiing*, p. 31.

11. Ibid., p. 21.

12. Ibid., pp. 11–12.

13. Ibid., p. 79.

14. Hal K. Rothman, *Devil's Bargains: Tourism in the Twentieth-Century American West* (Lawrence: University Press of Kansas, 1998), p. 186.

15. Ibid., pp. 187–89.

16. Ibid., p. 191.

17. Allen, *From Skisport to Skiing*, p. 171.

18. Rothman, *Devil's Bargains*, pp. 204–5.

19. *Fire on the Mountain*, prod. and dir. George Gage and Beth Gage, 72 min., First Run Features, 1996, videocassette.

20. Rothman, *Devil's Bargains*, p. 253.

21. Ibid., p. 198.

22. Ibid., p. 229.

23. Sureva Towler, *The History of Skiing at Steamboat Springs* (Steamboat Springs, Colo.: Routt County Research, 1987), pp. 165–68.

24. Rothman, *Devil's Bargains*, p. 259.

25. Ibid., p. 11.

26. Ibid., p. 259.

27. June Simonton, *Vail: Story of a Colorado Mountain Valley* (Vail, Colo.: Vail Chronicles, Inc., 1987), pp. 62–63.

28. Rothman, *Devil's Bargains*, pp. 243–44.

29. Ibid., p. 237.

30. Ibid., p. 246.

31. Ibid., p. 245.

32. Peggy Clifford, *To Aspen and Back: An American Journey* (New York: St. Martin's Press, 1980), pp. 107–8. Clifford is no relation to the author.

33. Rothman, *Devil's Bargains*, p. 240.

CHAPTER 2

1. "NSAA Model for Growth: The Next Steps," *NSAA Journal* (Oct./Nov. 2000), p. 3. The NSAA has created a "Model for Growth" to try to counteract what it believes will be an otherwise inevitable contraction in skier days. "Increasing the number of beginners isn't the answer," says Michael Berry, president of the National Ski Areas Association. "A 2.5 percent increase in beginners while keeping the current retention numbers results in a 37.9 percent decrease [in total skier days] in fifteen years [because increasing numbers of skiers are quitting the sport]. Even a 6 percent increase compounded annually sees a 13.3 percent decline over the same period." Bruce Lewis, "NSAA Leader Writes Prescription for Change in Ski Industry," *Park City (Utah) Record,* July 4, 2000.

2. Shannon Dortch, "Skiing, Skating, and Shredding," *American Demographics,* Feb. 1996, p. 4.

3. Brent Gardner-Smith, "Peering into Skiing's Crystal Ball," *Roaring Fork (Basalt, Colo.) Sunday,* April 18–24, 1999.

4. Estimated U.S. Ski Industry Skier/Snowboarder Visits by Regions, 1979–2000, National Ski Areas Association, Aug. 20, 2000.

5. Jason Blevins, "Nation's Ski Hills See Record Visits," *Denver Post,* May 9, 2001.

6. Brent Gardner-Smith, "U.S. Ski Visits Could Set Record, but Destination Resort Visits Flat," *Aspen Times,* May 4, 2001.

7. National Ski Areas Association Fact Sheet, updated Oct. 11, 2000.

8. National Demographic Study, Final Report, 1997–98, National Ski Areas Association, p. 11.

9. Ibid., p. 15, fig. 12.

10. Facts and Figures on the On-Snow Industry, SnowSports Industries America and National Ski Areas Association (Lakewood, Colo., June 1999), p. i.

11. Melinda Beck, "The Next Big Population Bulge: Generation Y Shows Its Might," *Wall Street Journal,* Feb. 3, 1997.

12. Juliet B. Schor, *The Overworked American: The Unexpected Decline of Leisure* (New York: Basic Books, 1991), p. 22.

13. Snow Sports Industry Intelligence Report, SnowSports Industries America and National Ski Areas Association (Lakewood, Colo., June 2000), p. 14.

14. Daniel Glick, *Powder Burn: Arson, Money, and Mystery on Vail Mountain* (New York: Public Affairs, 2000), p. 43.

15. Author interview with Andy Daly, president, Vail Resorts, July 24, 2000.

16. Author interview with Jim Spring, president, Leisure Trends Group, Sept. 18, 2000.

17. Author interview with Skip King, spokesman, American Skiing Company, Feb. 28, 2000.

18. "Resort Life," Intrawest annual report 1999, p. 15; Skier/Snowboarder Visits by Regions.

19. Adam Aron, CEO, Vail Resorts, interview by Christine Bushey, MSNBC Business Video, Sept. 9, 1997.

20. Author interview with Les Otten, founder, American Skiing Company, Feb. 27, 2000.

21. Ken Hulick, "An Inside/Outside View of Marketing," *Ski Area Management,* July 2000, pp. 15–16.

22. Spring interview.

23. American Skiing Company 1998–99 Media Guide, pp. 6–7.

24. Who Owns Which Mountain Resorts, National Ski Areas Association, Oct. 5, 2000.

25. King interview.

26. American Skiing Company 1998–99 Media Guide, pp. 19–20.

27. American Skiing Company annual report, Fiscal Year 1999, p. 2.

28. Author interview with Bob Ackland, general manager, Mad River Glen, Feb. 25, 2000.

29. Sureva Towler, *The History of Skiing at Steamboat Springs* (Steamboat Springs, Colo: Routt County Research, 1978), pp. 166–69.

30. Vail Resorts Media Guide, winter 1998–99, p. 24.

31. Author interview with Tom Clink, assistant sales manager for POMA's North American division, Oct. 11, 2000. The chairlift parameters were for a 6,000-foot detachable quad rising 1,400 feet and capable of carrying 2,400 skiers per hour. The gondola parameters specified an eight-place gondola, 9,000 feet long and rising 2,200 feet, carrying 2,400 people per hour.

32. Towler, *History of Skiing at Steamboat Springs,* p. 169.

33. Vail Resorts Annual Report, Fiscal Year 1998, p. 18; author interview with Hugh Smythe, vice president of resort operations, Intrawest Corporation, March 28, 2000.

34. Clink interview.

35. Bridger Gondola Builds Momentum, press release, Jackson Hole Ski Corporation, May 4, 1998.

36. Syd Kearney, "More Slopes, More Chairlifts and More Snow at Ski Resorts," *Aspen Times*, Oct. 21, 1998.

37. Erika Gonzalez, "Ski Areas Upgrading at Record Pace," *Rocky Mountain News* (Denver), Aug. 21, 1999; Towler, *History of Skiing at Steamboat Springs*, p. 169.

38. "Powder Play," *Dallas Morning News*, Feb. 7, 1999.

39. Spring interview.

40. Number of Ski Areas Operating in the United States, fact sheet, National Ski Areas Association, Aug. 2000.

41. Author interview with Michael Berry, president, National Ski Areas Association, July 8, 1997.

42. Snow Sports Industry Intelligence Report, p. 14.

43. Leisure Industry: Investment Trends for the 1999–2000 Ski Season, Bear, Stearns and Co. Consumer Equity Research, Dec. 1999, p. 13; David Rowan, "Are We All Still in the Same Business? An Exercise in Social Insecurity," *Ski Area Management*, May 2001, p. 44.

44. Jeff Berman, director, Colorado Wild, letter to Tere O'Rourke, district ranger for Dillon, Colorado, U.S. Forest Service, detailing Colorado Wild's scoping comments on the Jones Gulch expansion [undated], *Federal Register* 63, no. 217: pp. 63024–25.

45. Report from the White River National Forest Four-Season Resorts on Resort Trends and Their Potential Impact on Forest Planning, submitted by Arnold and Porter law offices, November 1997, p. 1.

46. "The Slippery Slope of Ski Resort Survival," *Denver Post*, April 8, 2001.

47. "Resorts Expand Despite Fewer Skiers," *Broomfield (Colo.) Enterprise*, Jan. 29, 2000.

48. Author interview with Dana Severy, vice president, Intrawest Mammoth Corporation, Nov. 12, 1999, and David Greenfield, president, mountain resort development group, Intrawest Corporation, March 27, 2000.

CHAPTER 3

1. Sandy Cortner, "A Crested Butte Journal," *Skier's Gazette*, Dec. 8, 1970, p. 13.

2. He acquired Killington, Mount Snow, Haystack, Waterville Valley, Sugarloaf, and Sugarbush by purchasing S-K-I Limited.

3. American Skiing Company 1999–2000 Media Guide, pp. 19–21.

4. Intrawest Corporation Annual Report to Shareholders for 1997, pp. 4–5; author interviews with Joe Houssian, CEO, and Hugh Smythe, vice president for operations, Intrawest Corporation, March 28, 2000.

5. "King of the Hill after an Epic Wipeout: Ski Mogul George Gillett Tackles the Slopes," *Time*, Dec. 12, 1997.

6. Booth Creek Ski Acquisition Corp. Prospectus Filed [with the United States Securities and Exchange Commission] Pursuant to Rule 424, June 26, 1998, p. 6. Booth Creek paid $17.5 million for Waterville Valley and Cranmore, and $121.5 million for the three California resorts. The Summit cost $14 million, Loon Mountain $29.9 million, and Grand Targhee $7.9 million (ibid., pp. 9–11). The bulk of the $162.5 million Gillett raised for this spree—$116 million—came from junk-rated bonds paying a steep 12.5 percent interest rate (ibid., p. 10, and "King of the Hill"). The reason for the high rates? Booth Creek was a significant credit risk that well might not have been able to make its payments (Booth Creek Ski Acquisition Corp. Prospectus, p. 20).

7. Emily Narvaes, "Gillett Still in Ski Business?" *Denver Post*, March 17, 2000.

8. Of this amount, sixty-four million dollars went to Apollo Ski Partners. Apollo Ski Partners is a holding of the Apollo Fund, a Delaware limited partnership that controls the bulk of Vail Resorts stock. Black is a partner in the Apollo Fund and, through this chain, effectively controls Vail Resorts. "King of the Hill" and Sheri Cole, "The French Connection: Who Owns Vail Resorts?" *Vail Trail*, March 13, 1998.

9. Vail Resorts Inc. Annual Report for 1999, p. 3.

10. Patrick Thorne, "2001: A Global Ski Odyssey," *Ski Area Management*, Nov. 2000, p. 69.

11. "The New Dream Home," *American Demographics*, May 1997.

12. Rebecca Piirto Heath, "Life on Easy Street," *American Demographics*, April 1997.

13. Hal Clifford, "It Takes a Village," *Ski*, March/April 1999, p. 104.

14. Ibid., p. 108.

15. Intrawest Corporation 1996 Annual Report to Shareholders, p. 3.

16. Vail Resorts 1997 Annual Report, p. 30.

17. David Rowan, "Are We All Still in the Same Business? An Exercise in Social Insecurity," *Ski Area Management*, May 2001, pp. 42–44.

18. Author interview with Gary Raymond, vice president for acquisitions and real estate, Intrawest Corporation, March 31, 2000.

19. Author interview with Michael Coyle, vice president for marketing, Intrawest Corporation, Nov. 17, 1998.

20. Promotional materials provided by American Skiing Company during March 2000.

21. American Skiing Company 1998 Annual Report, p. 1.

22. Julie Flaherty, "Picked Up and Dusted Off, a Ski Chain Starts Anew," *New York Times*, July 18, 1999.

23. American Skiing Company 2000 Annual Report, p. F-2.

24. Flaherty, "Picked Up and Dusted Off."

25. American Skiing Company 2000 Annual Report, pp. 4–5, 13–14.

26. American Skiing Company/Meristar Hotels and Resorts Document 425, filed with the Securities and Exchange Commission Dec. 11, 2000.

27. American Skiing to Sell Steamboat, Cut Costs, company press release dated May 30, 2001, posted on First Tracks!! Online Ski Magazine, www.firsttracksonline.com.

28. American Skiing Company Scores Ski Industry Record, company press release dated Aug. 4, 1998.

29. Hal Clifford, "Hot, Hot, Hot," *Ski*, Sept. 1998, p. 207.

30. Intrawest Sells $94 Million of Resort Real Estate, company press release dated April 6, 1998.

31. Intrawest Sells Out the Village at Squaw Valley USA, company press release dated April 19, 2000.

32. Keystone's Newest Neighborhood Sells $25 Million in Just 45 Minutes, company press release dated Aug. 16, 2000.

33. Edwin McDowell, "A Few Weeks to Call Your Own," *New York Times*, Jan. 29, 2000.

34. Beaver Creek Ski Enthusiasts Buy $4.75 Million in Vacation Ownership Property, Hyatt Mountain Lodge press release dated Dec. 8, 1997.

35. Intrawest Annual Report to Security Holders, fiscal year 1999, pp. 33–34.

36. Intrawest's 1999 Annual Report to Security Holders summed up the strategy of all the big operators:

The primary objectives of the Company's marketing strategy include (i) increasing the Company's market share of North American, European and Asian visitors, (ii) building demand during both peak and non-peak periods, (iii) increasing existing customers' use of the Company's network of resorts, (iv) expanding the summer- and shoulder-season businesses of the Company's resorts and (v) increasing the Company's total share of customer spending across each resort. (p. 15)

37. "Big Spenders: As a Favored Pastime, Shopping Ranks High with Most Americans," *Wall Street Journal*, July 30, 1987, cited in Olivia Mellan, *Overcoming Overspending* (New York: Walker and Company, 1995), pp. 18–19.

38. Clifford, "It Takes a Village," p. 104.

39. Maureen Drummey, "Hot Property," *Ski*, May/June 2001, p. 98.

40. Michele Conklin, "It Takes a Village," *Rocky Mountain News* (Denver), Feb. 27, 2000.

41. Hal Clifford, "Mount Millionaire," *Ski*, Feb. 1998, pp. 114–15.

42. Author interview with Les Otten, founder, American Skiing Company, Feb. 27, 2000.

43. American Skiing paid $288.3 million to Kamori International for both Steamboat ski area and Heavenly ski area in California. David Kesmodel, "Steamboat Eager for a Lift," *Rocky Mountain News* (Denver), Sept. 8, 2001.

44. Ibid.

45. Author interview with Michael Kinsley, Rocky Mountain Institute, June 11, 1999.

46. Intrawest Corporation Annual Information Form, fiscal year 1998, pp. 8–9; Vail Resorts Inc. Annual Report, fiscal year 1998, p. 6; American Skiing Company Annual Report, fiscal year 1998, pp. 7, 17; Who Owns Which Mountain Resorts, National Ski Areas Association, Oct. 5, 2000.

47. Forest Service Snowsport Fact Sheet, issued 1999.

48. Perhaps nobody makes money from this phenomenon so well as Vail Resorts, which has an interlocking relationship with East-West Partners, a Vail development company founded in 1986. East-West is principally held by Rod Slifer, Mark Smith, and Harry Frampton (Slifer is a former Vail mayor, Frampton a former president of Vail Associates, the forerunner of Vail Resorts), who also own 50 percent of the real estate firm Slifer, Smith and Frampton. SS&F is a Vail brokerage with ninety agents who handle the bulk of the Vail Valley retail real estate market, which in 2000 amounted to transactions worth more than a billion dollars. Who owns the other 50 percent of Slifer, Smith and Frampton? Vail Resorts, Inc., through its Vail Resorts Development Corporation. If VRDC sells raw property to a third-

party developer, and that developer then lists its retail products—say, condominiums—on the market with Slifer, Smith and Frampton, of which VRDC is half-owner, VRDC gets a kickback from SS&F known as an "override commission" on sales made to the public. This kickback ranges from .0075 percent to 2 percent above the normal commission. Keeping everything cozy, East-West Partners itself often buys development property from Vail Resorts. For instances, in late 1998 East-West entered a contract to buy 2.7 acres on Breckenridge's Main Street from Vail Resorts for $3.5 million. Clifford, "It Takes a Village," p. 115.

49. Houssian interview.

50. Robert Weller, "Railroad Joins Fight for Minturn Water," *Denver Post*, July 4, 1998; Steve Lipsher, "Minturn, Vail Lawsuit Settled, Ski Resort Gains Water in Dispute," *Denver Post*, Sept. 2, 1998.

51. Author interview with Scott Oldakowski, vice president for real estate and marketing, American Skiing Company, Nov. 17, 1998.

52. Author interview with Skip King, spokesman, American Skiing Company, Feb. 28, 2000.

53. Editorial, "Thoughts on Becoming an Asset," *Ski Area Management*, Sept. 2000, pp. 57–58.

54. "Theme Park Lessons Learned," *NSAA Journal*, June/July 2000, p. 1.

CHAPTER 4

1. Alex Markels, "Backfire," *Mother Jones*, March/April 1999, p. 63.

2. The one qualification to this assertion is it's possible Vail Resorts committed the arson against itself so that it would gain public sympathy, discredit environmentalists, and be able to rebuild older facilities in a bigger and better form. See Daniel Glick, *Powder Burn: Arson, Money, and Mystery on Vail Mountain* (New York: Public Affairs, 2000) for a detailed discussion of this possibility.

3. Genesis 1:28.

4. Charles Philips and Alan Axelrod, eds., *Encyclopedia of the American West*, vol. 3 (New York: Macmillan Reference USA/Simon and Schuster, 1996), pp. 138, 934–35.

5. Wallace Stegner's description of Gilpin's hyperbole is remarkable:

The Manifest Destiny which he had learned from [Senator Thomas Hart] Benton, and which was a creed and a policy of his generation, was a passionate vision to Gilpin. He saw the West through a blaze of mystical fervor, as part of a grand geopolitical design, the overture to global harmony; and his conceptions of its resources and its future as a home for millions was as grandiose as his rhetoric, as unlimited as his faith, as splendid as his capacity for inaccurancy. . . . Superlatives were futile for the description of the salubrity, richness, health, prosperity and peace this [Rocky Mountain] West offerred. . . . The painful struggles of earlier times and harsher climates would not be found. Even houses were unnecessary, so temperate were the seasons. . . . Agriculture was effortless: no forests needed clearing, manual tillage was not required, even the use of the plow was not essential, so eager were the seeds to germinate in this Paradise. As the plains were amply irrigated by underground and artesian waters, the plateau was watered by mountain streams of purest melted snow, and to arrange fields for irrigation was no more trouble than fencing, which the ditches here superseded. No heat or cold, no drouth or saturation, no fickle climate or uncertain yield, afflicted this extensive region, and no portion of the globe, even the Mississippi Valley with its potential eighteen hundred millions, would support so dense a population. San Luis Park would in time become as renowned as the Vale of Kashmir; South Pass would be a gateway more thronging than Gibraltar. And all up and down the length of the cordillera that stretched through two continents, the unlimited deposits of precious metals assured the people of a perennial and plentiful supply of coin. In a moment of caution, keeping his feet on the ground, Gilpin admitted that there were a few—a very few—patches of gravelly and unproductive soil in the mountain parks, but he hastened to add that these could be depended upon to contain placers of gold.

Wallace Stegner, *Beyond the Hundredth Meridian: John Wesley Powell and the Second Opening of the West* (New York: Penguin Books, 1953), pp. 1–5.

6. Henry David Thoreau, Journal [1906], entry from Jan. 5, 1856, cited in *Bartlett's Familiar Quotations*, 16th ed., p. 478.

7. Henry David Thoreau, *Walden; or Life in the Woods* (New York: Dover Thrift Editions, 1995), p. 53.

8. John Muir, "Save the Redwoods," *Nature Writings: The Story of My Boyhood and Youth, My First Summer in the Sierra, the Mountains of California, Stickeen, Selected Essays* (New York: The Library of America, 1977), p. 828.

9. The full title of the work is *A Modest Proposal for Preventing Children of Poor People from Being a Burthen to Their Parents, or Their Country, and for Making Them Beneficial to the Publick*.

10. Douglas S. Kinney, Gabriel D. Carter, Joshua M. Kerstein, *Values of the Federal Public Lands* (Boulder: Natural Resources Law Center, University of Colorado School of Law, 1998), p. 18.

11. Hal Clifford, *Longstreet Highroad Guide to the Colorado Mountains* (Atlanta: Longstreet Press, 1999), p. 141.

12. Aldo Leopold, *A Sand County Almanac, with Essays on Conservation from Round River* (New York: Oxford University Press, 2001), pp. xvii–xix.

13. U.S. Code title 16, chapter 23, section 1131 (c).1.

14. Kinney, Carter, and Kerstein, *Values of the Federal Public Lands*, p. 20.

15. Edward Abbey, *The Best of Edward Abbey* (San Francisco: Sierra Club Books, 1984), p. 293.

16. Kinney, Carter, and Kerstein, *Values of the Federal Public Lands*, p. 23. Of this amount, 35 million acres are on Forest Service land, 39 millions acres in national parks, 21 million acres on U.S. Fish and Wildlife refuges, and 1.4 million acres on BLM land.

17. Author interview with Sloan Shoemaker, conversation director, Aspen Wilderness Workshop, Aug. 29, 2000.

18. Eliot Porter, *The Place No One Knew: Glen Canyon on the Colorado* (San Francisco: Sierra Club Books, 1961).

19. Jim Steinberg, "A Mammoth Transformation—For the Better?" *Fresno Bee*, Nov. 6, 2000.

20. American Skiing Company Annual Report, Fiscal Year 1999, p. 2.

21. Vail Resorts Incorporated Annual Report, Fiscal Year 1998, p. 9.

22. Frank Clifford, "West's Recreation Faces Development Dilemma: Resorts May Be Less Invasive Than Mining and Logging, but Still Bring People," *Los Angeles Times*, Nov. 12, 1998. (Clifford is no relation to the author.)

23. Letter from Cynthia Cody, chief, EPA NEPA Unit, to Martha Ketelle commenting on the White River National Forest Plan draft environmental impact statement, May 9, 2000, p. 5 in EPA's detailed comments (sec. III. Recreation "A": Ski-based resorts). See http://www.fs.fed.us/r2/whiteriver/planning.

24. Author interview with Phil and Linda Miller and Joan May, Nov. 21, 2000.

25. Author interview with Joe Houssian, CEO, Intrawest Corporation, March 28, 2000.

26. Author interview with Andrea Mead Lawrence, Nov. 12, 1999.

27. Author interview with Dana Severy, vice president, Intrawest Mammoth Corporation, Nov. 12, 1999.

CHAPTER 5

1. Author interview with Gary Raymond, vice president for acquisitions and real estate, Intrawest Corporation, March 31, 2000.

2. Hal Clifford, "The Top 10 Tips for Buying Mountain Property," *Ski*, March/April 1998, p. 195.

3. Author interview with David Greenfield, president, mountain resort development group, Intrawest Corporation, March 27, 2000.

4. Federal Aviation Administration website, http://www.faa.gov/arp/aip_loc. Total investment by the FAA in the Eagle County Airport via the Airport Improvement Program amounted to $11,635,059 between 1990 and 1997, inclusive. Another $8,759,458 was invested via the same program during the next four years. Total FAA investment in Eagle from 1983 to 2000 was about $30 million.

5. Vail Resorts 1997 Annual Report, p. 33.

6. Wendi Grassechi, "Airport Update—'I Think I Can, I Think I Can . . . '," *Mammoth Times*, May 11, 2000.

7. Matt Rasmussen, "A Slippery Slope," *Inner Voice*, a publication of the Association of Forest Service Employees for Environmental Ethics (Eugene, Ore.), March/April 1999, p. 12.

8. Author interview with Michael Kinsley, Rocky Mountain Institute, June 11, 1999.

9. "Vail Merchants Struggling with Resort's Soaring Rents," *Aspen Times*, Dec. 14, 1999.

10. Author interview with Vail resident Elaine Kelton, July 26, 2000.

11. Hal K. Rothman, *Devil's Bargains: Tourism in the Twentieth-Century American West* (Lawrence: University Press of Kansas, 1998), p. 357.

12. Hal Clifford, "Vail vs. Whistler: Evolution of Two Ski Towns," *Ski*, Dec. 2000, p. 208.

13. Author interview with Andy Knudtsen, senior housing planner, Vail, July 2, 1998.

14. "Divided over Affordable Housing: Fierce Battle in Resort Town Prompts Mayor's Decision to Quit," *Washington Post*, Sept. 19, 1999.

15. Juliet B. Schor, *The Overspent American: Why We Want What We Don't Need* (New York: Harper Perennial, 1998), p. 31.

16. Plans for the cabins were dropped by Idarado in 2001 under pressure from the San Miguel County commissioners.

17. Sandy Cortner, "A Crested Butte Journal," *Skier's Gazette*, Dec. 8, 1970.

CHAPTER 6

1. Author interview with Gary Raymond, vice president for acquisitions and real estate, Intrawest Corporation, March 31, 2000.

2. This approach is weirdly evocative of what may be the most famous quote about the strategies of the Vietnam war. Following the destruction of the village of Ben Tre, an American army major told Associated Press correspondent Peter Arnett, "It become necessary to destroy the town to save it." Neil Sheehan, *A Bright Shining Lie: John Paul Vann and America in Vietnam* (New York: Random House, 1988), p. 719.

3. Hal Clifford, "Village Person," *Ski*, Nov. 1997, p. 189 et seq.

4. Author interview with Lorne Bassel, vice president of resort development, Intrawest Corporation, Jan. 19, 2001.

5. It can be a fat stream; at Mt. Tremblant, retail sales averaged $580 Canadian (US$406) per square foot in 2000, and totaled $87 million Canadian (US$61 million) for the village as a whole.

6. Bassel and the Dalai Lama may be on to something. A ski industry survey conducted in 2001 concluded that shopping was the number-one reason people visit ski resorts, followed by dining and skiing. Tim Schooley, "Survey Finds No. 1 Reason People Go to Ski Resorts Is for the Shopping: Seven Springs Plan Includes 130,000 Sq. Feet of Retail Space," *Pittsburgh Business Times*, July 13, 2001.

7. Author interview with Susan Byers, commercial leasing manager, Copper Mountain Resort, Jan. 19, 2001.

8. Hal Clifford, "Vail vs. Whistler: Evolution of Two Ski Towns," *Ski*, Dec. 2000, pp. 128, 208.

9. The Last Roundup? How Public Policies Facilitate Rural Sprawl and the Decline of Ranching in Colorado's Mountain Valleys, American Farmland Trust, 2000, p. 2.

CHAPTER 7

1. Vail Resorts Development Company Peaks 7 and 8 Master Plan Fact Sheet, pp. 2–3; Steve Lipsher, "Breckenridge Thinking Big," *Denver Post*, March 3, 1999, p. 1.

2. When an environmental assessment (EA) or environmental impact

statement (EIS) is to be written, the Forest Service hires an outside contractor to do much of the work and then reviews it. But internal documents in the Dillon, Colorado, ranger district sharply criticized this practice in 1998 and 1999, largely because rangers felt the contractors working on the EA for Breckenridge's Peak 7 expansion heavily favored the ski industry. The contractor, a company called Sno.engineering, had been selected by Vail Resorts after the Forest Service's regional office mandated that ski area developers choose from a list of Forest Service–approved contractors— rather than the traditional practice of the Forest Service being allowed to make that choice. Although paid by the developer, the contractor is obliged to work for the Forest Service and create an unbiased analysis—but, Forest Service officials complained, that didn't happen on Peak 7. District Ranger Tere O'Rourke wrote:

> This created a totally different atmosphere with the contractor and the ski areas. I seriously question the change in policy. The Forest Service had little say in the selection of the contractors and the relationship and product was very different. . . . The contractor chose to downplay material that did not favor the ski industry and highlighted comments or information that did favor the ski areas. . . . Many of the subcontractors work directly for the ski areas and are also employed by the third-party contractors. It is doubtful in my mind that they could do an analysis that would not favor their primary employer—the ski areas. (Memo from Tere O'Rourke to Martha Ketelle, Jan. 11, 1999.)

Quoting from other Dillon Ranger District staff reports about Sno.engineering, O'Rourke reported:

> Sno.e, in document preparation, attempted to put impacts in the best possible light or downplay impacts that are not favorable to the proponent. . . . It often appeared that the Sno.e staff was arguing for the position of the ski area rather than operating as an objective third-party contractor working for the Forest Service. . . . Overall, my perception of working with Sno.e was one of a proponent advocate, which does not seem appropriate given their role of unbiased and objective analysis and documents. (Letter from Tere O'Rourke to Martha Ketelle, Nov. 25, 1998.)

3. Author interview with Martha Ketelle, forest supervisor, White River National Forest, July 10, 2001.

4. Steve Lipsher, "Breckenridge Plan Draws Fire," *Denver Post*, Nov. 16, 1998.

5. Barrett wrote in his June 3, 1998, letter:

> The Forest Service has determined that site specific consideration of the Peak 7 expansion is appropriate to "increase skiing terrain, effectively distribute guests more evenly through the resorts . . .

and improve connectivity between the resorts." As none of these purposes or needs involves additional base area construction, the long-planned [on-mountain] improvements will occur with or without independent real estate development. . . . The precise layout of VRDC's subsequent site-specific development plans will still be influenced by unknown contingencies at the ski resort, but like many other private developers in the [Blue River] watershed, its plans would proceed with or without the ski mountain expansion.

6. EPA correspondence dated Sept. 25, 1998, to Colonel Dorothy F. Klasse, District Engineer, Sacramento District, Corps of Engineers.

7. Correspondence from Cynthia Cody to Tere O'Rourke, date stamped Nov. 25, 1997, Ref. 8EPR-EP. *Train wrecks* is a term popularized by former secretary of the interior Bruce Babbitt to describe an environmental policy debacle such as the judicial, administrative, social, economic, and environmental collision that resulted in the Pacific Northwest during the 1990s, when the northern spotted owl was put at risk by excessive logging of old-growth timber.

8. Correspondence from Cynthia Cody to Tere O'Rourke, date stamped May 11, 1998. Ref. 8EPR-EP.

9. "We believe it is within the Forest Service's NEPA responsibilities to fully disclose the environmental issues related to ski area expansion in the cumulative impact analysis," James E. Luey of the EPA's Ecosystem Protection Program wrote at the end of August. "We believe that the development of the base area and ski area configuration are inextricably tied by functional and economic dependence." Correspondence dated Aug. 31, 1998, from James E. Luey, Chief, Planning and Technical Unit, Ecosystem Protection Program, to Colonel Dorothy F. Klasse, Army Corps of Engineers.

10. Correspondence dated Sept. 25, 1998, to Colonel Dorothy F. Klasse, District Engineer, Sacramento District, Army Corps of Engineers, from William P. Yellowtail, Regional Administrator, EPA Region VIII.

11. Lipsher, "Breckenridge Thinking Big."

12. Stacy Malkan, "Vail Resorts Presents: The New Breckenridge," *Summit Free Press* (Breckenridge, Colo.), March 1999.

13. Letter from Martha J. Ketelle to Bill Jensen, Breckenridge Ski Resort, dated March 17, 1999.

14. Bob Berwyn, "USFS Go-Ahead for Peak 7 Road Draws Heat: Lack of Coordinated Planning Evident," *Ten Mile Times* (Frisco, Colo.), Oct. 4–10, 2000.

15. The USDA Forest Service and Ski Resorts: A Relationship Spanning Over 60 Years, undated fact sheet from USFS.

16. Author interview with Ed Ryberg, U.S. Forest Service, Aug. 27, 2001. Between twenty-four million and twenty-eight million skier days are counted annually on federal land.

17. Mark Obmascik, "Law Gives New Lease on Skiing," *Denver Post,* Dec. 27, 1999.

18. Tony Perez-Giese, "Getting a Lift: Environmentalists Cry Foul over the New Federal Ski Fee Bill," *Westword* (Denver, Colo.), Oct. 10, 1996.

19. Author interview, anonymous source, July 3, 2001.

20. One board foot, the standard unit of measure, is a piece of timber twelve inches by twelve inches by one inch.

21. From National Extension Tourism Conference 1998, Tourism Innovations: Developments, Policy, and Markets, May 17–19, 1999, cited on Wild Wilderness home page (www.wildwilderness.org).

22. Remarks of the Hon. James R. Lyons, Undersecretary for Natural Resources and Environment, U.S. Department of Agriculture, at the NSAA National Convention and OITAF International Congress, San Francisco, May 24, 1999, transcript p. 3.

23. August 2001 e-mail correspondence from Scott Silver to the author, citing a USFS internal document titled RHWR\Budget\FY99—Budget\ GAOALLOC. Appropriations for Recreation, Heritage, and Wilderness Resources were $372,247,000 in 1994, $263,105,000 in 1999.

24. Hal Clifford, "Land of the Fee," *High Country News* (Paonia, Colo.), Feb. 14, 2000, pp. 6, 10.

25. "The Next Commodity: Disneyfied Wreckretainment," essay by Scott Silver, founder, Wild Wilderness (www.wildwilderness.org).

26. August 2001 e-mail correspondence from Silver to author.

27. The Recreation Agenda, United States Department of Agriculture, Forest Service, FS-691, Sept. 2000, p. 2.

28. Ibid.

29. August 2001 e-mail correspondence from Silver to author.

30. Text of speech by Hon. James R. Lyons, presented at the American Recreation Coalition's Great Outdoors Week, June 8, 1998.

31. Memo from Janice McDougle, associate deputy chief, Washington Office, U.S. Forest Service, to Regional Forester, Region 2, dated Aug. 12,

1996, citing item "C (1): Effective Relationships with Ski Industry." (Emphasis added).

32. Letter from Michael Berry, NSAA, to James R. Lyons, dated Dec. 12, 1996.

33. National Winter Sports Partnership Budget Allocation, February 1997, pp. 2–3.

34. Challenge Cost-Share Agreement between National Ski Areas Association and USDA Forest Service, Rocky Mountain Region, dated Sept. 15, 1999; Challenge Cost-Share Agreement between USDA Forest Service, Rocky Mountain Region, and Colorado Ski Country USA, dated Dec. 17, 1997; Challenge Cost-Share Agreement between Rocky Mountain Region USDA Forest Service and SnowSports Industries of America, dated Nov. 24, 1998; Challenge Cost-Share Agreement between Rocky Mountain Region, USDA Forest Service and Sporting Goods Manufacturers Association, dated July 27, 1999; Challenge Cost-Share Agreement between USDA Forest Service, Rocky Mountain Region and SIRDAR, dated June 22, 2000.

35. National Winter Sports Partnership Budget Allocation, February 1997, pp. 2–3.

36. Leah Hogsten, "Forest Supervisor Brings Controversy," *Salt Lake Tribune*, March 29, 1998.

37. Forest Service Manual, Title 2300, Amendment no. 2300-94-1, effective June 17, 1994. Citations: 2343.11 and 2343.03.1.

38. Hogsten, "Forest Supervisor Brings Controversy."

39. Editorial, "Facing Ski Industry Realities," *Denver Post*, April 8, 2001.

40. This phenomenon is not limited to the self-sustaining tendencies of bureaucracies. In his seminal essay "Tragedy of the Commons," Garrett Hardin explained how individuals acting in their perceived best interests can degrade or destroy a common resource and thus ultimately harm themselves. As an example, consider a New England common, with a carrying capacity of ten sheep, and ten homeowners living around it. If each homeowner puts a single sheep on the common, he benefits from that sheep without damaging the common. Of course, if he wants to get a little richer, it makes sense for him to put two sheep on the common. Assuming all other things to be equal, each sheep will perhaps be a little smaller, since it doesn't have quite as much to eat, but the homeowner will still have the wool, meat, and milk of two sheep—more than he had with one. Thus, it is in each homeowner's perceived self-interest to maximize the number of sheep he puts on the common, with the result being that the common will be overgrazed, the grass will die, the dirt will be trampled to hardpan, and soon the common will be able to support no sheep at all, impoverishing everyone. This is the argument underlying the philosophy that government has a role in regulating and protecting

commonly shared resources such as public lands, air, and waters. There is, then, a certain irony in the way each national forest is now promoting ski-area expansion without considering the overall impacts on the commons—in this case, the totality of Forest Service land and of the ski industry. Garrett Hardin, "The Tragedy of the Commons," *Science* 162, pp. 1243–48 (1968).

41. Steve Lipsher, "Vail Wires Slopes for Stock E-Trading," *Denver Post,* Dec. 7, 1999.

42. Christopher Smith, "Forest Boss Got Free Lift Ticket before OK'ing Snowbird Plans," *Salt Lake Tribune,* May 23, 2000.

43. Forest Service Manual Title 2300—Recreation, Wilderness, and Related Resource Management, R-4 Supplement 2300-91-1, effective Nov. 13, 1997.

44. Information on the identity of pass holders and Forest Service policy was obtained by the author via a Freedom of Information Act request to various U.S. Forest Service offices.

45. Jeff Burch to Sheep Mountain Alliance board members, Oct. 24, 1996.

46. The deal prohibited snowmaking in the expansion area, protected several rare fens, moved the ski area boundaries back from private land that had development potential, eliminated a planned restaurant and "interpretive center," raised minimum in-stream flow levels by restricting drawdowns for existing snowmaking, and banned the widening of a narrow road.

47. Matt Rasmussen, "A Slippery Slope," *Inner Voice,* a publication of the Association of Forest Service Employees for Environmental Ethics (Eugene, Ore.), March/April 1999, p. 12.

48. Personal communication to the author from Matt Rasmussen, editor, *Inner Voice.*

49. "Sinclair Oil Corporation Company Capsule," Hoover's Online (www.hoovers.com), downloaded Jan. 4, 2002.

50. Charles F. Trentelman, "Section of Snowbasin Road Still Sliding Down; Experts Don't Know What It Will Take to Fix the Problem," *Standard-Examiner* (Ogden, Utah), May 4, 2001.

51. Christopher Smith, "Holding: Maverick Entrepreneur Has Made a Fortune through Hard Work and Patience," *Salt Lake Tribune,* Feb. 13, 2000; Christopher Smith, "Politicians Paved Way for Road to Snowbasin," *Salt Lake Tribune,* Feb. 13, 2000; Christopher Smith, "Holding Gave Forest Service Employees Freebies: But Snowbasin Owner Denies Buying Influence," *Salt Lake Tribune,* Feb. 13, 2000.

52. BLM and the Forest Service Land Exchanges Need to Reflect Appropriate Value and Serve the Public Interest, General Accounting Office GAO/RCED-00-73, June 2000, p. 41.

53. Ibid., pp. 4, 6.

54. J. Robb Brady, "Table Targhee Land Swap," *Idaho Falls Post-Register,* June 14, 2000.

55. Jennifer Langston, "Land Swap Generates Public Discussion," *Idaho Falls Post-Register,* March 19, 2000.

56. "The environmental impact expected from base-area development plans . . . must be disclosed in detail to allow the public a complete understanding of the direct, indirect and cumulative effects from these proposed actions," the EPA wrote. Correspondence from Carol L. Campbell, Director, Ecosystems Protection Program, EPA Region VIII, to Jerry B. Reese, Forest Supervisor, Grand Targhee National Forest, dated Oct. 20, 1999.

57. A Critique of the Squirrel Meadows Grand Targhee Land Exchange Proposal Draft Environmental Impact Statement, Peter Morton, Ph.D., the Wilderness Society, Sept. 17, 1999.

58. Jennifer Langston, "Forest Service Approves Targhee Land Swap," *Idaho News,* Dec. 13, 2000.

59. Court Rejects Grand Targhee Land Exchange, press release from Greater Yellowstone Coalition, Aug. 9, 2001. GYC was one of six plaintiffs who had sued the Forest Service to stop the land trade.

60. Langston, "Forest Service Approves Targhee Land Swap."

61. U.S. Forest Service and Sugarbush Exchange Land, First Tracks!! Online Ski Magazine (www.firsttracksonline.com), July 26, 2000.

62. "5,500 Acres of New National Forest Lands in Colorado: Crested Butte, Forest Service, Colorado State Land Board Successful in First Ever Three-Way Land Exchange," Crested Butte Mountain Resort Press Release, Nov. 18, 1998.

63. "Sugarbush Completes and Vail Pursues Land Exchanges," *Ski Area Management,* Sept. 2000, p. 16.

64. Jane Reuter, "Intrawest Seeks to Expand Resort with USFS Land Exchange," *Summit Daily News* (Breckenridge, Colo.), Sept. 9, 1998.

65. Correspondence from Cindy Cody, EPA Region VIII, to Jeff Hyatt, Winter Sports Administrator, Leadville Ranger District of the San Isabel National Forest, dated Jan. 13, 2000.

66. Colorado Wild Fall/Winter 2000–2001 newsletter.

CHAPTER 8

1. Ed Quillen, "The Starving Lynx Are Just Pawns in a Statewide Chess Game," *Denver Post,* April 18, 1999.

2. Mark Eddy, "Lynx Killer Skinned for Crime: Hunter to Pay $18,000, Give Up Gear," *Denver Post*, Dec. 18, 1999. Mulkey was ordered by a judge to pay $13,328 in costs to the Colorado Division of Wildlife and another $5,000 to the Division's Operation Game Thief program. He forfeited his rifle and all-terrain-vehicle to the division, was sentenced to perform one hundred hours of community service, and was banned for life from hunting in Colorado.

3. Quillen, "The Starving Lynx Are Just Pawns."

4. Hal Clifford, "Vail vs. Whistler: Evolution of Two Ski Towns," *Ski*, Dec. 2000, p. 128; U.S. Census Bureau, State and County QuickFacts (http://quickfacts.census.gov/qfd/).

5. Author interview with Bill Heicher, field officer, Colorado Division of Wildlife, July 26, 2000.

6. Author interview with Ron Younger, former field biologist, U.S. Bureau of Land Management, July 8, 1997.

7. Michael Jamison, "Whitefish-Area Growth May Be Funneling Grizzlies into Town," *The Missoulian* (Mont.), Nov. 23, 1999.

8. Frank Clifford, "West's Recreation Areas Face Dilemma," *Los Angeles Times*, Nov. 12, 1998.

9. "Ski Resort Offices Raided by EPA in Alleged Violations," *Contra Costa Times* (Calif.), June 25, 2000; "Regulators Call for AG Probe of Squaw Valley Ski Resort," *Contra Costa Times* (Calif.), May 12, 2001. California attorney general Bill Lockyer did sue Squaw Valley on behalf of the Lahontan Regional Water Quality Control Board in January 2002. "Squaw Valley Olympics Host Sued by California," *Oakland* (Calif.) *Tribune*, Jan. 26, 2002.

10. "I-70 Like a Berlin Wall for Wildlife, Biologists Say," *Denver Post*, May 21, 2000.

11. In an unusual but illustrative incident in January 2000, a delivery man mistakenly pumped seventy thousand gallons of diesel fuel into a water-quality-monitoring well, rather than a storage tank, at Copper Mountain. Only 150 gallons were recovered; the balance is somewhere underground. Said one EPA official: "Everything goes downhill, so you expect it will eventually get to the streams." Catherine Lutz, "Missing: One Truckload of Fuel," *High Country News* (Paonia, Colo.), July 2, 2001.

12. "Announcing the Initiation of a Comprehensive Study and Analysis of the Impact of Ski Resort Development on Biodiversity Values," call for submissions from Biodiversity Legal Foundation, Boulder, Colo., Jan. 1999, p. 11.

13. Scott G. Miller, Coordinator, Partners for Wildlife Program, U.S. Fish and Wildlife Service, "Environmental Impacts: The Dark Side of Outdoor

Recreation?" paper presented at Outdoor Recreation: Promise and Peril in the New West, June 8–10, 1998 Natural Resources Law Center, University of Colorado School of Law, Boulder, Colo., pp. 2–3.

14. U.S. Fish and Wildlife Service Conference Opinion, Vail Ski Area Category III Expansion, March 16, 1999, pp. 11–13.

15. Ibid., p. 16.

16. Ibid., p. 30.

17. Ibid., p. 6.

18. Ibid., p. 9.

19. Ibid., p. 46.

20. "I-70 Like a Berlin Wall for Wildlife, Biologists Say."

21. U.S. Fish and Wildlife Service Conference Opinion, pp. 39–42.

22. Ibid., pp. 49–50.

23. Letter from James S. Mandel, Vail Resorts attorney, to LeRoy W. Carlson and Gary Patton, U.S. Fish and Wildlife Service, Nov. 10, 1998.

24. U.S. Fish and Wildlife Service Conference Opinion, p. 57.

25. Ibid., p. 62.

26. Ibid., p. 9.

27. E-mail from Richard Hannan, Endangered Species Office, U.S. Fish and Wildlife Service, to Joe Webster, Associate Regional Director, U.S. Fish and Wildlife Service, Nov. 4, 1998.

28. E-mail from LeRoy Carlson, Colorado Field Office Supervisor, U.S. Fish and Wildlife Service, to Joe Webster, Associate Regional Director, U.S. Fish and Wildlife Service, Nov. 23, 1998.

29. E-mail from Gary Patton, biologist, U.S. Fish and Wildlife Service, to John Hamill, Colorado Regional Office, U.S. Fish and Wildlife Service, Nov. 24, 1998.

30. Author interview with Gary Patton, biologist, U.S. Fish and Wildlife Service, July 4, 2001.

31. Steve Lipsher, "Slip-Up Possible in Ski Lift Rift," *Denver Post*, Dec. 14, 1998.

32. Letter from Wendell Wood, Oregon Natural Resources Council, to Robert Castaneda, Winema National Forest Supervisor, Feb. 24, 1999, pp. 2–4.

33. Letter from John Bunyak, Chief, Policy, Planning, and Permit Review

Branch, National Park Service, to Robert Castaneda, Winema National Forest Supervisor, Feb. 22, 1999.

34. Letter from Wendell Wood, Oregon Natural Resources Council, to Robert Castaneda, Feb. 24, 1999, p. 13.

35. Letter from Richard B. Parkin, Chief, Geographic Implementation Unit, U.S. Fish and Wildlife Service, to Robert Castaneda, Feb. 26, 1999.

36. Deborah Frazier, "Snowmaking Forecast: Cloudy," *Rocky Mountain News* (Denver), March 27, 2000.

37. Keystone Announces Ribbon-Cutting for Environmentally Friendly Information Center on Earth Day, FirstTracks!! Online Ski Magazine (www.firsttracksonline.com) press release, April 10, 2001.

38. Letter from Melinda Kassen, Trout Unlimited, to William P. Yellowtail, Regional Administrator, U.S. EPA Region VIII, Feb. 15, 2000.

39. Steve Lipsher, "Ski Area Creeks Tainted; Federal Officials Blame Snow-maker," *Denver Post*, Jan. 28, 2000. An acre-foot is enough water to cover one acre of land one foot deep, or about enough to sustain a typical household of four Americans for a year.

40. Letter from Melinda Kassen, Trout Unlimited, to Michael Claffey, U.S. Army Corps of Engineers, and Phil Hegeman, Colorado Department of Health, June 9, 2000.

41. Bob Berwyn, "Jones Gulch Plan Faces Water Quality Hurdles," *Summit Daily News* (Breckenridge, Colo.), undated draft article.

42. Robert Braile, "Critics Say Ski Areas a Drain on Resources," *Boston Globe*, Jan. 28, 2000.

43. Letter from U.S. senators Patrick Leahy (D-Vt.) and Robert Bennett (R-Utah) to Dan Reicher, Assistant Secretary for Energy Efficiency and Renewable Energy, Department of Energy, Aug. 6, 1999.

44. E-mail to the author from Randy Udall, Director, Community Office of Resource Efficiency, Aspen, Colo.

45. Mark Eddy, "Power Plants Killing Wilderness, USGS Says," *Denver Post*, April 10, 1997.

46. Breckenridge Final Environmental Assessment, White River National Forest, U.S. Forest Service, p. C-4, item 11.

47. *Sustainable Slopes: The Environmental Charter for Ski Areas*, National Ski Areas Association, June 2000, p. 1.

48. Ibid., p. 8.

49. Ibid., p. 14.

50. Air quality is another area where ski areas claim to do well, but don't. Air quality suffers from traffic in ski towns; during the 1980s and 1990s, Aspen and Telluride, for example, repeatedly violated federal air quality standards because of fireplace smoke, traffic-induced road dust, and restaurant grill smoke. Even when resorts do meet clean air standards, they are only meeting the same standards to which major urban areas are held. And the fossil fuel consumption associated with ski resorts is staggering. A single snowmobile, used by ski patrollers, lift operators, or for tours, emits as much pollution as thirty modern passengers cars. Enormous quantities of fuel go into making snow, running heated sidewalks and driveways, powering snow-grooming machines and ski lifts, and keeping an endless chain of supplies and tourists running uphill. The visitors most coveted are those who come from far away, burning untold amounts of jet fuel and gasoline to do so.

51. Glick presentation to Sheep Mountain Alliance, March 23, 2001, Telluride, Colo.

52. Author interview with Jim Spring, president, Leisure Trends Group, Sept. 18, 2000.

CHAPTER 9

1. Author interview with Myles Rademan, planning director and director of public affairs, Park City, Utah, March 15, 2000.

2. *Aspen Times*, Aug. 26–27 edition, 2000.

3. Robert H. Frank, "Traffic and Tax Cuts," *New York Times*, May 11, 2001.

4. Comparative Socioeconomic Data in the Summit County Region, Fall 1998, report issued by Northwest Colorado Council of Governments, p. 13.

5. In 1999, the median sales price for a Pitkin County home topped $2.4 million. In Eagle County it was $631,000, Summit County, $212,000. Rural Resort Region 2000 Benchmark Report, prepared by RST Associates and Third Sector Innovations, Inc., for Eagle, Garfield, Lake, Pitkin, and Summit Counties, p. 28. No 1999 data was available on home sales for Lake County.

6. Steve Lipsher, "Ski Areas' Labor Gap Expanding: Projections Show 2 of 3 Jobs Could Go Unfilled by Year 2020," *Denver Post*, April 9, 2000.

7. Tom Winter, "Colorado's Last Resort," *Ski*, May–June 2001, p. 95 et seq.

8. 2000 Rural Resort Region Benchmark Report, p. 37.

9. Steve Lipsher, "Mountain Housing Costs Peak," *Denver Post*, April 9, 2001.

10. 2000 Rural Resort Region Benchmark Report, p. 28. No 1999 data was available on home sales for Lake County.

11. Scott Condon, "Habitat Breaks Ground on First Affordable Home," *Aspen Times,* Aug. 7, 2000.

12. Hal Clifford, "For Resort Staff, Cost of Rocky Mountain Living High," *Boston Globe,* May 30, 1995.

13. Hal Clifford, "Ski Town Workers Find Homes in the Hills," *High Country News* (Paonia, Colo.), Sept. 11, 2000, p. 4.

14. Author interview with George Sheers, sheriff, Lake County, Colo., May 16, 2001.

15. Steve Lipsher, "Hispanics a Growing Force in Mountains," *Denver Post,* April 15, 2000.

16. Author interview with Alice Pugh, director, Full Circle, Leadville, Colo., May 15, 2001.

17. Jeff Dick, "Lake County, Copper Mtn. at Odds over Employee Housing", *Leadville (Colo.) Herald Democrat,* March 18, 1999; Amy Kemp, "Copper Development = Lake Problems," *Leadville (Colo.) Chronicle,* March 18, 1999.

18. 2000 Rural Resort Region Benchmark Report, p. 37.

19. Ibid., pp. 16 (graduation rates), 17 (revenues per pupil), 24 (health insurance), 25 (Medicaid), 37 (wages).

20. Comparative Socioeconomic Data in the Summit County Region, pp. 15–16.

21. Lake County Risk Assessment, 1996–97, report by Lake County Build a Generation, pp. 1–2.

22. Dick, "Lake County, Copper Mtn. at Odds over Employee Housing"; Kemp, "Copper Development = Lake Problems" (quotation).

23. Author interview with Elena and Jesús García, May 16, 2001.

24. Author interview with Captain Scott Friend, Colorado State Patrol, Aug. 27, 2000.

25. E-mail correspondence with the author. The law officer communicated on condition of anonymity.

26. Louis Uchitelle, "How to Define Poverty? Let Us Count the Ways," *New York Times,* May 26, 2001.

27. Author interview with Steve Carcaterra, executive director, LIFT-UP, Aug. 30, 2000.

28. "Yearning to Ski: Coming to America 2," *The Economist*, Feb. 3, 1996, pp. 22–23.

29. Ray Ring, "The New West's Servant Economy," *High Country News* (Paonia, Colo.), April 17, 1995.

30. Michael Janofsky, "Immigrants Flood Border in Arizona, Angering Ranchers," *New York Times*, June 18, 2000.

31. This problem is not limited to border areas. Vans loaded with undocumented workers are regularly intercepted by law officers in Colorado. Some aren't so lucky. On March 12, 2001, six such workers died on Interstate 76 in eastern Colorado when their Chevy van, packed with twenty people, was hit by an out-of-control truck. This sort of carnage is no longer rare (Jim Hughes, "I-76 Crash Kills Six Immigrants," *Denver Post*, March 13, 2001). Nor is the danger limited to highways. In late May 2001, fourteen immigrants died from heat and dehydration in Arizona's Cabeza Prieta Refuge, out of a group of twenty-eight who crossed the border on May 19. Thousands of immigrants have suffered similar fates in the deserts of the Southwest. On average, one immigrant a day dies in a U.S. desert after crossing the border (James Sterngold, "Rights Groups Urge Change in Border Policy," *New York Times*, May 26, 2001).

32. "An Arizona Mayor Condemns the New West's Thirst for Servants," *High Country News*, Sept. 27, 1999, p. 9, letter reprinted from *Aspen Daily News*, July 8, 1999.

33. Editorial, *Denver Post*, Jan. 3, 2000, quoted in Sam Dillon, "Agua Prieta Journal: Boom Turns Border to Speed Bump," *New York Times*, Jan. 18, 2000.

34. Author interview with Michael Kinsley, Rocky Mountain Institute, June 6, 2000.

35. Hal K. Rothman, *Devil's Bargains: Tourism in the Twentieth-Century American West* (Lawrence: University Press of Kansas, 1998), p. 11.

CHAPTER 10

1. Author interview with Aaron Brill, cofounder, Silverton ski area, April 6, 2001.

2. "Has the Les Otten Saga Ended?" *Ski Area Management*, May 2001, p. 95.

3. "Vail Resorts' Skier Visits Up 7.6 Percent," *Aspen Times*, June 7, 2001; Scott Condon, "Vail Follows Skico's Lead, Eliminates 37 Positions," *Aspen Times*, May 4, 2001; Tom Ross, "Resort Tightens Belt after Slim Winter," *Steamboat (Colo.) Pilot*, May 5, 2001.

4. "Aspen Prices 'Insane'" (letter to the editor), *Aspen Times,* April 21, 1999.

5. Author interview with Johnathan Stauffer, former Vail resident, Jan. 3, 2001.

6. Jim Spring, "Who's on the Slopes?" *Ski Area Management,* May 2001, p. 61.

7. Author interview with Myles Rademan, director of public affairs, Park City, Utah, March 15, 2000.

8. *Points West Chronicle,* newsletter from Center for the New West, Winter 1997–98, p. 1.

9. "The Roaring Fork Silicon Valley" (letter to the editor), *Aspen Times,* June 6, 2001, p. 9.

10. Author interview with Juli Beth Hoover, executive director, Mad River Planning District, Feb. 25, 2000.

11. Author interview with Terry Minger, Aug. 1, 2000.

12. Author interview with Mike Shirley, CEO, Bogus Basin ski area, April 24, 2001.

13. Author interview with Doug Wales, director of marketing, Bridger Bowl, May 3, 2001.

14. Author interview with Bob Ackland, general manager, Mad River Glen, Feb. 25, 2000.

15. That may be changing. Local officials in Basalt, Colorado, spent part of the spring of 2001 investigating the possibility of opening a local ski hill behind their high school.

16. "Winter Park Man Proposes Sale of Ski Area Stock," *Telluride Watch,* July 6, 2001, reprinted from *Winter Park Manifest,* June 27, 2001.

17. Bogus Basin Is Your Winner for Best Program to Grow the Sport to New Participants, Bogus Basin press release, undated.

18. Jason Blevins, "Nation's Ski Hills See Record Visits," *Denver Post,* May 9, 2001; Spring, "Who's on the Slopes?"

19. Allen Best, "Are There Casualties of the Season Pass Wars in Colorado?" *Ski Area Management,* May 2001, pp. 75–76.

20. Leslie B. Otten Resigns; William J. Fair Named CEO of American Skiing Company, American Skiing Company press release, March 28, 2001.

21. Marty Basch, "Abram a Family Value: New Owner Keeps Area Kid-Friendly," *Boston Globe,* March 1, 2001.

INDEX

Cooley, John, 16
Copper Mountain, Colo.: accidental pumping of diesel fuel into water-quality-monitoring well at, 260n11; condominiums sold at, 50; control exercised by Intrawest over businesses in New Ski Villages at, 115–22; land trade proposed at, 157; New Ski Villages concept implemented at, 110, 111, 114; owners of, 14, 41; proposed filling in of wetlands at, 179; reduced price on season passes at, 233
costs: of airport upgrade at Mammoth Lakes, 93–94; of average lift ticket, 31–32; of buying/renting condominiums, 49, 50, 86, 108, 193, 194; of fractional ownership, 47; of home sites in ski resorts, 46, 50, 53; of installing and operating chairlifts and gondolas, 30–31; of Intrawest's Discovery Center at Mammoth Lakes, 88; of legal fees for Minturn to fight Vail Resorts, 58; of real estate in ski towns, 86, 192–93; reduced, for lift tickets/season passes, 229–31, 233–34; rising, of skiing, 23–24, 25–28, 27n, 32, 218, 221, 221n; for ski areas to lease U.S. Forest Service land, 135–36; of ski equipment, 25, 32; 221n; of ski instruction, 32, 221n; of ski vacations, 27n, 221, 221n; of snow grooming machines, 30; of snowmaking, 29, 30; of stock of Big Three, 219; to taxpayers for Forest Service in Winter Sports Partnership, 144, 145; to Telski for obliterating wetlands (EPA fine), 179; of time shares, 50; of town homes, 86; of Yellowstone Club membership, 53

Coyle, Michael, 46
Crested Butte, Colo.: "golden age" of, 37; housing for workers in, 196; lack of accessibility of, 92; land trade at, 157; layoffs at, 220; New Ski Villages concept being embraced by, 109; opening of, 14
Crown family, 80n
customers, lack of marketing research on, 26–27

Dalai Lama, 121, 253n6
Daly, Andy, 21–22
Davis, Rick, 85–87, 88, 89
day visitors, spending by, vs. by destination visitors, 117
Deer Valley, Utah, 19, 31, 49
demographics: behind declining number of skiers, 19–20, 222–23; increasing wealth of skiers, 32–33
destination ski resorts: first, 6, 11–12; skier days at, 14, 19
destination visitors, spending by, vs. by day visitors, 117
Disney Corporation: contemplated purchase of Intrawest, 61; ski industry's marketing approach as similar to, 60
Disneyland, New Ski Villages contrasted to, 128
Dolores River basin, lynx reintroduced in, 159–61, 260n2
Dombeck, Mike, 138
Drexel Burnham Lambert, 42
Durango Mountain Resort, Colo. (Purgatory), 14, 92, 109

Eagle County, Colo.: cost of housing in, 195, 263n5; development and growth of, 162–63; official poverty line in, 206; in Rural Resort Region of Colorado, 190; upgrading of airport in, 92–93,

public lands (continued)
71–73, 251n16; "tragedy of the commons" on, 147, 257n40; under control of federal government, 72. See also land use; U.S. Forest Service
Pugh, Alice, 200–201
Purgatory, Colo. (Durango Mountain Resort), 14, 92, 109

Quillen, Ed, 160–61

Rademan, Myles: on empty houses in ski towns, 212–13; on future of skiing/ski towns, 224, 228, 235, 236, 238, 240; on income disparity in ski towns, 191
Radisson, time-share sales by, 50
Ralston-Purina, 6, 14, 43
Raymond, Gary, 46, 91–92
real estate development: effect on neighboring areas, 126; golden age of ski towns ended by, 39, 59–60, 103–5; Janss and Seibert's new approach to, 15–17; land trades facilitating, 153–58; massive scope of, in ski towns, 76–77; migratory routes of elk interrupted by, 63–64; money made from, 49–51, 53; ski industry's shift to emphasis on, 7–9, 15, 17, 43–49, 222. See also housing; New Ski Villages
recreation: as business of U.S. Forest Service, 137–40; industrial, environmental impacts of, 77; partnerships between U.S. Forest Service and corporations in business of, 141–47; user fees for, 140
rental real estate, New Ski Villages: commercial, developer's control over, 115–22; hot-beds concept of (condominiums), 108
rental real estate, ski towns: com-

mercial, 96–97; spiral of impossibility of, 95–96; workers unable to afford, 97–98, 104, 104n, 193
Reynolds, Grey, 154
river otters, 132
road kills, 168
Roaring Fork Valley: cost of housing in, 192–93, 195, 196, 263n5; racism in, 210; wildlife and habitat problems in, 166
Rocky Mountain Institute, 54, 95, 213
rope tows, 30
Rothman, Hal K., 13, 214
Rural Resort Region, Colo.: counties in, 190; disjunct between tax collection and social services needs in, 199–201
rural-urban model of ski towns, 223–29, 237–38, 237n, 240

A Sand County Almanac (Leopold), 71
Schaffgotsch, Felix, 11, 239
Schneider, Hannes, 241n6
Schniebs, Otto, 10
Schor, Juliet, 98
Schull, Rob, 152–53
season passes: given by ski areas to U.S. Forest Service employees, 148–49, 258n44; reduced prices for, 229–31, 233–34. See also lift tickets
second homes. See vacation homes
Seibert, Pete, 239; control exercised by, 111, 113; development model pioneered by, 15, 16, 51
Severy, Dana, 83–84
Sheep Mountain Alliance (SMA), 78, 149–51
Sheers, George, 197
Shirley, Mike, 229–30, 233
Shoemaker, Sloan, 74–75
shopping, 52, 111, 121, 253nn5–6

Sierra-at-Tahoe, Calif., 42
Sierra Club, 76, 77, 131
Silver Creek, Colo., 194
Silverman, Rick, 38, 81, 102
Silver, Scott, 141, 142–43
Silverton Mountain, Colo., ski area, 216–18, 238–39
S-K-I Limited, 246n2
Ski Area Citizens Coalition, 147
ski areas: complimentary season passes given to U.S. Forest Service employees by, 148–49, 258n44; first large public, being built since 1980, 216–18; land leased from U.S. Forest Service by, 135–37, 256n16; locally owned, 229–36, 240, 266n15; purchased by American Skiing, 40, 246n2; purchased by Booth Creek Ski Holdings, 42, 246n6; purchased by Intrawest, 40–41; purchased by Vail Resorts, 24, 42–43; small, decline of, 23, 32; total number of, 14, 32. *See also* ski resorts
ski business. *See* ski industry
ski club, first, 10
Ski Cooper, Colo., 157–58, 162, 233
ski corporate conglomerates, 6, 39. *See also* Big Three; Booth Creek Ski Holdings
ski equipment, cost of, 25, 32, 221n
skier days: at destination ski resorts, 14, 19; at resorts owned by ski corporate conglomerates, 39; at ski areas on land leased from U.S. Forest Service, 135, 256n16; in Colorado, 6, 14; defined, 6; increase in, with snowmaking, 28; minimal number of, for area to interest Big Three, 92; nationwide decline in, 18–19, 243n1
skiers: day vs. destination, 14, 19; demographics behind declining

number of, 19–20, 222–23; disconnect between growth in number of, and capital investments, 31, 33–35; increasing wealth of, 32–33, 78; price of skiing too high for, 26–27, 217–18, 221, 221n; protection vs. development of environment favored by, 75, 77
ski industry: colonial behavior by corporations in, 211, 214, 223; consolidation in, 8, 23, 43; decline of, 18–19, 23, 32, 219, 243n1; environment-friendly image of, 182, 186–87; history of, 6, 9–17; negative effects of, on environment, 178–86, 263n50; partnerships between U.S. Forest Service and, 143–47; reasons for decline of, 19–21, 22–23, 25–28, 219–23; shift to real estate development emphasis in, 7–9, 15, 17, 43–49, 222; standardization of visitor experiences by, 60–61; Tenth Mountain Division veterans' role in creating, 12–13; U.S. Forest Service as compromised in oversight and regulation of, 137, 142–47, 149, 155, 158
skiing: difficulties of learning and going, 22–23; early history of, in America, 9–12; future role of, in ski towns, 228–36, 239–40; marginalization of, by Big Three, 45–49, 102–3, 109; rising price of, 23–24, 25–28, 27n, 32, 221, 221n; as way of life, 9–10, 36–39
ski-in/ski-out home sites, 46, 46n, 78
ski instruction, cost of, 32, 221n
ski lifts. *See* lifts
ski resorts: air access to, 92–94, 95, 252n4; annual investment

U.S. Army Corps of Engineers, and base development at Peak 7 in Breckenridge, 131, 133–34, 254n5

U.S. Bureau of Land Management (BLM): land trades of property of, 155; public lands controlled by, 72; wilderness-designated lands of, 251n16

U.S. Department of Justice: antitrust settlement of American Skiing with, 42; demanded ski area at Arapahoe Basin be sold by Vail Resorts, 43

U.S. Environmental Protection Agency: alleges environmental violations at Squaw Valley, Calif., 167–68, 260n9; and approval of expansion at Breckenridge's Peak 7, 131–35, 255n9; comments on White River National Forest revised forest management plan, 77, 152; penalized Telluride Ski and Golf Company for obliterating wetlands, 179, 179n; U.S. Forest Service's position on land trades questioned by, 155–56, 158, 259n56

user days. *See* skier days

U.S. Fish and Wildlife Service: no-jeopardy decision by, on lynx in Vail's Category III expansion area, 170–78; wilderness-designated lands of, 251n16

U.S. Forest Service: Big Three's leasing of lands of, 5, 55–56; complimentary ski area season passes given to employees of, 148–49, 258n44; compromised in role of overseeing and regulating ski industry, 137, 142–47, 149, 155, 158; developers pay for salaries for certain employees

of, 130–31, 253n2; examples of pro-development bias of, 152–54; land trades (exchanges) between developers and, 153–58; oversight by, of Telluride Company's expansion plans, 79, 149–52, 258n46; partnerships between recreation/ski industry and, 141–47; position on snowmaking, 185–86; "positive externalities" created by ski area development on lands of, 56, 64, 135, 248n48; proposed expansions by Colorado ski resorts into lands of, 33–34; public lands controlled by, 72; shift from logging to recreation as business of, 137–40; ski areas leasing land from, 135–37, 256n16; Vail Resort's expansion at Breckenridge's Peak 7 approved by, 129–35, 253n2, 254n5, 255n9; wilderness-designated lands of, 71, 251n16

U.S. General Accounting Office (GAO), recommendation by to discontinue land trades, 155

U.S. Skiing, 143

vacation homes: Baby Boomers' buying of, 44–45; fractional ownership of, 47; money made from selling, 49–51; ski towns' high number of, 97–98, 103–4, 193, 212; time-share ownership of, 50

Vail Associates, 42–43

Vail, Colo.: air access to, 92–93, 252n4; as company town, 55; downtown retail rental rates in, 97; in Eagle River Valley, 166; high percentage of vacation homes in, 193; housing for workers in, 97–98, 193, 196;

price of ski trip to, 24, 221; urban sprawl at, 126

Vail Mountain, Colo.: Adventure Ridge mountain-top amusement park at, 147; amount paid to lease U.S. Forest Service land, 136; development model pioneered at, 51, 110, 111, 126; environmental arson on, 65, 249n2; first detachable quad chairlift at, 30; history of, 14, 15, 16, 42; lynx habitat disturbed by Category III expansion at, 65, 74, 169–78; proposed expansion into Blue Sky Basin, 33; wealth of skiers at, 32

Vail Resorts Development Company (VRDC), 45–46, 131, 248n48

Vail Resorts Incorporated: before-tax profits (2000) of, 5, 241n1; business strategy of, 7; capital investments by, 31, 52; corporate offices of, 21–22; and decision by U.S. Fish and Wildlife Service on lynx in area proposed for expansion by, 160–61, 170–78; history of, 42–43, 246n8; interlocking relationship with East-West partners, 248n48; land trade proposed by, 157; Latino workers for, 188–90; layoffs by, 219; Minturn's water-rights dispute with, 57–58; ownership of, 246n8; partnered with Intrawest at Keystone, 41, 77, 115; portion of ski market controlled by, 7, 43; rate of growth of (1997), 23–24; reduced prices for season passes of, 233; skiing vs. real estate as business of, 45–46; ski resorts of, 24, 42–43; stock offerings, price of, 43, 219, 246n8. *See also* Big Three; *specific ski areas/resorts*

Vermont, snowmaking's environmental effects in, 184

Vistabahn, 30

Wales, Doug, 230–31, 234, 236

Walter, John, 84–85

Wasatch-Cache National Forest, Utah: complimentary season ski passes for employees of, 148, 149; land trade by Snowbasin in, 153–54; ski resorts seeking expansion in, 146

water: quality of, impact of ski resort development on, 132, 168, 260n11; required for snowmaking, 181–84, 262n39; rights to, dispute between mountain town and Vail Resorts over, 57–58

Waterville Valley, N.H., 40, 42, 246n2, 246n6

wealth: increasing disparity of, 104–5, 191–92; public land development to increase, 78; of skiers today, 32–33, 78

Webster, Joe, 175

Weingardt, Bernie, 146, 148, 149

Whistler Mountain, B.C.: financial problems at, 40; marketing of lifestyle for Creekside development at, 100; New Ski Villages concept at, 110; purchased by Intrawest, 41

White River National Forest, Colo.: complimentary ski season passes for employees of, 149; developer funding of staff positions in, 130–31; EPA comments on U.S. Forest Service's revised forest management plan for, 77, 152; expansion at Peak 7 in Breckenridge approved by, 133–35

wilderness: lands designated as, 71–73, 251n16; origin of concept of, 71